MW00448509

Teaching Political Theory

ELGAR GUIDES TO TEACHING

The Elgar Guides to Teaching series provides a variety of resources for instructors looking for new ways to engage students. Each volume provides a unique set of materials and insights that will help both new and seasoned teachers expand their toolbox in order to teach more effectively. Titles include selections of methods, exercises, games and teaching philosophies suitable for the particular subject featured. Each volume is authored or edited by a seasoned professor. Edited volumes comprise contributions from both established instructors and newer faculty who offer fresh takes on their fields of study.

Titles in the series include:

Teaching Entrepreneurship, Volume Two
A Practice-Based Approach
Edited by Heidi M. Neck, Candida G. Brush and Patricia G. Greene

Teaching Environmental Impact Assessment
Angus Morrison-Saunders and Jenny Pope

Teaching Research Methods in Political Science
Edited by Jeffrey L. Bernstein

Teaching International Relations
Edited by James M. Scott, Ralph G. Carter, Brandy Jolliff Scott and Jeffrey S. Lantis

Teaching Marketing
Edited by Ross Brennan and Lynn Vos

Teaching Tourism
Innovative, Values-based Learning Experiences for Transformative Practices
Edited by Johan Edelheim, Marion Joppe and Joan Flaherty

Teaching Sports Economics and Using Sports to Teach Economics
Edited by Victor A. Matheson and Aju J. Fenn

Creating Inclusive and Engaging Online Courses
A Teaching Guide
Edited by Monica Sanders

Teaching Undergraduate Political Methodology
Edited by Mitchell Brown, Shane Nordyke and Cameron G. Thies

Teaching Graduate Political Methodology
Edited by Mitchell Brown, Shane Nordyke and Cameron G. Thies

Teaching Political Theory
A Pluralistic Approach
Nicholas Tampio

Teaching Political Theory
A Pluralistic Approach

Nicholas Tampio

Professor of Political Science, Fordham University, USA

ELGAR GUIDES TO TEACHING

Edward Elgar
PUBLISHING

Cheltenham, UK • Northampton, MA, USA

© Nicholas Tampio 2022

Cover image: NASA

All rights reserved. No part of this publication may be reproduced, stored in a retrieval system or transmitted in any form or by any means, electronic, mechanical or photocopying, recording, or otherwise without the prior permission of the publisher.

Published by
Edward Elgar Publishing Limited
The Lypiatts
15 Lansdown Road
Cheltenham
Glos GL50 2JA
UK

Edward Elgar Publishing, Inc.
William Pratt House
9 Dewey Court
Northampton
Massachusetts 01060
USA

A catalogue record for this book
is available from the British Library

Library of Congress Control Number: 2022941151

This book is available electronically in the **Elgar**online
Political Science and Public Policy subject collection
http://dx.doi.org/10.4337/9781800373877

Printed on elemental chlorine free (ECF)
recycled paper containing 30% Post-Consumer Waste

ISBN 978 1 80037 386 0 (cased)
ISBN 978 1 80037 387 7 (eBook)

Printed and bound in the USA

Contents

List of boxes   vi
Preface   vii

1   Teaching political theory: a pluralistic approach   1

PART I   DESIGNING A POLITICAL THEORY COURSE

2   Crafting a syllabus, with illustrations from American
     political thought   23

3   Writing lectures, with illustrations from Chinese and
     European political thought   43

4   Making assignments, with illustrations from Indian and
     African American political thought   76

PART II   TEACHING POLITICAL THEORY TODAY

5   Teaching Greek political thought, with a focus on Sextus
     Empiricus   119

6   Teaching Chinese political thought, with a focus on Zhuangzi   140

7   Teaching neuroscience in a political theory course   166

8   Teaching the public, with examples from education policy   190

Index   204

Boxes

1.1 Invite students into a conversation   5

2.1 How to bring your politics into the classroom   26

3.1 Use images   46

4.1 Watch movies   78

5.1 Stage debates   121

6.1 Run simulations   142

7.1 Go on field trips   167

8.1 Play to the back of the room   193

Preface

One of the most exciting moments in my life was taking my first political theory class in college. I was amazed that one could take a course reading, discussing, and writing about what the greatest minds had to say about politics. I loved reading *The Republic*, *The Prince*, *On Liberty*, and *The Communist Manifesto*. My mind was racing, thinking about the nature of justice, how to acquire and hold onto political power, how to sharpen our thinking by learning the arguments of our opponents, and how the ruling ideas tend to be those of the ruling class. I took every political theory class I could in college and relished the conversations and debates. I then spent a decade in graduate school at Indiana University and Johns Hopkins University, watching and learning from political theorists at the top of the profession. After a fellowship at the University of Virginia, and visiting positions at George Mason University and Hamilton College, I started a tenure track job at Fordham University, the Jesuit university of New York, where I am now a full professor and teach courses and units on classical Greek political thought, classical Chinese political thought, the European Enlightenment, American political thought, the politics of the Marvel Cinematic Universe, global justice, education policy, economic philosophy, contemporary political theory, and science and politics. This book shares insights about teaching political theory based on my own experience and learning about others'. Theorists teach in the classroom, but we also teach whenever we write academic work or speak to the public. This book, then, is also about how to do political theory, or think profoundly about politics, now.

I wish to thank my teachers who have left an imprint on this book's treatment of how to teach the history of political thought (Eugene Lewis, Russell L. Hanson, Anthony Pagden, Giulia Sissa), the relationship between political science and political theory (Jeffrey C. Isaac), the political importance of neuroscience (William E. Connolly, Jane Bennett), and the political repercussions of skepticism (Richard E. Flathman). My economics professor at New College, Catherine Elliott, showed me how to teach a college course with structure, passion, and attention to students. I hope that my students feel pride in this book and recognize that I could not have written it without their energy, questions, responses, objections, looks of puzzlement, feedback, and friendship.

I presented chapters of this book at conferences of the American Political Science Association, the Association for Political Theory, and the John Dewey Society. Tongdong Bai, Adrian Blau, Kennan Ferguson, Jennifer Forestal,

Katherine Goktepe, Jeffrey C. Isaac, Tao Jiang, Sabina Knight, John Christian Laursen, Jared Loggins, Thomas Merrill, Anindya Sekhar Purakayastha, and Peng Yu offered feedback on chapters that improved the entire book.

I thank Caroline Kracunas at Edward Elgar Publishing for inviting me to write this book, to Matthew Moore for giving her my name, and the reviewer for encouragement and advice. I thank Bert Ulrich at NASA for granting permission to use the image on the cover. I wrote this book during the COVID-19 pandemic, which meant that I was often working at home close to my wife Gina and our sons Giuliano, Luca, Nicola, and Giorgio. We moved into a new house, built bike trails in the woods, sat around fires, discussed European and American history, played games, cooked meals, volunteered at a food pantry, and made each other laugh. I hope that the book expresses the joy I felt while writing it as well as concern about what is happening in the world.

1. Teaching political theory: a pluralistic approach

INTRODUCTION

When I teach a course in political theory, I start by writing the day's headlines on the board. Looking with the class at *The New York Times* homepage, I find stories about American race relations, political developments in China, India, Saudi Arabia, Europe, and Latin America, scientific breakthroughs, economic debates, and education policy.

The day's headlines, I tell my class, are like waves. Every day, the news is filled with developments that matter to individuals affected. Journalists perform a valuable function in educating the public. If you are swimming with your children, surfing in a tournament, or fishing for the day, you want the most recent, accurate description of how high the waves are. Similarly, if you are thinking about which candidates to vote for, which foreign policies to support or oppose, whether to teach in person or online, or whether to support an education initiative or not, you want to follow current events. In middle school, I delivered newspapers to homes in my neighborhood and would read the front section of the newspaper every morning. Keeping up with the news is a valuable exercise for people who care about the world.

One day, my grandfather told me why he didn't read the newspaper. He said that if you picked up a newspaper from 100 years ago, you would see that the headlines are nearly the same. For example, there have been a spate of articles about COVID-19 that could, with a few minor changes, describe the 1918 influenza pandemic. One hundred years ago, people died, states and countries learned lessons, or didn't, and people praised and criticized leaders. Reading the newspaper, by itself, can become repetitive over time. Sometimes people want to get a deeper understanding of events.

Beneath waves, there are tides. More precisely, tides are big waves that cause the sea to rise and fall along the shorelines across the world. The wind affects waves; the sun and moon affect the tides. If you are going out for a day on the ocean, particularly if you're on a canoe or a kayak, you want to know the schedule of the tides. The social sciences, I tell my students, investigate the tides of human affairs. Underneath the current events on the board, I identify the topics that social scientists would study to make sense of the day's developments. The American presidency. Housing policy. Foreign policy. The rise of populism around the world. Natural science. Economics. Education policy.

It is easy, particularly for the young, to think that everything that happens is unique, but social scientists can identify patterns across time and place. Social scientists collect and analyze data, sometimes scrutinizing a small number of cases, other times surveying a large number, sometimes alone, sometimes as part of a team. People look for patterns in how leaders make decisions, in how countries learn from one another, in the relationship between politics and markets, and whether publics listen to experts. Political scientists typically investigate one aspect of human affairs, but the borders between sociology, economics, history, and other social sciences are as fluid as the lines demarcating where one sea ends and another begins. In *How Social Science Got Better*, Michigan State political professor Matt Grossmann commends recent developments in the social sciences, including "the triumph of empiricism over grand theory, the rise of open and big data, the specification of causal identification strategies, and the rise of team science" (Grossmann 2021: 28). Many social scientists today aspire to be more like natural scientists, including running experiments and collecting data that other social scientists can access and replicate.

According to scientists, there is a level to the ocean beneath tides: currents. I learned about ocean currents after a ship carrying bath toys lost part of its cargo in the Pacific Ocean in 1992. This flotilla of blue turtles, green frogs, red beavers, and yellow ducks began to circle the globe in ways that fascinated oceanographers, environmentalists, and the general public. By tracking these bath toys, people could visualize the "circulation pumps" that bring water around the planet. In the Labrador Sea, warm water approaches the Arctic, freezes, and the saltier remains sink to the bottom of the ocean, pushing the Gulf Stream towards the equator. Human beings normally cannot see or feel ocean currents, but the lost bath toys helped people visualize mesoscale eddies that exercise a profound effect on the weather of the Labrador Sea, Greenland, and the rest of the world (Hohn 2011). In light of global climate change, scientists study currents even if, as of yet, there are many unanswered questions about what happens at the bottom of the oceans.

I think of political theory as the study of the ocean currents of political life. Stories in the news are about human beings. If they are not about human beings, then they are about human beings encountering, experiencing, and learning about nonhuman things. Beneath the social sciences is the topic of human nature. What is it in human nature that makes people strive for elected office, become scientists, idolize powerful leaders, read books, march, protest, support the police and military, think or not think? What is it that human beings can know, and what must always remain out of reach? What is the nature of reality, and what does that mean for whether human beings may somehow transcend their environment to choose and act otherwise? Does God exist, and if so, what does that mean for what human beings should do? How should we act as individuals towards other people—the topic of ethics—and how should we act as a collective body—the topic of politics? What does it mean to think, and how can one do it well? The German word for "profound" is *tiefste*: deep. Political theory, at least the conception of it that is the focus of this book, addresses the deep questions of politics—the ones that flow beneath every investigation of what leaders, voters, states, institutions, parties, organizations do or should do.

Political theorists are often lodged in political science departments, and, when relations are healthy, both parties benefit from their exchanges about the different levels of political life. Take the study of democracy. Political scientists study the causes of democratization and how a democratic political system affects political stability, economic growth, the protection of human rights, and foreign policy. Political theorists argue about whether and why democracy is better than other forms of governance and how democracies should create space for religious freedom, distribute resources, protect civil liberties, and interact with other countries on the world stage. When things are going right, there is "cross-fertilization" between colleagues researching what is and what ought to be, with political scientists keeping theorists grounded in reality, and political theorists imagining new things to research and advocate (Oprea 2020). Political theorists are also often in conversation with theologians, philosophers, historians, natural scientists, sociologists, journalists, and other people inside and outside the academy. In various ways, we all want to understand the deepest layers of social life, which sometimes brings us far away from the surface of the news cycle.[1]

Political theory is a tradition. As a political theorist, my job in the university, and the world at large, is to inherit a stack of books and pass it on to the next generation. As a teacher, I assign students Plato's *Republic*, Machiavelli's *Prince*, Kant's *Toward Perpetual Peace*, W. E. B. Du Bois's *The Souls of Black Folk*, Sayyd Qutb's *Social Justice in Islam*, Hannah Arendt's *Human Condition*, Leo Strauss's *Natural Right and History*, John Rawls's *Theory of Justice*, Martha Nussbaum's *Sex and Social Justice*, and Tongdong Bai's *Against Political Equality: The Confucian Case*. I teach students certain ways to read texts and how to write research papers on authors, political themes, and ongoing political developments. The word tradition comes from the Latin root *traditio*, "a handing over," which is also the root of the word treason (Coles 2001). Political theorists keep alive a certain way of studying and thinking about political affairs, but they also constantly change it by adding and dropping authors and themes from their syllabi and research agendas (Moore 2010). John G. Gunnell has documented how German émigrés shaped academic political theory after World War II as a humanistic and historical vocation at odds with the rest of political science's commitments to liberalism, democracy, and the scientific method (Gunnell 1988). Gunnell is right to challenge the view there is a "grand tradition" running from Plato to the most recent issue of *Political Theory*, and theorists in a globalizing world may wonder whether we should still believe in "a body of political theory that constitutes some privileged or canonical repository of wisdom" (Isaac 1995: 643). Nevertheless, political theorists may assemble a usable history for themselves that gives meaning to their work and an archive to reconstruct. For political theorists today, that archive includes lived experiences, rituals, oral traditions, cuisines, clothing, and the visual arts (Behl 2022; Freeden 2021; Rollo 2021; Thomas 2010).[2]

Here is an example from what my students may learn from taking a sequence of my courses. In Introduction to Political Philosophy, I teach *A Treatise of Human Nature*, in which David Hume argued that human beings have sympathy for those that are closest to them. Human beings are not so much selfish as partial, and justice arises as a social convention to manage human partiality. In American Political Thought, I teach my students that James Madison studied the Scottish Enlightenment with John Witherspoon as an undergraduate at the College of New Jersey, and Madison's argument about factions in *Federalist No. 10* reconstructs Hume's insight that people tend to be partial to people with whom they share ideas, passions, history, and geography and that a representative republic may extend over a large territory (Thompson 1976). In Education Politics and Policy, we learn how the Constitution distributes education power at the federal, state, and local levels to prevent any one faction from controlling public schools. I teach *A Treatise of Human Nature*, in other words, to illuminate the deeper philosophical issues flowing beneath debates about things like how schools choose curricula or whether there is a constitutional right to education (Tampio 2021).

"The only reason to teach political theory," Judith Shklar explains, "is the conviction that a complete person must be able to think intelligently about government, and the only way to rise above banality is to learn to think one's way through the works of the great writers on the subject and to learn to argue with them" (Shklar 2019: 215). Political theory can be an exhilarating effort to engage in a conversation (see Box 1.1) across time and place about who we are, what we can know, the nature of reality, and what people can do right now to make the human experience richer. And once they refine their ideas in this conversation, political theorists may leave the academy to enter political debates, whether through their scholarship, teaching, activism, meeting with politicians, or public-facing writing.

BOX 1.1 INVITE STUDENTS INTO A CONVERSATION

Political education is not merely a matter of coming to understand a tradition, it is learning how to participate in a conversation: it is at once initiation into an inheritance in which we have a life interest, and the exploration of its intimations. (Oakeshott 1991: 62)

How do political theorists heed Michael Oakeshott's advice to bring students into a conversation? How do we teach students about an accumulated body of wisdom in such a way that students will continue their own political education once the class is done?

In the summer of 2021, I began my Introduction to Political Theory course by discussing the metaphor of the political ocean and then asked students to show how one could study the same political topic from the perspective of journalism, political science, and political theory. Teaching the course online, I placed the students in breakout rooms in groups of three.

I thought it would be easy. Students would find a newspaper article about a president giving a speech, a political science article about presidents, and a political theory article about human nature. I was surprised, however, that students had trouble with the assignment. Students did searches on the Internet and found articles about a topic, but they did not know the difference between journalism, political science, and political theory.

When the class reconvened, I offered examples of how to read a newspaper article, find political science articles on the topic, and then read political theory articles. I explained how double-blind peer review works and the different kind of work published in *The Washington Post*, the *American Political Science Review*, and *Political Theory*. I showed them how to do a search on the library homepage and explained how it is better as a rule to cite recent sources. I said that the purpose of the course is to help them think about the deepest level of politics that sometimes seems far removed from the daily news cycle.

Will I continue to ask students to do this assignment? Maybe. But this episode reinforced for me that I am not simply teaching students about a static tradition. Rather, I am displaying what it means, and why it matters, to pursue the vocation of political theory.

POLITICAL THEORY AND POLITICAL SCIENCE

Political theory is one of the main subfields of political science in the United States alongside American politics, comparative politics, international relations, and public policy. Political scientists sometimes argue that political theory is closer to a humanities discipline and thus should not be housed in political *science* departments.[3] Fortunately, many political scientists believe that "we have an epistemologically pluralistic profession, which we should encourage, protecting as an asset the strength of our divergent voices" (Box-Steffensmeier, Sinclair-Chapman and Christenson 2021). In this section, I argue that political science capaciously understood should welcome people who make it their vocation to study the obscure but powerful ocean flows of politics. Just as a sports team needs players with diverse skill sets, political scientists may appreciate that political theorists often use different literatures, methods, and styles to study political affairs. I tell my students that many political theorists study the history of ideas to help us understand and shape contemporary politics. Political theory is the subfield of political science that foregrounds the question of what political affairs *should* be. Students often take political theory courses with the hope that they will gain clarity about the *why* questions. Why should I be a Republican or a Democrat? Why should the U.S. intervene in other countries' affairs, if at all? Why should the government tax people, build walls, run schools, pay reparations to descendants of enslaved Americans, or clean the air? What are the normative considerations that undergird political science's commitments to polling ordinary people? Political theorists can teach popular classes that help students make sense of developments in the world, their other political science courses, and their lives.

Political theory, however, has an embattled place in political science. To understand why, we may turn to Gary King, Robert O. Keohane, and Sidney Verba's influential conception of political science in their book, *Designing Social Inquiry: Scientific Inference in Qualitative Research*. According to King et al., political science at its best is a combination of creativity and discipline in order to describe and explain facts about the real world. On the one hand, political scientists should raise hard questions, venture bold hypotheses, think creatively about how to conduct research, and be prepared to challenge common-sense interpretations of politics. On the other, political scientists must also identify their method, show their data, and make their analyses transparent. "A dynamic process of inquiry occurs within a stable structure of rules" (King et al. 1994: 12). The more they articulate the nature of political science, however, King et al. make demands that will be almost impossible for a political theorist to follow:

> Scientific research uses explicit, codified, and public methods to generate and analyze data whose reliability can therefore be assessed... If the method and logic of a researcher's observations and inferences are left implicit, the scholarly community has no way of judging the validity of what was done. We cannot evaluate the principles of selection that were used to record observations, the ways in which the observations were processed, and the logic by which conclusions were drawn. We cannot learn from their methods or replicate their results. Such research is not

a *public* act. Whether or not it makes good reading, it is not a contribution to social science. (King et al. 1994: 8)

In their sharp distinction between science and good reading, King et al. marginalize many kinds of research and researcher from political science. I understand the appeal of running experiments like in a laboratory, but many political scientists who use qualitative methods, mixed methods, or interpretive approaches study things that cannot be replicated, nor can they render explicit their steps—a demand, incidentally, that may be impossible to meet for political scientists who draw upon "tacit knowledge" in choosing their objects or methods of inquiry (Polanyi 2009). There is no fact that can settle a debate about why democracy is better than meritocracy or vice versa, whether the United States should commit to defending human rights around the world, or whether authoritarian measures are legitimate to address climate change. Though King et al. don't necessarily want to banish political theorists from political science departments, they envision political science as continuing to move in the direction of teams collaborating on the analysis of "big data" (King 2014).[4]

In this situation, it is important to recuperate Sheldon Wolin's case for political theory in his famous 1969 article, "Political Theory as a Vocation." A professor at the University of California-Berkeley and then Princeton University, Wolin authored *Politics and Vision* and influenced many political theorists, particularly on the left (Cane 2016). Wolin, alongside John Dewey and Hannah Arendt, held that philosophy's venerable quest for eternal truths no longer made sense, and he associated his task with defending democracy against the totalitarian trends present even in nominally liberal democratic societies. In the mid-twentieth century, political scientists were trying to emulate the natural sciences; for Wolin, this approach did not work in a realm imbued with meaning that required interpretation rather than data analysis, an exploration of "what is politically appropriate rather than towards what is scientifically operational" (Wolin 1969: 1071).

Wolin's essay is a polemic against what he calls "methodism," the belief that political science is a science only insofar as it stipulates and follows rigorous methods. According to Wolin, methodists, or behaviorists, analyze data about the world. Yet, as the etymology of statistics indicates, the state collects and uses much of this data. As I have learned from researching education policy, the state often does not collect data that might provide evidence for critics of its policies, such as the number of field trips, guest speakers, or outdoor activities. Political science that uses ready-made procedures, and plugs in data provided by the state, may exhibit status-quo bias methodologically and politically. Methodological "assumptions are such as to re-enforce an uncritical view of existing political structures and all that they imply" (Wolin

1969: 1064). Wolin's approach is compatible with reflections on how to do political theory—including using game theory, thought experiments, conceptual analysis, and modeling—but Wolin objects to a "vending machine" model of political science in which researchers enter inputs, push the start button, and then collect the neatly packaged output (Blau 2017b; Johnson 2021).

Wolin's warning retains its urgency in the current debates about the "reproducibility crisis" in the social sciences. In 2018, *Nature Human Behaviour* published an article by Colin F. Camerer and 19 co-authors in which they replicated social science experiments in *Nature* and *Science* between 2010 and 2015. The team found that there is widespread "systematic bias" in the social sciences whereby authors identify false positives on their hypothesis, overestimate effect sizes of true positives, and tweak the model until it reaches the required significance level ("p-hacking" or "data fishing"). "These systematic biases can be reduced by implementing pre-registration of analysis plans to reduce the likelihood of false positives and registration and reporting of all study results to reduce the effects of publication bias inflating effect sizes" (Camerer et al. 2018: 643). I attended a lecture by one of the co-authors of this paper, Anna Dreber, a professor of economics at the Stockholm School of Economics, who described a paper in which multiple teams were given the same dataset and asked to determine whether soccer referees are more likely to give red cards to players with a darker skin tone, and the teams reached wildly different conclusions (Silberzahn et al. 2018). The way to solve the reproducibility crisis, for Dreber and others, is to standardize data collection and analysis so that researchers find the same results when they rerun experiments or analyze datasets.

From the perspective of this political theorist, however, I noted that many of the experiments that Dreber described included analysis of data that could be collected quickly and cheaply using the polling service Amazon Mechanical Turk (MTurk). As Wolin observed in the 1960s, this kind of analysis takes an ahistorical, acontextual view of politics in pursuit of timeless natural laws, even though we live in a world where people's minds and behavior often change. To be fair, methodologically rigorous research on huge datasets can illuminate, for instance, how the Chinese government uses social media posts to distract the public rather than to engage critics (King, Pan and Roberts 2017). Nevertheless, an insistence on methodological rigor discourages certain kinds of research that shed light on political affairs in ways that elude reproducible, quantitative social science. According to American Political Science Association president Rogers M. Smith in his 2020 Presidential Address, political science was slow to recognize big developments like the civil rights movements in the 1950s and 1960s, the rise of religious fundamentalists in the 1970s and 1980s, and the distrust of the political establishment in the late twentieth century (Smith 2020). Kristen Renwick Monroe, a comparativist, notes that standardizing research data and transparency has a "chilling effect" on certain kinds of research approaches, including interviewing people in vulnerable situations (Monroe 2018). An emphasis on rigor, transparency, methods, and the like may lead to political science ignoring important questions that can only yield approximate answers. In the constructive side of Wolin's essay, he explains the vocation of political theory as the pursuit of political wisdom:

> Political life does not yield its significance to terse hypotheses, but is elusive and hence meaningful statements about it often have to be allusive and intimative. Context becomes supremely important, for actions and events occur in no other setting. Knowledge of this type tends, therefore, to be suggestive and illuminative rather than explicit and determinate. (Wolin 1969: 1070)

When you are studying something like the founding of the United States, you are investigating a singular event that cannot be replicated. Many political theorists will read figures such as John Adams to understand the threat that wealth poses to democracy (Mayville 2018), but there is no method as such that political theorists use when deciding what authors, texts, ideas, or historical eras to study. They have a feel for the game, as it were, that says that reading these texts will help us more than reading those ones. Political theorists pursue intimations—that is, they hear their mentors or peers discussing something and have a hunch that learning more about the topic will pay dividends for making sense of our current predicament. To be sure, there are political theorists who do not think that an apprenticeship in the history of ideas is the best or only way to fashion ideas to understand contemporary politics. In a short essay on how to write analytic political theory, for instance, Robert E. Goodin, the founding editor of *The Journal of Political Philosophy*, emphasizes "thinking through a problem" rather than immersing oneself in the history of political thought (Goodin 2017: 18). But the conception of political theory presented in this book maintains that studying the history of ideas helps us craft political lenses through which to look at political life (Thiele 2018: 3–5).

Wolin distinguishes political science and political theory by their respective orientations to history. Political scientists do specialized research that will in turn be superseded by future research; it makes more sense for them to read recent journal articles and learn the latest statistical techniques than to, say, peruse old issues of the *American Political Science Review*. For political theorists, on the contrary, reading old books can be an appropriate way to understand how things developed the way they did and how they might be different. One reads past political theories "not because they are familiar and therefore confirmative, but because they are strange and therefore provocative" (Wolin 1969: 1077). Wolin's historical scholarship, and that of his students, is careful and accurate, but its main purpose is to get us in the habit of looking for new

vantage points on the present. Unlike, say, Leo Strauss, who reads classical
political philosophers because they "see the political things with a freshness
and directness which have never been equaled" (Strauss 1988: 27), Wolin
reads classical philosophers to explore "the way in which new theoretical
vistas are opened" (Wolin 1969: 1077). In the 1960s, Sheldon Wolin and Leo
Strauss had a heated exchange in the *American Political Science Review*. With
the benefit of hindsight, we can appreciate that they were both trying to protect
a style of political thinking, rooted in the past but with an eye to the present, at
risk of being supplanted by behavioralist positivism (Barber 2006).

One of Sheldon Wolin's graduate students, Wendy Brown, makes a persuasive case for how the vocation of political theory has changed in recent
years. Political theorists today confront a series of new developments: a world
that is increasingly interconnected because of the Internet and the ease and
relative cheapness of international travel, communication, and commerce;
the investigation of political themes in other academic disciplines such as art
history, anthropology, rhetoric, geography, and literature; and the increasing
professionalization of political theory where rising scholars make their mark
in ever-shrinking research areas. In his 1969 article, Wolin invoked "epic
political theorists" who "inaugurate a new way of looking at the world, which
includes a new set of concepts, as well as new cognitive and normative standards" (Wolin 1969: 1078). In her 2002 *Political Theory* article, "At the Edge,"
Brown in a similar spirit calls for political theorists to engage in "deliberate
and careful transgression, risk, and interdisciplinary adventurousness" (Brown
2002: 570). For Brown, political theorists need to take stock of the most
important developments in recent world history, including the expansion of
economic ways of thinking to traditionally noneconomic aspects of life, a trend
often called "neoliberalism." She also reminds political theorists that their
vocation is to imagine how things could be, not just represent how they are.
"Theory is never 'accurate' or 'wrong'; it is only more or less illuminating,
more or less provocative, more or less of an incitement to thought, imagination, desire, possibilities for renewal" (Brown 2002: 574). In a similar vein,
Jeffrey C. Isaac worries that focusing on methodological rigor drains political
science of "intellectual vitality" and "the willingness to take intellectual risks
in the name of being interesting" (Isaac 2015: 276).

Political theorists are responsible for lecturing on certain books, but doing
political theory well means attuning oneself to the time and place in which
one lives. This can mean going for walks in the neighborhood, talking with
friends, being careful about one's diet and physical exercise routine, going to
museums and concerts, and doing other activities that the Jesuits call "spiritual
exercises" and Michel Foucault called "techniques of the self." Teaching political theory does not just mean lecturing on books to students; it also entails

showing students how to cultivate oneself in such a way that one may think deeply about politics.

KINDS OF POLITICAL THEORY

One way to access the ocean currents of politics is to read profound political thinkers. One way to differentiate kinds of political theories is to consider how they read canonical texts.

Contextual Studies

When I teach an author, I begin my lectures by giving a short biography of the author and say a little about the time and place in which they lived. One reason I do this is because it helps make the argument come alive if you can visualize the person who wrote the book at hand. Another is because you cannot make sense of an author unless you know what problems in the academy and the world they were addressing when they wrote. When teaching American political thought, for instance, students should learn that Alexander Hamilton and James Madison were concerned about extra-constitutional direct action such as Shays' Rebellion in Massachusetts and the Whiskey Rebellion in Pennsylvania (Wilson 2021). Without this knowledge, students may not realize why Publius favored republicanism, or rule by representatives, over direct democracy.

Cambridge historian Quentin Skinner has made a powerful case that you need to situate a book in its historical context to understand its meaning. "Any statement…is inescapably the embodiment of a particular intention on a particular occasion, addressed to the solution of a particular problem" (Skinner 2002: 88). To make sense of a text, you must know something about the context in which the author wrote. What were the raging intellectual and political debates at the time? Who else was writing on the topic in that milieu and what were they saying? What did the author intend to do with their text? Arguments are time bound, and scholars should not infer meanings that are simply not there. Better, Skinner counsels, for us to understand authors in their time and then think for ourselves in our time. Though Skinner disavows the term "the Cambridge school," it is the common term to describe a method of "locating texts in their precise historical context" (Charette and Skjönsberg 2020). The Cambridge school has performed a valuable service in explaining the relationship between text and context in work by Machiavelli, Thomas Hobbes, John Locke, Immanuel Kant, and more recently, twentieth-century Black intellectuals thinking about nation building and worldmaking after colonialism (Getachew 2020).

Although I appreciate contextual scholarship in the history of political thought, I am, in the words of Michael Frazer, "a presentist," somebody who reads and teaches intellectual history to better contribute to ongoing political debates (Frazer 2019). In Chapter 3, for instance, I discuss how teaching Machiavelli alongside Han Feizi illuminates a realist strand in political thinking that flows beneath both the Italian Renaissance and the Warring States period. This method sacrifices a deep investigation of how Machiavelli and Han Feizi were in conversation with their contemporaries, but I believe it pays dividends in shedding light on the deepest currents of contemporary U.S. and Chinese politics.

The Straussian History of Political Philosophy

What defines the context in which a writer thinks? For Skinner and other members of the Cambridge school, the answer is often the author's immediate milieu. Skinner is right that one gains insight into *The Prince* if one compares it to other mirror-for-princes tracts written during the Italian Renaissance. On the other hand, Machiavelli conducts a conversation with many Greek and Latin authors, some of whom he cites such as Livy and Xenophon, as well as others whom he does not cite but seems to have in mind such as Plato and Aristotle. For Leo Strauss and his disciples, political philosophers should read, teach, and write about the giants of political philosophy and their most important books.

Leo Strauss explains his thinking in his book, *Thoughts on Machiavelli*: "One cannot see the true character of Machiavelli's thought unless one frees himself from Machiavelli's influence. For all practical purposes this means that one cannot see the true character of Machiavelli's thought unless one recovers for himself and in himself the pre-modern heritage of the western world, both Biblical and classical" (Strauss 1995b: 12). When I teach a course on modern political thought, I often start with Paul's *Letter to the Romans* for students to appreciate what is blasphemous in Machiavelli's discussion of the soul and God. I also explain Plato and Aristotle's defense of the philosophical life to bring out the shock factor in Machiavelli's statement that "in this world there are none but the vulgar." Given the time constraints professors face in a course, I side with Strauss that the priority should be to assign and stage conversations between profound political thinkers across human history. For all my Straussian proclivities as a teacher, however, Adrian Blau has identified limits to Strauss's readings in the history of political thought, including drawing conclusions with insufficient evidence, dismissing alternate explanations, and constructing fanciful esoteric interpretations that rely on dubious techniques such as counting names and numbers and looking in the middle of texts and chapters (Blau 2012, 2019). I also think that Strauss attributes too much world-historical power to great books and not enough to, for example, inventions such as the printing press and the pamphlets they made possible (Trueman 2021).

Comparative Political Theory

Like many political theorists nowadays, I recognize that it is important to teach authors, books, and perspectives from across the world. In the lead article for the journal *Comparative Political Theory*, which I presently co-edit, Michael Freeden explains why it is valuable to do this:

> Mecca, Moscow, Mogadishu, Manila, Mexico City, or Montreal all offer comparative insights on matters relating to, say, lending or withholding support for political collectivities. Monarchs, mayors, chieftains, generals, parliamentarians, and trade union heads offer comparative instances of leadership practices that shed light on the intricacy of decision-making procedures embraced by discrete communities. (Freeden 2021: 4)

Political theorists can, Freeden concedes, study historically marginalized groups because of a sense of outrage or an attempt to redress historical wrongs. But this approach almost makes the texts props for our own moral outrage at, say, British imperialism and its aftermath. Far better, Freeden maintains, to read these texts because of the wisdom they contain about matters of perhaps universal concern about the sources of legitimacy or the nature of political leaders. Leo Strauss once remarked that "it is merely an unfortunate necessity which prevents us from listening to the greatest minds of India and China" (Strauss 1995a: 7). Political theorists arguably from the start of the tradition have traveled to other parts of the world to see how they do things (Euben 2008; March 2009); translations, exchange programs, and scholarship have now made it easier for political theorists to access the thoughts of people in other times and places. In several chapters of this book, I elucidate what North Atlantic political theorists gain by reading William Apess, Han Feizi, Zhuangzi, Gandhi, Savarkar, and other authors who are not (yet) at the center of the canon. The goal is not to shame students into learning subaltern perspectives; it is to invite them to read authors who provide alternate accounts of the ocean flows of politics.

Timely Interventions

In his famous 1837 speech, "The American Scholar," Ralph Waldo Emerson counsels scholars to put down their books and be attentive to what is happening in the world right now, in science, politics, art, and so forth. Emerson thinks it is fine to study the great thinkers of the past, but it is not proper to worship statues. Scholars may read Cicero, Bacon, and Locke, but they should emulate, not regurgitate, them. "Books are for the scholar's idle times. When he can read God directly, the hour is too precious to be wasted in other men's transcripts of their readings." Emerson counsels scholars to live in the world and not just the library: "Life lies behind us as the quarry from whence we get tiles and copestones for the masonry of today" (Emerson 1983: 58, 62). Emerson calls for scholars to see things as they are and not through inherited lenses.

Jeffrey C. Isaac brings Emerson's counsel into political theory in his 1995 article, "The Strange Silence of Political Theory." Isaac opens his article by observing how few political theory articles in leading journals have addressed the 1989 democratic revolutions in Central Europe. For Isaac, this "strange silence" is an indictment of the professionalization of academic political theory. Too many theorists, on Isaac's account, focus on trendy and arcane topics and authors rather than fulfilling their mission of being what Emerson called "the world's eye." Isaac enjoins political theorists to stop navel gazing and start explaining and offering guidance about how to navigate current events that "present serious choices regarding moral responsibility, political membership, and constitutional foundations" (Isaac 1995: 649).

I appreciate Isaac's reminder about the importance of political theorists doing timely work. I often lecture for a few classes on an author and then have students present research papers on what the author would say about a current event. The purpose of my classes is not just to have students plumb the ocean depths of politics—though I do think that students appreciate getting insight into what has shaped the environment in which they live. I also want students to see why political theory matters, how Xunzi's view of the ruler needing to steam flat the crooked wood of his subjects, for instance, illuminates what Chinese leaders may be thinking when they use big data and a social credit system to shape people into good subjects. That said, I agree with William E. Connolly that political theorists tend to do better work when they alternate between timely and untimely meditations—that is, when they sometimes contribute to a current policy debate and at other times study a more arcane subject of interest mostly to other scholars (Tampio 2016b).

A Pluralistic Approach

In this book, I advocate a conception of political theory that takes a pluralistic approach, which draws upon European, American, Chinese, and Indian intellectual traditions, which cites material inside and outside the text, and strives to accurately interpret authors and ideas but which ultimately cares about getting to the bottom of political things. What is the political vision that animates this pluralist approach to political theory? The short answer is that it strives to express what the political theorist William E. Connolly has called the ethos of pluralization.

Pluralism is the notion that people tend to congregate into groups, and politics involves the ongoing collaboration of and conflict between groups. Connolly participates in a pluralist tradition that includes, in the twentieth century, political scientists such as Robert Dahl, Charles Lindblom, David Truman, and David Easton (Wenman 2015). Connolly also maintains that pluralist political theory tends to prioritize groups that are currently in existence rather than welcome new constituencies as they cross the threshold of public recognition. Therefore, the ethos of pluralization aims to "translate the pluralist appreciation of established diversity into active cultivation of generosity to contemporary movements of pluralization" (Connolly 1995: xv). In this book, I strive to exercise an ethos of pluralization that reaches out to constituencies that have not held center stage in Euro-American academic political theory.

Pluralists disagree with each other about politics, philosophy, pedagogy, and all sorts of other topics. Pluralism as such will resolve few difficulties. However, pluralists do tend to agree that no one philosophical or religious school has a monopoly on truth, that no political faction ought to hold unchecked power, and that pluralism tends to support liberal democracy, or the notion that majorities should rule while minorities have the right to dissent. As the book proceeds, I will sympathetically portray many schools of thought that are not pluralistic. In my political vision, I want to create room for many groups that will not be able to attain their deepest strivings; from their perspective, my political theory is intolerant of what they deem most essential. Liberalism is historically and conceptually tied to skepticism, and to some of its religious and philosophical opponents, liberalism is a skepticism that hides its dogmatism (Strauss 1959: 390). I concede Strauss's point: I do not present the truth as lived by Confucians, medieval Christian theologians, Islamic political philosophers, or other existential faiths. I am interested in the question of how different traditions can help us make sense of the deepest flows of politics, animated by the conviction that the emerging global order requires cooperation and mutual respect among these traditions. There will still be debates and conflicts; there will still be politics.

* * *

No one researcher or teacher can meaningfully use every approach to political theory. I will mention two that I respect but do not often use in my own research or teaching.

Analytic Political Philosophy

According to its adherents, analytic philosophy uses reason, method, and science to explore a reality that exists independent of human knowledge of it. Continental philosophy, on the other hand, is skeptical of science's claims to objective knowledge; orients itself by Romantic thinkers such as Rousseau and Herder; shares Kierkegaard and Nietzsche's wariness of systematic thinking; and maintains that philosophy is entwined with religion, culture, and politics (Pettit 2017: 5). Continental and analytic political theory differ in how they envision the relationship between philosophy and history and whether philosophy is more of a humanities or natural science discipline. Continental theory treats "social and political philosophy as a historically situated practice of reasoning," while analytic theory "rarely engages in any depth with historical approaches to the history of political ideas" (Owen 2016: 8). Continental theory is more like the history of art, dominated by classic figures, and analytic theory aspires to be like a natural science, making steady progress over time (Harman 2017).

In this book, I cite articles in top political science and political theory journals, but I rarely cite articles in political philosophy journals such as *Ethics*, *The Journal of Political Philosophy*, and *Philosophy & Public Affairs*. I use a few of the methods deployed in analytic political theory—including comparative political thought and interpreting texts—but I do not use, or teach, positive political theory, rational choice theory, or "wacky" thought experiments that clarify our normative principles (Brownlee and Stemplowska 2017; List and Valentini 2016). "Academia works best when we study what we love and there is rigorous and robust discussion of whether there are gaps or under-emphases in our collective focus" (Blau 2017a: 14). I agree. Political theory students should learn from academics with different loves and specialties, including those not discussed in this book.

Political Theory in an Ethnographic Key

According to Matthew Longo and Bernardo Zacka, comparative political theory can provide a fresh vantage point on political phenomena; enrich our political thinking by introducing us to new values, concepts, and meanings; and alert us to harms that our categories may have on other people in the world. I agree with all of that. They add the stipulation—familiar from other methodological statements about comparative political theory (Godrej 2009; Jenco 2014)—that scholars must "attain proximity with the subjects of study, paying close attention to details—someone's posture, the placement of furniture, their choice of words—with the presumption that such details are meaningful, and their meaning depends on context" (Longo and Zacka 2019: 1067).

I am grateful to learn from area specialists who master other intellectual traditions from the inside. But, as a professor and a parent with responsibilities to raise my children, I cannot realistically do ethnographic political theory, nor do I understand why I would want to discipline myself by another tradition (March 2015) or adopt methods that have been "either abandoned or fiercely disputed *within* the Confucian context" (Jin 2021: 18; original emphasis). Theorists may travel to other countries, through texts or in person, but making the entry cost to another tradition too high makes it inaccessible to all but a few (privileged) scholars. I would rather teach foreign political theorists as best I can with translations and the help of secondary literature.

* * *

In an essay categorizing approaches to the history of political thought, Adrian Blau argues that methodological boxes "constrain our ability to think freely about how we do and should interpret texts" (Blau 2021: 114). I agree. If I wrote this book five years ago, or revise it in the future, it would be a different book; political theory is a living discipline alert to the dangers and possibilities of its time. Political theorists share an abiding concern about getting to the roots, the bottom of things, the ocean currents, whatever metaphor you like for the most profound things in political life. The book succeeds if it entices more people to study, do, and teach political theory.

NOTES

1. W. E. B. Du Bois succeeded in having one foot in the empirical social sciences and one foot in political theory. He collected and studied quantitative and qualitative data, and he anticipated earlier than many political scientists the utility of using data visualization techniques to convey statistical findings to academic and popular audiences (Gordon-Reed 2021; Kastellec and Leoni 2007). Du Bois also recognized that evidence by itself would not answer important questions about how to achieve a more just, egalitarian world.

2. Ella Baker argued for a conception of philosophy that recognizes that organizers advance "self-conscious theories of how society works and changes" (Inouye 2022: 533). On the one hand, theorists should have a wide conception of who to read and teach for insights on the ocean flows of politics. On the other, the term *philosophy* carries baggage, and sometimes it does not make sense to burden other thinkers with that baggage (Tampio 2016a).

3. Andrew Rehfeld makes an "offensive" argument that political theory should either do falsifiable social science or leave political science: "Humanistic research, like dermatology or music theory, is not political science and as such should find another home" (Rehfeld 2010: 465). Ross Corbett replies that Plato and Aristotle discussed music in their political works because "styles of music affect the passions, which in turn form the basis of education" and "political society relies on its members' having received a particular education" (Corbett 2011: 569). I agree with Corbett that political science benefits from having

people who specialize in things like the pedagogical effects of music and gymnastics.

4.   In his article, "Political Science is a Data Science," Jeff Gill observes that governments are using big data to monitor and control the population, but "I hope that this is a temporary trend and that people around the world can keep some control over their data as challenging world events unfold" (Gill 2021: 1). From whence comes this hope? Why should people be concerned about things like individual liberty or privacy? No matter how much political science becomes a data science, it still needs a place for people who work on normative ("should") questions.

REFERENCES

Barber, B. (2006), "The Politics of Political Science: 'Value-Free' Theory and the Wolin–Strauss Dust-Up of 1963," *American Political Science Review*, **100** (4), 539–45.

Behl, N. (2022), "Situated Citizenship: A Theoretical and Methodological Intervention," *Comparative Political Theory*, **2** (1), 21–30.

Blau, A. (2012), "Anti-Strauss," *The Journal of Politics*, **74** (1), 142–55.

Blau, A. (2017a), "Introduction: A 'How-to' Approach," in A. Blau (ed.), *Methods in Analytical Political Theory*, New York: Cambridge University Press, pp. 1–17.

Blau, A. (ed.) (2017b), *Methods in Analytical Political Theory*, New York: Cambridge University Press.

Blau, A. (2019), "Review: *Hobbes's Kingdom of Light: A Study of the Foundations of Modern Political Philosophy*," *Notre Dame Philosophical Reviews*, 20 May.

Blau, A. (2021), "How Should We Categorize Approaches to the History of Political Thought?," *Review of Politics*, **83** (1), 91–114.

Box-Steffensmeier, J., V. Sinclair-Chapman and D. P. Christenson (2021), "Promoting Pluralism: 2021 APSA Annual Meeting Theme Statement," *Apsanet*, accessed January 12, 2021 at https://connect.apsanet.org/apsa2021/theme-statement/.

Brown, W. (2002), "At the Edge," *Political Theory*, **30** (4), 556–76.

Brownlee, K. and Z. Stemplowska (2017), "Thought Experiments," in A. Blau (ed.), *Methods in Analytical Political Theory*, New York: Cambridge University Press, pp. 21–45.

Camerer, C. F., A. Dreber and F. Holzmeister et al. (2018), "Evaluating the Replicability of Social Science Experiments in *Nature* and *Science* between 2010 and 2015," *Nature Human Behaviour*, **2** (9), 637–44.

Cane, L. (2016), "Sheldon Wolin, *Politics and Vision*," in J. T. Levy (ed.), *The Oxford Handbook of Classics in Contemporary Political Theory*, Oxford: Oxford University Press, accessed April 8, 2020 at https://doi.org/10.1093/oxfordhb/9780198717133 .013.41.

Charette, D. and M. Skjönsberg (2020), "State of the Field: The History of Political Thought," *History*, **105** (366), 470–83.

Coles, R. (2001), "*Traditio*: Feminists of Color and the Torn Virtues of Democratic Engagement," *Political Theory*, **29** (4), 488–516.

Connolly, W. E. (1995), *The Ethos of Pluralization*, Minneapolis, MN: University of Minnesota Press.

Corbett, R. J. (2011), "Political Theory within Political Science," *PS: Political Science & Politics*, **44** (3), 565–70.

Emerson, R. W. (1983), "The American Scholar," in R. W. Emerson, *Emerson: Essays & Lectures*, ed. J. Porte, New York: Library of America, pp. 51–72.

Euben, R. L. (2008), *Journeys to the Other Shore*, Princeton, NJ: Princeton University Press.

Frazer, M. L. (2019), "The Ethics of Interpretation in Political Theory and Intellectual History," *The Review of Politics*, **81** (1), 77–99.

Freeden, M. (2021), "Comparative Political Thought: What Are We Looking At?," *Comparative Political Theory*, **1** (1), 3–7.

Getachew, A. (2020), *Worldmaking After Empire: The Rise and Fall of Self-Determination*, Princeton, NJ: Princeton University Press.

Gill, J. (2021), "Political Science is a Data Science," *The Journal of Politics*, **83** (1), 1–7.

Godrej, F. (2009), "Towards a Cosmopolitan Political Thought: The Hermeneutics of Interpreting the Other," *Polity*, **41** (2), 135–65.

Goodin, R. (2017), "How to Write Analytical Political Theory," in A. Blau (ed.), *Methods in Analytical Political Theory*, New York: Cambridge University Press, pp. 18–20.

Gordon-Reed, A. (2021), "The Color Line," *The New York Review of Books*, **68** (13), 26–8, August 19.

Grossmann, M. (2021), *How Social Science Got Better: Overcoming Bias with More Evidence, Diversity, and Self-Reflection*, New York: Oxford University Press.

Gunnell, J. G. (1988), "American Political Science, Liberalism, and the Invention of Political Theory," *American Political Science Review*, **82** (1), 71–87.

Harman, G. (2017), "The Enduring Importance of the Analytic/Continental Split," *Gavagai*, No. 3, 160–62.

Hohn, D. (2011), *Moby-Duck: The True Story of 28,800 Bath Toys Lost at Sea & of the Beachcombers, Oceanographers, Environmentalists & Fools Including the Author Who Went in Search of Them*, New York: Penguin.

Inouye, M. (2022), "Starting with People Where They Are: Ella Baker's Theory of Political Organizing," *American Political Science Review*, **116** (2), 533–46.

Isaac, J. C. (1995), "The Strange Silence of Political Theory," *Political Theory*, **23** (4), 636–52.

Isaac, J. C. (2015), "For a More Public Political Science," *Perspectives on Politics*, **13** (2), 269–83.

Jenco, L. K. (2014), "Histories of Thought and Comparative Political Theory: The Curious Thesis of 'Chinese Origins for Western Knowledge,' 1860–1895," *Political Theory*, **42** (6), 658–81.

Jin, Y. (2021), "What Confucianism and for Whom? The Value and Dilemma of Invoking Confucianism in Confucian Political Theories," *The Journal of Value Inquiry*, 1–21, accessed December 2, 2021 at https://doi.org/10.1007/s10790-021 -09858-2.

Johnson, J. (2021), "Models-As-Fables: An Alternative to the Standard Rationale for Using Formal Models in Political Science," *Perspectives on Politics*, **19** (3), 874–89.

Kastellec, J. P. and E. L. Leoni (2007), "Using Graphs Instead of Tables in Political Science," *Perspectives on Politics*, **5** (4), 755–71.

King, G. (2014), "Restructuring the Social Sciences: Reflections from Harvard's Institute for Quantitative Social Science," *PS: Political Science and Politics*, **47** (1), 165–72.

King, G., R. O. Keohane and S. Verba (1994), *Designing Social Inquiry: Scientific Inference in Qualitative Research*, Princeton, NJ: Princeton University Press.

King, G., J. Pan and M. E. Roberts (2017), "How the Chinese Government Fabricates Social Media Posts for Strategic Distraction, Not Engaged Argument," *American Political Science Review*, **111** (3), 484–501.

List, C. and L. Valentini (2016), "The Methodology of Political Theory," in H. Cappelen, T. Szabó Gendler and J. Hawthorne (eds), *The Oxford Handbook of Philosophical Methodology*, Oxford: Oxford University Press, pp. 525–53.

Longo, M. and B. Zacka (2019), "Political Theory in an Ethnographic Key," *American Political Science Review*, **113** (4), 1066–70.

March, A. F. (2009), "What is Comparative Political Theory?," *The Review of Politics*, **71** (4), 531–65.

March, A. F. (2015), "On the Will to Be Disciplined: Response to Jenco," *Political Theory*, **43** (2), 234–41.

Mayville, L. (2018), *John Adams and the Fear of American Oligarchy*, Princeton, NJ: Princeton University Press.

Monroe, K. R. (2018), "The Rush to Transparency: DA-RT and the Potential Dangers for Qualitative Research," *Perspectives on Politics*, **16** (1), 141–8.

Moore, M. (2010), "Political Theory Today: Results of a National Survey," *PS: Political Science & Politics*, **43** (2), 265–72.

Oakeshott, M. (1991), *Rationalism in Politics and Other Essays*, Indianapolis, IN: Liberty Fund.

Oprea, A. (2020), "Pluralism in Political Philosophy: A Reply to Dowding and Walsh," *Australian Journal of Political Science*, **55** (4), 456–62.

Owen, D. (2016), "Reasons and Practices of Reasoning: On the Analytic/Continental Distinction in Political Philosophy," *European Journal of Political Theory*, **15** (2), 172–88.

Pettit, P. (2017), "Analytical Philosophy," in R. E. Goodin, P. Pettit and T. Pogge (eds), *A Companion to Contemporary Political Philosophy* (2nd edition), Chichester: John Wiley & Sons, pp. 1–35.

Polanyi, M. (2009), *The Tacit Dimension*, Chicago, IL: University of Chicago Press.

Rehfeld, A. (2010), "Offensive Political Theory," *Perspectives on Politics*, **8** (2), 465–86.

Rollo, T. (2021), "Back to the Rough Ground: Textual, Oral and Enactive Meaning in Comparative Political Theory," *European Journal of Political Theory*, **20** (3), 379–97.

Shklar, J. N. (2019), "Why Teach Political Theory?," in S. Ashenden and A. Hess (eds), *On Political Obligation*, New Haven, CT: Yale University Press, pp. 213–19.

Silberzahn, R., E. L. Uhlmann and D. P. Martin et al. (2018), "Many Analysts, One Data Set: Making Transparent How Variations in Analytic Choices Affect Results," *Advances in Methods and Practices in Psychological Science*, **1** (3), 337–56.

Skinner, Q. (2002), *Visions of Politics: Regarding Method: Volume 1*, New York: Cambridge University Press.

Smith, R. M. (2020), "What Good Can Political Science Do? From Pluralism to Partnerships," *Perspectives on Politics*, **18** (1), 10–26.

Strauss, L. (1959), "The Liberalism of Classical Political Philosophy," *The Review of Metaphysics*, **12** (3), 390–439.

Strauss, L. (1988), *What Is Political Philosophy? And Other Studies*, Chicago, IL: University of Chicago Press.

Strauss, L. (1995a), *Liberalism Ancient and Modern*, Chicago, IL: University of Chicago Press.

Strauss, L. (1995b), *Thoughts on Machiavelli*, Chicago, IL: University of Chicago Press.

Tampio, N. (2016a), "Not All Things Wise and Good Are Philosophy," *Aeon*, September 13, accessed October 4, 2021 at https://aeon.co/ideas/not-all-things-wise -and-good-are-philosophy.

Tampio, N. (2016b), "Political Theory and the Untimely," *Political Theory*, 1–7, accessed April 13, 2020 at https://journals.sagepub.com/doi/pdf/10.1177/ 0090591716628624.

Tampio, N. (2021), "The Misguided Quest for a Constitutional Right to Education," *Phi Delta Kappan*, **102** (6), 50–55.

Thiele, L. P. (2018), *The Art and Craft of Political Theory*, New York: Routledge.

Thomas, M. C. (2010), "Orientalism and Comparative Political Theory," *The Review of Politics*, **72** (4), 653–77.

Thompson, D. F. (1976), "The Education of a Founding Father: The Reading List for John Witherspoon's Course in Political Theory, as Taken by James Madison," *Political Theory*, **4** (4), 523–9.

Trueman, C. R. (2021), "Lessons from the Reformation's Pamphlet War," *First Things*, November 4, accessed January 2, 2022 at https://www.firstthings.com/web -exclusives/2021/11/lessons-from-the-reformations-pamphlet-war.

Wenman, M. (2015), "William E. Connolly: Resuming the Pluralist Tradition in American Political Science," *Political Theory*, **43** (1), 54–79.

Wilson, J. L. (2021), "Constitutional Majoritarianism against Popular 'Regulation' in the *Federalist*," *Political Theory*, accessed January 30, 2022 at https://doi.org/10 .1177/00905917211043796.

Wolin, S. S. (1969), "Political Theory as a Vocation," *The American Political Science Review*, **63** (4), 1062–82.

PART I

Designing a political theory course

2. Crafting a syllabus, with illustrations from American political thought

INTRODUCTION

One of the joys and responsibilities of teaching a political theory course is deciding what to put on the syllabus. In a well-designed course, students learn about profound authors, texts, and ideas; gain the ability to read complicated texts; earn cultural capital; think more deeply about current events; participate in energetic debates about ideas and politics; and have fun. When teaching a topic as big as American political thought, the list of possible names and topics is too long to cover in a course, and growing.[1] The goal instead should be to teach students *how to think about* the subject (Germano and Nicholls 2020: 70). My course introduces students to the archive of American political thought that informs contemporary American political debates; nurtures the disposition to consider a political question from multiple points of view; and gives students confidence that they can pick up a classic or new text in American political theory and make sense of it.[2]

I tell students that it is not a history course per se, though I will mention dates and events to situate the conversation. Rather, I assign work to help them understand key authors, texts, ideas, and arguments from the past so that they may more thoughtfully contribute to conversations in their lifetime. In her 1990 American Political Science Association Presidential Address, "Redeeming American Political Theory," Judith Shklar says that "for the study of democratization few eras in American history are more revealing than the first four decades of the last century" (Shklar 1991: 8–9). I agree. In the early nineteenth century, political thinkers argued about what it means to be an American using language that still supports contemporary debates about immigration, naturalization, and education. I structure my American political thought course as a series of debates. By juxtaposing authors with different answers to the same question, you help students get in the habit of looking at political things from multiple angles. The chapter then identifies the main lessons I want students to take from reading the French aristocrat Alexis de Tocqueville, the Pequot Methodist minister William Apess, and the civil rights activists Frederick Douglass and Sojourner Truth. In a word, I want students to be critically responsive to constituencies that would like a larger role in the ever-evolving American identity (Connolly 1995). In conclusion, I suggest that as the pace of globalization continues to accelerate, teachers of nineteenth-century American political thought may want to assign more Mexican, Central American, South American, and Caribbean authors.

MAJOR AND MINOR AUTHORS ON THE READING LIST

I am, with caveats, a great books teacher. Leo Strauss wrote two essays in which he articulated how reading great books enriches the life of the individual and society (Taylor 2021). Political philosophy aims to gain a profound understanding of political affairs. Teachers and students, naturally, want to enlist the help of the deepest thinkers they can. It is a rare gift to meet such people in person. More frequently, students can only talk with them, as it were, through their writings. The task of a political theorist, then, is to teach "with the proper care the great books which the greatest minds have left behind" (Strauss 1989: 311–12). The greatest minds disagree with each other, and a good teacher will assign books to prompt students to forge their own combination of elements from diverse thinkers. "It is merely an unfortunate necessity which prevents us from listening to the greatest minds of India and of China" (Strauss 1989: 317). I read this line as leaving open the possibility that the great books tradition may encompass thinkers from around the world who write in different genres. It is a mistake to assume that assigning great books imparts a conservative political sensibility. Leftist political theorist Wendy Brown writes, "In academe, I'm the kind of conservative who loves the classics and believes the old and great books ought to be absolutely central in a college education" (Brown 1998). Students experience personal fulfillment, and are politically wiser, if they engage in a conversation, via print, with profound political thinkers. The canon ought to have porous and flexible borders that can incorporate, for example, formerly enslaved people such as Sojourner Truth who were never taught to read or write. Given that instructors and students are pressed for time, what principles should guide the selection of which texts to assign?

In my classes, I assign a mix of authors to inculcate the habit of looking at political questions from at least two angles. To envision this mix, think of a tradition as a circle of books, authors, ideas, arguments, and schools. The left side of the circle is drawn with a mostly solid line and is composed of authors, texts, and ideas that tend to reinforce the reigning order of ideas and policies. In American politics, these are the kinds of texts that are cited in official pronouncements by presidents, members of Congress, or Supreme Court justices: the Declaration of Independence, *The Federalist Papers*, Supreme Court decisions, political party platforms, and the like. These texts are central to the "public political culture" (Rawls 2005).

In any political order, there are elements that seek to change or escape the existing intellectual and political establishment. These are the authors that are on the right side of the circle with a perforated border. If major authors support those who currently hold power in society, minor authors "trigger uncontrollable movements and deterritorializations of the mean or majority" (Deleuze and Guattari 1987: 106). As a teacher, I often find that a course comes to life when we discuss authors who challenge the prevalent positions with which I begin a course. Minor authors challenge the status quo and break open the canon to new perspectives. The goal of assigning minor authors is not simply to expand the size of the majority but also to press students to seek out new voices about what America is and can become. What perspectives and ways of life are being silenced and oppressed in the current arrangement of forces? How can we generate a more vibrant pluralism if we create space for eccentrics—that is, individuals and groups who do not agree with people at the center of power?

Major and minor authors can both plumb the deepest political waters. The distinction is not between smarter and dumber or better and worse thinkers. The distinction is between those who affirm the current distribution of power and those who challenge it, though many thinkers combine both impulses (Honig 1993: 201). These terms are not permanently attached to authors: when African American thinkers such as Thurgood Marshall and Martin Luther King, Jr. led the civil rights movement in the 1950s and early 1960s, they were minor thinkers, but after the passage of the Civil Rights Act of 1964, the Voting Rights Act of 1965, and Marshall's ascension to the Supreme Court, they could be viewed as major thinkers ensconced in the heart of American political culture and law (Moak 2021). There is a difference between thinkers breaking the law and making the law. Nonetheless, political life often requires a balance between authors who want to conserve the political-intellectual regime and those who want to rearrange elements or pierce a country's walls (Mill 2003: 113). The major and minor distinction is mostly a heuristic for political theorists to teach authors that habituate students to think with and against common sense. A good class, I've found, introduces students to authors that confirm and challenge their ideological commitments.

In this chapter, I trace the thought process by which I assign authors for my course on American political thought. Most students identify as Democrat or Republican, and I assign texts to give students an understanding of the philosophical principles that flow beneath these two political parties. Politicians come and go, but political philosophies have a certain consistency that deserve scrutiny. College can be a perfect time for students to think about the deeper issues involved with being on the political left or the political right (see Box 2.1 for O'Shea's view on this). Students may also realize that political partisan identification can restrain thinking as well as support it. Identifying with a political party is like hanging onto a life preserver in the turbulent sea of politics. Theorists relinquish that life preserver when they dive deep into the political ocean.

When I teach American political thought, I begin the course by identifying a set of basic questions that we will ask each author:

- What are the problems facing the country?
- What does it mean to be an American?
- What are the principles of American politics?

Once we discern each author's answers to these questions, the class can then bring the authors into a conversation, where we imagine how the authors would go back and forth between each other. Finally, students present research papers on what each author would say about a current event, bringing themselves into the conversation.

BOX 2.1   HOW TO BRING YOUR POLITICS INTO THE CLASSROOM

Political theorists tend to choose this vocation because they care deeply about politics. Often, we have strong commitments to a political party, a movement, or even antipathy towards politics as such. One way or another, it is tempting to encourage, subtly and not so subtly, our students to agree with us.

In *Political Science Pedagogy*, the political theorist William Sokoloff recommends that theorists deploy a critical, radical, and utopian pedagogy. It is critical because it exposes the things that block a vibrant democracy. It is radical because it exposes the contingency of what many of us take for granted about our shared world. And it is utopian because it explores the possibility of a democratic future that includes "substantive equality, meaningful work, the abolition of prisons, the protection of our environment, universal health care, guaranteed housing, the end of imperialism, quality education for all and putting an end to the war machine" (Sokoloff 2020: 18).

Based on his descriptions of his classes and feedback from his students, I believe that students are lucky to have Sokoloff as a professor. That said, I think that professors should exercise restraint when presenting their own point of view in class. Even radically egalitarian professors are normally older and more credentialed than their students, and, most importantly, professors hold the power to give students grades.

On October 27, 2021, Tom O'Shea tweeted on why left-wing philosophers should teach conservative, libertarian, and right-wing thought. "I feel we need to look the right square in the face to beat those ideas, as well as inoculating some students against their seductions. And if it gets us down or pushes a few of them rightward, that's the price of intellectual autonomy" (O'Shea 2021). That is a great way to put it. As political theorists, we ought to teach the authors, books, traditions, themes, and so forth, that we love. Students can probably glean what we ourselves think, particularly if they check our social media feeds and public-facing writing. That said, we owe it to our students to present other sides of the issue in their strongest form so that they may freely choose for themselves. Political theory teachers should inculcate thoughtfulness—a habit of looking at things from multiple perspectives—rather than partisanship.

ALEXIS DE TOCQUEVILLE ON WHITE AMERICANS

Political theorists on the right and the left maintain that Tocqueville is a major political thinker (Tocqueville 2002: xvii; Wolin 2003: 4). Many social scientists, regardless of field, subfield, or political bent, mine *Democracy in America* for insights such as the role of civil associations in generating social bonds and political solidarity (Putnam 2000). Tocqueville is a common point of reference for many political scientists, theorists, and commentators. Tocqueville also makes a profound argument about how the Puritan legacy shaped the New England character that still influences certain American habits such as our egalitarianism, restlessness, and indifference to much European history, philosophy, and theology.

Tocqueville (1805–59) was a French aristocrat with an ambivalent relationship to democracy. He compared democracy to a raging river that could not be dammed: "one finds so to speak no great events in seven hundred years that have not turned to the profit of democracy" (Tocqueville 2002: 5). At the same time, Tocqueville thought that the French could learn lessons from America about how to steer a country towards democratic liberty rather than democratic tyranny, a political regime in which individual greatness could still shine through rather than be subsumed by mediocrity. Tocqueville's journey to America in 1831–32 generated a book that aimed "to instruct democracy," "purify its mores," and "to substitute little by little the science of affairs for its inexperience" (Tocqueville 2002: 7).

According to Tocqueville, American identity began when the Pilgrims landed at Plymouth Rock in 1620. "There is not one opinion, one habit, one law, I could say one event, that the point of departure does not explain without difficulty" (Tocqueville 2002: 29). What makes American identity different than European identities? The Pilgrims were political and religious dissidents, and they did not bring monarchy or aristocracy with them to America. They founded a religious-political order based on radical Protestantism and a kind of republicanism. The Constitution rejected titles of nobility, and the mores of the country became egalitarian. If the Spanish or French had landed on the coast of New England, the trajectory of the United States would have headed in a different direction. But they did not, and Tocqueville sees "the whole destiny of America contained in the first Puritan who landed on its shores" (Tocqueville 2002: 267).

An Irish friend in graduate school told me that in World War I, German snipers were told to shoot American officers, but they couldn't do it because all Americans walk like officers. I don't know if this story is true, but I tell my class that, even if it is not, it illustrates Tocqueville's point that Americans carry themselves differently than people do in hierarchical cultures. I also discuss how the rich barricade themselves off from the poor in this country— by flying in helicopters, for example—to illustrate Tocqueville's point that an industrial aristocracy could arise in the country and corrupt its egalitarian character.

The Pilgrims bequeathed the American identity a commitment to political participation nourished in the township. "In the heart of the township one sees a real, active, altogether democratic and republican political life reigning... Affairs that touch the interest of all are treated in the public square and within the general assembly of citizens, as in Athens" (Tocqueville 2002: 40). According to Tocqueville, democracy educates people to participate in politics. Democracy does not assume that human beings are smart; it assumes that, with exercise, they can grow their civic muscles.

Finally, Tocqueville argues that the Pilgrims founded American Christian *mores*, or habits of the heart and mind. For Tocqueville, Christian mores permeate American orientations to the family, work, and community. "All the sects in the United States are within the great Christian unity, and all the morality of Christianity is everywhere the same" (Tocqueville 2002: 278). This class gives us an opportunity to discuss whether Tocqueville's thesis about widespread Christian mores in America still applies or should apply (Connolly 1995).

Tocqueville's ideal American is white, a New Englander, a man, a newspaper reader, an active citizen, business minded, restless, and with Protestant mores. Tocqueville also offers insight into slave-owning whites who disdain work and like to hunt, the kind of men who brought Andrew Jackson to the presidency and who still exert power in American politics (Glasser 2018).

For years, I would teach Tocqueville's chapter on the "three races" that inhabit the United States. I appreciate Tocqueville scholars who identify minor notes in his major text, such as his critique of American racism and colonialism (Ikuta and Latimer 2021; McQueen and Hendrix 2017; Tillery

2018). Tocqueville condemned the English colony in Jamestown for bringing slavery to the colonies and thereby introducing "idleness into society, and with it, ignorance and haughtiness, poverty and luxury" (Tocqueville 2002: 31). Tocqueville's America is primarily an idealized picture of New England, but he still acknowledges the lasting effects of the American slave trade that began in 1619. Nowadays, I prefer to teach Native American and African American authors on the topic of American identity (Ferguson 2016).

WILLIAM APESS ON NATIVE AMERICANS

There is a certain logic to determining what minor authors to read. Minor political theorists are at the margins of the canon. At the same time, if you assign somebody that few people have heard of, you risk having a conversation by yourself. Ideally, you want to teach minor authors who have one foot in the mainstream tradition, or who other political theorists are already engaging with in productive ways. Recently, there has been a spate of first-rate work on the Native American author William Apess (1798–1839) (Connolly 1995: 194–229; Dahl 2016; Hendrix 2011; Hirsch 2017). Reading Apess is important for understanding the situation of Native Americans in the early nineteenth century, but I primarily teach the text to press my students to think about how we ought to listen to those harmed by policies we support or go along with now.

In *A Son of the Forest*, Apess tells his story. "My grandfather was a white man and married a female attached to the royal family of Philip, king of the Pequot tribe of Indians" (Apess 1992: 3). Apess presents himself as a Native American, a descendant of one of the most famous and feared Native American leaders in early American history, and an adopted member of the Mashpee tribe whom he led in their efforts to nullify a Massachusetts law governing the tribe. Here is one place where he explains the proper terms to describe his people: "I know of nothing so trying to a child as to be repeatedly called by an improper name. I thought it disgraceful to be called an Indian; it was considered as a slur upon an oppressed and scattered nation… The proper term which ought to be applied to our nation, to distinguish it from the rest of the human family, is that of '*Natives*'" (Apess 1992: 10; original emphasis). Apess also had white ancestors, served as a Methodist minister, wrote in the modern genre of the autobiography, and dressed in a suit rather than Native American clothing while delivering his famous "Eulogy on King Philip" in the Odeon Theater in Boston in 1836. Apess's life is a rebuke to Tocqueville's view that Indians are a noble race whose pride prevents them from adjusting to the modern world.

Apess, like Tocqueville, thinks that the Pilgrims hold the key to American identity, but he tells the story from the perspective of the Natives. When the

Pilgrims arrived on American shores, they were cold, hungry, and at risk of death unless the Native Americans helped them, which they did. "Had it not been for this humane act of the Indians [in 1622], every white man would have been swept from the New England colonies" (Apess 1992: 280). In response to this kindness, Apess documents, the Pilgrims committed acts of treachery and violence against the Natives, including terrorizing women and children at night and extorting rent from the people who once owned the land and sold it to them for a pittance. The "Eulogy on King Philip" brings tears to your eyes.

Part of what makes Apess interesting is his complex relationship with European/American culture. Apess thanks the white people who helped raise him when his parents abused and neglected him, becomes a Christian and is grateful for Christians who are indifferent to skin color, and asserts that Natives deserve to govern themselves because of republican principles. When his mother broke his arm in an alcohol-fueled rage, he was taken in by their neighbors, the Furmans. "Mrs. Furman was a kind, benevolent, and tenderhearted lady—from her I received the best possible care" (Apess 1992: 6). Apess describes what it was like to attend a Methodist meeting: "I felt convinced that Christ died for all mankind—that age, sect, color, country or situation made no difference. I felt an assurance that I was included in the plan of redemption with all my brethren" (Apess 1992: 19). Apess opens his book on Indian nullification by comparing the Mashpees stopping people from taking wood from their land to America's Founding Fathers who "threw the tea overboard" (Apess 1992: 167). Later Indigenous resistance movements would not ask for recognition by white people in this way (Coulthard 2014).

Apess also expresses frustration at whites who do not live up to their principles. He is furious at whites who gave the Natives rum rather than food and clothing (Apess 1992: 33). He accuses whites of being false Christians when they only worship with people of the same skin color, and his call for the Mashpees to secede from Massachusetts reminds Americans of what the colonists did when they broke away from England. He asks his readers to imagine all the races of humanity sitting before God. "Now suppose these skins were put together, and each skin had its national crimes written upon it—which skin do you think would have the greatest?" (Apess 1992: 157).

One could read Apess as wanting Native Americans to simply be assimilated into the American identity. The "Eulogy on King Philip" excoriates the Pilgrims for their words and deeds and seems to suggest that Native Americans, or those who remain, should go to war against Americans: "We want trumpets that sound like thunder, and men to act as though they were going at war with those corrupt and degrading principles that robs one of all rights, merely because he is ignorant and of a little different color" (Apess 1992: 307). However, the speech ends on a conciliatory note: "while you ask yourselves, 'What do they, the Indians, want?' you have only to look at the unjust laws made for them and say, 'They want what I want,' in order to make men of them, good and wholesome citizens" (Apess 1992: 307). *They want what I want.* Is Apess simply asking for whites to treat Natives as different-colored versions of themselves? No. Rather, in the words of Alexander Hirsch, William Apess is doing "Indigenous counter-actualization," retelling the story of America's past to open up a new future shaped by Native Americans (Hirsch 2017: 396). Apess, like later postcolonial and decolonial theorists, wants to address the wrongs of settler colonialism and envision new arrangements for Indigenous self-rule (Ivison 2002; Temin 2021; Tully 1995; Young 2000). White Americans want to govern themselves. The Natives want the same thing. The task now is to negotiate between these two competing desires to control the water, soil, and air, to rule a territory and make treaties with other powers, and to determine which mores deserve respect.

Is assigning Apess an example of decolonizing the curriculum? Eve Tuck and K. Wayne Yang criticize this kind of language because changing the authors on a syllabus does not change the reality of hundreds of years of settler colonialism. What they want is nothing less than "repatriation of Indigenous land and life" (Tuck and Yang 2012: 21). I do not see how this is possible.[3] Political theorists and political actors should, however, listen to Natives who want a greater say over control of their land and contribute to ongoing state and federal debates—for instance, over the use and protection of natural resources (Rose, Geroux and Ferguson 2020).[4] It is also important to read authors with the goal of envisioning alliances between people whose interests sometimes but don't always overlap, including Creoles and Blacks contesting the legacies of colonization and racialized slavery (Sealey 2020).

FREDERICK DOUGLASS ON BLACK AMERICANS

Tocqueville's America originates in Plymouth, Massachusetts in 1620. Journalists and scholars have rightly suggested that it is as important to date America's founding to the first sale of slaves in Jamestown, Virginia in 1619 (Hannah-Jones 2019). To think about the relationship between American identity and the fact and legacy of slavery, I assign Frederick Douglass's famous speech, "What to the Slave is the 4th of July?". Douglass (1818–95) overlapped in time and place with Tocqueville and Apess; political theorists are still writing about his work; and he remains a part of America's public political culture. Like Apess, Douglass spurs us to envision an American identity that includes, but also changes because of this inclusion, different races. Douglass is an American exceptionalist who believes that America has a distinct, perhaps providential, role in human history and global affairs; but he is also an *aspirational* exceptionalist who "espouses honest, bold, and sometimes biting critique" to prompt Americans to keep thinking about how best to live up to their ideals (Williams 2020: 375).

Douglass's life story was entangled with the arguments he made throughout his life about freedom (Bennett 2016). Douglass was born into slavery in Maryland; fought Edward Covey, a slave-breaker, nearly to the death; led the abolitionist movement in Massachusetts and New York; traveled to Ireland and Great Britain; befriended the radical abolitionists William Lloyd Garrison and John Brown; and wrote three autobiographies that, along with his speeches, have become "essential to the canon of African American and American political thought" (Shulman 2014: 959).

In his famous 1852 speech in Rochester, New York, Douglass starts from the center of the American political tradition, and then calls upon the listener or reader to move away from it without renouncing it entirely. In this respect, the speech is a model for how students can draw upon the archive of American political thought to contribute to current political debates.

Douglass opens the speech by praising his audience for celebrating the 4th of July and the ideals embedded in the Declaration of Independence. The 4th of July is "the birthday of your National Independence, and of your political freedom. This, to you, is what the Passover was to the emancipated people of God" (Douglass 2016: 50–51). The Declaration of Independence is "the very ringbolt in the chain of your yet undeveloped destiny... The principles contained in that instrument are saving principles. Stand by those principles, be true to them on all occasions, in all places, against all foes, at whatever cost" (Douglass 2016: 53). These sentences are rhetoric to move Douglass's largely white audience over to his side. Douglass is also advancing the Declaration of Independence's philosophical case for political equality (Allen 2014).

After praising American founding ideals, Douglass says that America fails to live up to them. "What, to the American slave, is your 4th of July? I answer; a day that reveals to him, more than all other days in the year, the gross injustice and cruelty to which he is the constant victim" (Douglass 2016: 60). Like Apess, Douglass asks that we look at American history from the perspective of those dispossessed, enslaved, tortured, or killed to generate wealth, institutions, mores, and cultural artifacts. For students doing presentations on Douglass, I might suggest that they look at the case for reparations or protests against police violence.

Douglass, like Apess, invokes republicanism and Christianity to change how people view and treat people of different races. Douglass criticizes the Fugitive Slave Act for paying judges to send slaves back to their owners: "Let it be thundered around the world that in tyrant-killing, king-hating, people-loving, democratic, Christian America the seats of justice are filled with judges who hold their offices under an open and palpable bribe" (Douglass 2016: 63). He criticizes Christians who do not protest this law: "I take this law to be one of the grossest infringements of Christian Liberty, and, if the churches and ministers of our country were not stupidly blind, or most wickedly indifferent, they, too, would so regard it" (Douglass 2016: 63). Ultimately, Douglass thinks that it is a waste of time to *argue* about the legitimacy or not of slavery: "There is not a man beneath the canopy of heaven that does not know that slavery is wrong for him" (Douglass 2016: 59).

Douglass recommends that his audience use the Constitution to advance the cause of creating a more egalitarian society. In his 1852 speech, Douglass argues that the Constitution can be read as a "liberty document." The document does not use the words *slavery*, *slave-holding*, or *slave*; instead, the preface and purpose of the Constitution in general is to spread the blessings of liberty to more and more people. Douglass holds that "every American citizen has a right to form an opinion of the Constitution, and to propagate that opinion, and to use all honorable means to make his opinion the prevailing one" (Douglass 2016: 69). Douglass does not think that slavery is in the country's DNA, that it constitutes America's original sin, or that it is somehow woven into the country's identity in ways that cannot be repaired moving forward. Rather, Douglass thinks that the Constitution can justify the cause of freedom for enslaved people—a prescient idea given how the Reconstruction amendments buttressed the egalitarian claims of African Americans.

As with Apess, Douglass can be read as an assimilationist, somebody who wants African Americans to fit into the American identity of Christian, republican, hard-working individualists.[5] One work where this theme rings loud is "Self-Made Men" (1894), one of Douglass's last speeches in which he enjoins African Americans to "WORK! WORK!! WORK!!! WORK!!!!" and white Americans to simply let African Americans do so. "The nearest approach to justice to the Negro for the past is to do him justice in the present. Throw open to him the doors of the schools, the factories, the workshops, and of all mechanical industries. For his own welfare, give him a chance to do whatever he can do well. If he fails, let him fail!" (Douglass 2016: 340, 341). Douglass here sounds like Booker T. Washington, who in his 1895 Atlanta Address advised African Americans to "cast down their bucket," to make the best of their situation as laborers until such point that other doors may open for their own children. Douglass, like his biographer Washington, knew that Black people needed to acquire wealth and power in white America if they ever hoped to overthrow Jim Crow (Jagmohan 2021).

One could also read Douglass as envisioning a new American identity that changes because of the inclusion of African Americans, as well as other races. It is to this possibility we now turn.

FREDERICK DOUGLASS ON CHINESE AMERICANS

While writing this chapter, David W. Blight, a historian at Yale, published an article in *The Atlantic* on Frederick Douglass's 1869 speech, "Our Composite Nationality." The timing was fortuitous, as the country was again confronting a wave of aggression towards Asian Americans. Theorists may teach Douglass to introduce students to an early debate about Chinese immigration; more importantly, we read this text because it gives us a language with which to oppose hostility towards ethnic minorities and envision a "pluralist utopia" (Blight 2019).

The proximate cause of Douglass's speech was the Burlingame Treaty, negotiated between the United States and China in 1868, in which the American government permitted Chinese immigration but denied Chinese the right to be naturalized as citizens. In his speech, Douglass considers the objection that white people own the continent and may reasonably prevent other races from entering their territory. Against this nativist sentiment, Douglass gives three responses:

- The first response is an appeal to the human right of migration. "I submit that this question of Chinese immigration should be settled upon higher principles than those of a cold and selfish expediency. There are such things in the world as human rights. They rest upon no conventional foundation, but are eternal, universal and indestructible" (Douglass 2016: 225).
- The second response is that Chinese immigrants are skilled workers and may contribute to the country's wealth. "Let the Chinaman come; he will help to augment the national wealth; he will help to develop our boundless resources; he will help to pay off our national debt; he will help to lighten the burden of our national taxation; he will give us the benefit of his skill as manufacturer and as a tiller of the soil, in which he is unsurpassed" (Douglass 2016: 230). Furthermore, Douglass suggests that the Chinese will eventually abandon their allegiance to their country of origin and become full-fledged Americans: "As to the superstitious attachment of the Chinese to China, that, like all other superstitions, will dissolve in the light and heat of truth and experience" (Douglass 2016: 221).
- The third response is that Americans should welcome the Chinese precisely because they have different beliefs and mores. Douglass considers the objection of people who want America to retain Christianity at the heart of its identity and do not want to welcome people with a different faith. He asks: "shall we send missionaries to the heathen and yet deny the heathen the right to come to us? I think a few honest believers in the teachings of Confucius would be well employed in expounding his doctrines among us" (Douglass 2016: 230). One reason that Douglass welcomes Confucians

is that religious diversity hinders the exercise of majority tyranny: "We should welcome all men of every shade of religious opinion, as among the best means of checking the arrogance and intolerance which are the almost inevitable concomitants of general conformity" (Douglass 2016: 230). In addition, "each race of men has some special faculty, some peculiar gift or quality of mind or heart, needed to the perfection and happiness of the whole" (Douglass 2016: 270). America flourishes, and becomes a great civilization, when it draws upon the talents of many kinds of people.

What is the difference between races? Douglass says that the Chinese "are industrious, docile, cleanly, frugal; they are dexterous of hand, patient in toil, marvelously gifted in the power of imitation, and have but few wants" (Douglass 2016: 223). One ought to be wary of attributing personality traits to another race; race can be a crude category to distinguish groups of people; and racial characteristics may reflect the condition of the people in a particular historical context. Still, what is exciting about this speech is that it expresses a "vision of a pluralist future of human equality in the recently re-United States" (Blight 2019). Douglass's America has room for Europeans, African Americans, and Chinese; it may also welcome people that Americans do not even know about yet. To fulfill the country's destiny, "we should welcome to our ample continent all the nations, kindreds, tongues, and peoples, and as fast as they learn our language and comprehend the duties of citizenship, we should incorporate them into the American body politic" (Douglass 2016: 228).

What will America look like with "all the nations, kindreds, tongues, and peoples" living in the same territory? What will be the politics, novels, food, churches, or games in a country with people from around the world? How will Americans balance the competing pulls of unity and diversity, order and freedom? Douglass's speech provides a launching pad for conversations about whether America should reclaim a past era of greatness or move confidently into a pluralist future.

SOJOURNER TRUTH ON RELIGIOUS AMERICANS

One cannot tell the history of the United States in the early nineteenth century without discussing slavery, and one cannot make sense of contemporary political discourse without understanding the concept of intersectionality. For both historical and contemporary reasons, it is vital to assign things about Sojourner Truth (1797–1883), the only formerly enslaved Black woman "with sufficient strength, poise, and self-confidence to become a public presence over the long term" (Painter 1997: 4). Sojourner Truth knew Frederick Douglass, and famously asked him when he called for violence to free enslaved people whether God was dead. Famed as an orator and itinerant preacher, she was not taught to read or write, which means that the only accounts we have of her are mediated by other people, including educated white women such as Harriet Beecher Stowe and Frances Dana Barker Gage (Painter 1997: 174). Be that as it may, Sojourner Truth's speech "Ain't I A Woman?"—although filled with inaccuracies such as a Southern dialect that Truth, raised speaking Dutch in New York, did not have—has entered the archive of American political thought as a powerful call for racial and gender equality. In *Sojourner Truth and Intersectionality*, Katrine Smiet also contends that this speech may contribute to contemporary discussions about the role of religion as an empowering force for social justice.

Sojourner Truth, according to Smiet, is rightly identified as a precursor to intersectional theorists who study the complex interplay between race, gender, and oppression. Smiet identifies this theme in the reception of Sojourner Truth in the work of queer feminist author bell hooks, womanist theologian Jacquelyn Grant, and feminist philosopher Donna Haraway. Though these readings have value, Smiet says, they downplay the religious themes in Truth's work. Secular feminists appreciate her critique of patriarchal Christianity, but they do not then recognize that her "faith not only *inspired* her to fight against injustices that she lived through in her own life and that she witnessed around her, it also provided her with *tools* to do so" (Smiet 2020: 88; original emphasis). Isabella Baumfree changed her name to "Sojourner Truth" because she felt that she was divinely called to travel around the country and preach (Smiet 2020: 88). According to her biographer Nell Irvin Painter, "Without doubt, it was Truth's religious faith that transformed her from Isabella, a domestic servant, into Sojourner Truth, a hero for three centuries—at least" (Painter 1997: 4). Modern feminists should recognize the religious dimension of Sojourner Truth's being and thinking.

With one's students, one can watch videos on the Internet of Black women such as Kerry Washington and Alfre Woodard reading Truth's famous speech. It only takes a few minutes of class time. Then, on the board, one can write down religious images that appear in the speech (Smiet 2020: 88). When Truth watched her children sold into slavery, she says, "I cried out with my mother's grief" and "none but Jesus heard me!" An audience member supposedly yelled out that Jesus was a man. Truth replied: "Where did your Christ come from? Where did your Christ come from? From God and a woman! Man had nothing to do with him!" She considers the objection that Eve turned the world upside down, and replies that shows that women have power indeed: "If the first woman God ever made was strong enough to turn the world upside down all alone, these women together ought to be able to turn it back, and get it right upside up again!" (Truth 2020: 3–4). These argumentative moves suggest that religious feminists may understand "religious traditions as sites *both* of oppression and of liberation" (Smiet 2020: 104; original emphasis). One can further complicate the narrative by discussing how Sojourner Truth's religious life included elements of animist West Africa, pagan Europe, the Calvinist Dutch Reformed Church, and the Arminian Methodists (Painter 1997: 24–5).

If my students and I are in the process of reconstructing the American identity, it matters that we read authors from different subject positions. It is important that Americans read Black women in the nineteenth century. Sojourner Truth is a resource for intersectional theorists. She also poses a challenge to secularists who insist that the public sphere be governed by the principles of public reason. In *Political Liberalism*, John Rawls permits religious discourse with the "proviso" that it can be translated into secular political terms. For Rawls, abolitionists in the antebellum South "could have seen their actions as the best way to bring about a well-ordered and just society in which the ideal of public reason could eventually be honored" (Rawls 2005: 250). This interpretation of the abolitionist movement does not fit Sojourner Truth's speech. I teach "Ain't I A Woman?" to spark conversations about whether modern secular political orders can and should bracket religiosity.

HEMISPHERIC AMERICAN POLITICAL THOUGHT

When I was an undergraduate, I spent a month in Costa Rica, and a man on the street of San José asked me where I was from. I told him America. He told me that he too was American. He was right: I was being parochial. In this chapter, I have focused on U.S. American political thought, but American political thought includes the work of people living in Mexico, the Caribbean, Central America, and South America. As somebody who has lived and worked most of his life on the Eastern seaboard of the United States, I tend to teach American political thinkers from the same region. However, I recognize that it is important, for political and intellectual reasons, to teach political thinkers from around the country. In an article on the "Republicans of Nacogdoches," Arturo Chang shows how Indigenous, Mestizo, and white actors on the Mexico–U.S. borderlands justified the founding of the Republic of Texas.

Chang's portrayal of the Republicans of Nacogdoches attends to their ideological code-switching. Republicans such as Jose Gutiérrez de Lara took a cue from U.S. Federalists such as James Madison and Alexander Hamilton that the novelty and justice of republican institutions justified independence from European powers—Spain in the case of Mexico. The Republicans of Nacogdoches "instrumentalized popular investments in Pan-American emancipation to involve Indigenous, Mestizo, Creole, and White actors in the pursuit of Mexican independence" (Chang 2021a). In documents such as *Address of Colonel Bernardo, to the Republican Volunteers at Nacogdoches* (1812), Gutiérrez called upon a transnational community of Americans to oppose Spanish authorities enslaving Mexicans in Texas. At the same time, the Republicans of Nacogdoches were calling for a new kind of colonialism or imperialism in which they would be the beneficiaries. Gutiérrez promises "mines of gold, silver, or what nature soever" to whoever joins his cause (Chang 2021a: 15). Trying to recruit U.S. Americans, Mexicans, Indigenous peoples, and Creoles, the Republicans of Nacogdoches used both anti- and neocolonial argumentative moves.

Chang is critical of the way the Republicans of Nacogdoches reproduced the hierarchies, extractive policies, racial subjection, and ethnic persecution of the colonial state. This ambivalence is seen in other scholars of American political thought who worry that theorists of *mestizaje* perpetuate racial hierarchy *within* Latin America (Hooker 2014); that the Creole elites who led the Latin American independence movements exploited and excluded Indigenous, African, and mixed-race populations (Simon 2017); and that the leaders of the Haitian Revolution espoused a society founded on universal racial equality but reproduced social inequalities to preserve the plantation system (Ravano 2021). Though there are scholars who appreciate Latin American contributions to political thought—including the notions of democratic Caesarism (Vacano 2012) and radical left populism, or Chavismo (Ciccariello-Maher 2020)—I have noticed that few political theorists do so without reservations. But you do not need to agree with authors to assign them.

We study political theory to gain a deeper understanding of political developments and envision better futures. People on both sides of the Rio Grande are thinking about how to better manage territories that fall within a single watershed (Espejo 2020). Policymakers and the public debate the right way to help Haiti after a natural disaster and respect its political autonomy. The United States is grappling with how to recognize the elections of Latin American countries such as Nicaragua and Venezuela and prevent those countries from abusing human rights and aligning with U.S. strategic competitors (Guillermoprieto 2021; Naim 2021). By assigning authors from Mexico, the Caribbean, Central America, or South America, political theorists are teaching students that they should take an expansive view of what it means to be an American and the sphere of American politics. We also demonstrate that political theorists may search for wisdom from people and traditions that "operate beyond the conventional parameters of Western archives and epistemologies" (Chang 2021b: 12).

NOTES

1.   In the fall of 2020, I invited students in my American intellectual history class at Cooper Union for the Advancement of Science and Art, New York to present on authors that we did not cover in the class but could have. Students gave excellent presentations on Hannah Arendt, Jason Brennan, Adrienne Maree Brown, Robert

Caro, Angela Davis, Emma Goldman, Pope John Paul II, Adrian Piper, Coco Schutz, Rebecca Solnit, Harriet Beecher Stowe, Jia Tolentino, Phyllis Wheatley, and Andrew Yang.

2. One of the best parts of teaching is hearing from former students. Here is a note I received while drafting this chapter:

> You really were the best professor I could have asked for at Fordham. I never truly enjoyed or looked forward to a class like I did political philosophy. I am very convinced the reason I succeeded in law school was because of the analytical skills I gained from two semesters of class with you!!

3. In the summer of 2020, my family visited Plimoth Plantation in Massachusetts and met a young woman who was studying the Native American language Wampanoag, who told us that the language had effectively disappeared though there were a few dozen people trying to recover knowledge of it.

4. Louise Erdrich, a member of the Turtle Mountain band of Chippewa, raises a series of questions that resemble Apess's in her novel, *The Night Watchman*. This passage describes the reflections of a man working with his tribe to oppose a congressional plan to terminate their rights to the land:

> Who was an Indian? What? Who, who, who? And how? How should being an Indian relate to this country that had conquered and was trying in every way possible to absorb them?… How could Indians hold themselves apart, when the vanquishers sometimes held their arms out, to crush them to their hearts, with something like love? (Erdrich 2020: 98)

5. Sharon R. Krause observes that for all of Douglass's celebration of heroic individuals, he still recognized that Black people needed certain social and political conditions to exercise agency, including suffrage, the rights to political office, public education, economic provisions, and a culture of equal respect and recognition (Krause 2020). Krause's essay exemplifies how political theorists may reconstruct the history of ideas to participate in contemporary debates—in this case, about whether the market or the government are the proper sites of Black freedom. For Krause's Douglass, the answer is both.

REFERENCES

Allen, D. S. (2014), *Our Declaration: A Reading of the Declaration of Independence in Defense of Equality*, New York: Liveright.

Apess, W. (1992), *On Our Own Ground: The Complete Writings of William Apess, a Pequot*, ed. B. O'Connell, Amherst, MA: University of Massachusetts Press.

Bennett, N. (2016), "To Narrate and Denounce: Frederick Douglass and the Politics of Personal Narrative," *Political Theory*, **44** (2), 240–64.

Blight, D. W. (2019), "Frederick Douglass's Vision for a Reborn America," *The Atlantic*, December.

Brown, W. (1998), "Left Conservatism, I," *Theory & Event*, **2** (2), accessed June 6, 2022 at http://muse.jhu.edu/article/32501.

Chang, A. (2021a), "Languages of Transnational Revolution: The 'Republicans of Nacogdoches' and Ideological Code-Switching in the U.S.–Mexico Borderlands," *Contemporary Political Theory*, accessed June 6, 2022 at https://doi.org/10.1057/s41296-021-00527-4.

Chang, A. (2021b), "Restoring Anáhuac: Indigenous Genealogies and Hemispheric Republicanism in Postcolonial Mexico," *American Journal of Political Science*, accessed September 28, 2021 at https://doi.org/10.1111/ajps.12660.

Ciccariello-Maher, G. (2020), "Populism, Universalism, and Democracy in Latin America," in L. K. Jenco, M. Idris and M. C. Thomas (eds), *The Oxford Handbook of Comparative Political Theory*, Oxford: Oxford University Press, pp. 504–24.

Connolly, W. E. (1995), *The Ethos of Pluralization*, Minneapolis, MN: University of Minnesota Press.

Coulthard, G. S. (2014), *Red Skin, White Masks: Rejecting the Colonial Politics of Recognition*, Minneapolis, MN: University of Minnesota Press.

Dahl, A. (2016), "Nullifying Settler Democracy: William Apess and the Paradox of Settler Sovereignty," *Polity*, **48** (2), 279–304.

Deleuze, G. and F. Guattari (1987), *A Thousand Plateaus: Capitalism and Schizophrenia*, Minneapolis, MN: University of Minnesota Press.

Douglass, F. (2016), *The Essential Douglass: Selected Writings and Speeches*, ed. N. Buccola, Indianapolis, IN: Hackett Publishing Company.

Erdrich, L. (2020), *The Night Watchman*, New York: Harper.

Espejo, P. O. (2020), *On Borders: Territories, Legitimacy, and the Rights of Place*, New York: Oxford University Press.

Ferguson, K. (2016), "Why Does Political Science Hate American Indians?," *Perspectives on Politics*, **14** (4), 1029–38.

Germano, W. and K. Nicholls (2020), *Syllabus: The Remarkable, Unremarkable Document That Changes Everything*, Princeton, NJ: Princeton University Press.

Glasser, S. B. (2018), "The Man Who Put Andrew Jackson in Trump's Oval Office," *POLITICO Magazine*, January 22.

Guillermoprieto, A. (2021), "Nicaragua's Dreadful Duumvirate," *New York Review of Books*, **68** (20), December 16.

Hannah-Jones, N. (2019), "America Wasn't a Democracy, Until Black Americans Made It One: The 1619 Project," *The New York Times*, August 14.

Hendrix, B. (2011), "What to the Indian is the Fourth of July?—William Apess in Democratic Context," *APSA 2011 Annual Meeting Paper*, accessed May 21, 2020 at https://papers.ssrn.com/abstract=1900054.

Hirsch, A. K. (2017), "Agonism and Hope in William Apess's Native American Political Thought," *New Political Science*, **39** (3), 393–411.

Honig, B. (1993), *Political Theory and the Displacement of Politics*, Ithaca, NY: Cornell University Press.

Hooker, J. (2014), "Hybrid Subjectivities, Latin American Mestizaje, and Latino Political Thought on Race," *Politics, Groups, and Identities*, **2** (2), 188–201.

Ikuta, J. and T. Latimer (2021), "Aristocracy in America: Tocqueville on White Supremacy', *The Journal of Politics*, **83** (2), 547–59.

Ivison, D. (2002), *Postcolonial Liberalism*, New York: Cambridge University Press.

Jagmohan, D. (2021), "Booker T. Washington and the Politics of Deception," in M. L. Rogers and J. Turner (eds), *African American Political Thought: A Collected History*, Chicago, IL: University of Chicago Press, pp. 167–91.

Krause, S. R. (2020), "Frederick Douglass: Nonsovereign Freedom and the Plurality of Political Resistance," in M. L. Rogers and J. Turner (eds), *African American Political Thought: A Collected History*, Chicago, IL: University of Chicago Press, pp. 116–41.

McQueen, A. and B. A. Hendrix (2017), "Tocqueville in Jacksonian Context: American Expansionism and Discourses of American Indian Nomadism in Democracy in America," *Perspectives on Politics*, **15** (3), 663–77.

Mill, J. S. (2003), *On Liberty*, eds D. Bromwich and G. Kateb, New Haven, CT: Yale University Press.

Moak, D. (2021), "Thurgood Marshall: The Legacy and Limits of Equality Under the Law," in M. L. Rogers and J. Turner (eds), *African American Political Thought: A Collected History*, Chicago, IL: University of Chicago Press, pp. 386–412.

Naim, M. (2021), "Venezuela's Fatal Embrace of Cuba," *The Wall Street Journal*, December 10.

O'Shea, T. (2021), "As a Marxist…," *Twitter*, October 27, accessed October 28, 2021 at https://twitter.com/DrTomOShea/status/1453430153019805701.

Painter, N. I. (1997), *Sojourner Truth: A Life, A Symbol*, New York: W. W. Norton & Company.

Putnam, R. D. (2000), *Bowling Alone: The Collapse and Revival of American Community*, New York: Simon & Schuster.

Ravano, L. (2021), "The Borders of Citizenship in the Haitian Revolution," *Political Theory*, **49** (5), 717–42.

Rawls, J. (2005), *Political Liberalism* (expanded edition), New York: Columbia University Press.

Rose, D., R. Geroux and K. Ferguson (2020), "LandBody: Radical Native Commitments," *Theory & Event*, **23** (4), 973–6.

Sealey, K. (2020), "Roots and Routes: Negotiations between Creolizing and Indigenous Identities in the Americas," presentation, Fordham University Social & Political Philosophy Workshop, October 13.

Shklar, J. N. (1991), "Redeeming American Political Theory," *The American Political Science Review*, **85** (1), 3–15.

Shulman, G. (2014), "Douglass, Frederick (1818–95)," in M. T. Gibbons et al. (eds), *The Encyclopedia of Political Thought* (8 vols), Oxford: Wiley-Blackwell, pp. 959–62.

Simon, J. (2017), *The Ideology of Creole Revolution: Imperialism and Independence in American and Latin American Political Thought*, New York: Cambridge University Press.

Smiet, K. (2020), *Sojourner Truth and Intersectionality: Traveling Truths in Feminist Scholarship*, New York: Routledge.

Sokoloff, W. W. (2020), *Political Science Pedagogy: A Critical, Radical and Utopian Perspective*, New York: Palgrave Macmillan.

Strauss, L. (1989), *An Introduction to Political Philosophy: Ten Essays*, Detroit, IL: Wayne State University Press.

Taylor, F. (2021), "Michael and Catherine Zuckert on Leo Strauss's 'What is Liberal Education?' and 'Liberal Education and Responsibility'," *The Enduring Interest Podcast*, November 1, accessed November 21, 2021 at https://enduringinterest .podbean.com/e/michael-and-catherine-zuckert-on-leo-strauss-s-what-is-liberal -education-and-liberal-education-and-responsibility/.

Temin, D. M. (2021), "Our Democracy: Laura Cornelius Kellogg's Decolonial-Democracy," *Perspectives on Politics*, **19** (4), 1082–97.

Tillery, A. B. (2018), "Reading Tocqueville behind the Veil: African American Receptions of Democracy in America, 1835–1900," *American Political Thought*, **7** (1), 1–25.

Tocqueville, A. de (2002), *Democracy in America*, eds and trans. H. C. Mansfield and D. Winthrop, Chicago, IL: University of Chicago Press.

Truth, S. (2020), *Ain't I A Woman?*, New York: Penguin Books.

Tuck, E. and K. W. Yang (2012), "Decolonization is Not a Metaphor," *Decolonization: Indigeneity, Education & Society*, **1** (1), 1–40.

Tully, J. (1995), *Strange Multiplicity: Constitutionalism in an Age of Diversity*, New York: Cambridge University Press.

Vacano, D. A. von (2012), *The Color of Citizenship: Race, Modernity and Latin American/Hispanic Political Thought*, New York: Oxford University Press.

Williams, L. (2020), "Blasting Reproach and All-Pervading Light: Frederick Douglass's Aspirational American Exceptionalism," *American Political Thought*, **9** (3), 369–95.

Wolin, S. S. (2003), *Tocqueville between Two Worlds: The Making of a Political and Theoretical Life*, Princeton, NJ: Princeton University Press.

Young, I. M. (2000), "Hybrid Democracy: Iroquois Federalism and the Postcolonial Project," in D. Ivison, P. Patton and W. Sanders (eds), *Political Theory and the Rights of Indigenous Peoples*, New York: Cambridge University Press, pp. 237–57.

3. Writing lectures, with illustrations from Chinese and European political thought

INTRODUCTION

Your responsibility as a political theory teacher is to take a stack of books from your predecessors and hand them on, with modifications, to the next generation. Your teachers tell you to read Plato's *Republic*, Machiavelli's *Prince*, and Hannah Arendt's *Human Condition*, and when it is your turn you explain to college students—or alumni, or the community, or people who watch videos or listen to podcasts on the Internet—what they contribute to making sense of the deepest levels of political life. The books are in many languages—Sanskrit, Chinese, Arabic, Greek, French, German, English—and sometimes you are responsible for teaching traditions that are transmitted in forms other than great books. How can you balance the desire to teach students material that is already somewhat familiar to them with a desire to open their minds to new traditions, books, authors, and ideas? In this chapter, I explain the framework I use to teach the history of political philosophy. If you ask each author a few basic questions, then you can stage in your mind a conversation between them. "The greatest minds utter monologues. We must transform their monologues into a dialogue, their 'side by side' into a 'together'" (Strauss 1989: 317).

In this chapter, I walk through how I construct this dialogue by asking each author about their biographies, the problems they see in the world, the flaws they see in other philosophies, their views of human nature, the principles they think should govern political life, and how they justify their views. To illustrate this process and its payoff, I stage a conversation between the pre-Qin master Han Feizi (d. 233 bce) and the Italian Renaissance philosopher Niccolò Machiavelli (1469–1527 ce), two realists who challenge us to look beneath the moralistic rhetoric of politicians and see how the gears of power turn based on perceived self-interest.

CONSTRUCTING A DIALOGUE

In *The Design of the University*, Heinz-Dieter Meyer explains how the lecture (*Vorlesung*) became a part of the German research university and then migrated to the United States and the rest of the world. "Writing a lecture was a new thing. It meant making a survey of available knowledge in a field and organizing it so that students could absorb the latest developments in their area of study" (Meyer 2016: 69). A proper lecture serves two functions. It educates students about the history and present knowledge of a field of inquiry, and it inspires the lecturer and listeners to advance the pursuit of knowledge. Based on the original German model, graduate seminars—from the Latin word for seed—are the places where faculty grow new ideas. I learned from watching William E. Connolly at Johns Hopkins University that political theorists should use every teaching opportunity as an occasion to grow as a thinker.

A good lecture has structure and room for spontaneity. In my own undergraduate experience, my political theory professor used to begin class by asking students what they thought of the readings. I still hear about professors using this technique, which can work if the students are curious about the material, have already had some exposure to it, and have the work ethic and academic skills to teach themselves the material. One of the slogans of my alma mater New College of Florida is: "In the last analysis, each individual is responsible for his or her own education." I believe that. However, only 400 students attended New College when I was there, and most teachers need to figure out a way to convince students to invest time and energy in reading difficult texts. As a student, I became annoyed when other students, who often had more confidence than knowledge, used valuable class time to express their opinions. Students want to hear experts share their knowledge, so I believe in the value of an old-fashioned lecture. At the same time, I read the room when I'm lecturing, and I have an interactive style where I pause lectures to ask students for questions or to share what they're thinking. And I rarely lecture for longer than 45 minutes, making sure to leave time at the end of class for open-ended discussion. The ideal, then, is for the lecture to be a framework you can modify and add to as you teach each iteration of the course.

In his *Prison Lectures*, the Italian Marxist Antonio Gramsci explained that students learn the history of philosophy to construct "in a systematic, coherent and critical fashion one's own intuitions of life and the world" (Gramsci 2000: 328–9). When students spend two weeks on an author, they should be able to hear that thinker in their minds; when a class goes well, students should end the course with several voices in their head. If a student joins a political debate, they should be able to imagine what Machiavelli, Kant, and others might say. The way to think for oneself is not to be ignorant of other voices but to participate in a conversation in one's own head. A lecture can help students to acquire more internal interlocutors and thus to become more thoughtful. A political theory course stages a kind of play in which thinkers talk with one another and invite the audience to participate.

Political theorists face the challenge that canonical authors live in different times and places and write in disparate languages and genres. Plato wrote dialogues in which readers must glean what Plato himself thinks based on clues in the text. What we have from Aristotle are apparently his lecture notes. Thucydides wrote a history of the Peloponnesian War, and the Greek orators, poets, and playwrights conveyed political ideas in different genres. The difficulty becomes amplified once political theorists start teaching authors outside the European canon. The *Analects* is a collection of stories about and sayings of Confucius that is difficult to parse without a guide or reconstruction (Chin 2007). The great Daoist texts—the *Daodejing* and the *Zhuangzi*—are often enigmatic and elusive. The *Mengzi, Xunzi,* and *Han Feizi* texts make arguments and offer advice to rulers in ways that are somewhat familiar to scholars trained in European philosophy. Political theorists need to figure out a way to teach profound texts in ways that enable meaningful conversations between people living in ancient Greece, Warring States China, the Italian Renaissance, eighteenth-century Prussia, the United States founding, and today.

One concern about this approach is that it stages conversations that would have been meaningless for the people involved. Political thinkers tend to write for the readers of their time and place. R. G. Collingwood articulates an intuition that guides the Cambridge school of political thought: "what is thought to be a permanent problem P is really a number of transitory problems p_1, p_2, p_3…whose individual peculiarities are blurred by the historical myopia of the person who lumps them together under the one name P" (Collingwood, cited in McQueen 2017: 16). It is true that scholars learn a great deal about thinkers by situating them in their intellectual and political milieu and should be attentive to how thinkers frame the problem as one way, p_1, rather than another, p_2. And yet virtually every political thinker must explain why they are writing their books and essays, and in so doing they identify real-world problems and inadequacies in the intellectual responses on offer. We may pose the same questions to diverse authors and compare answers to see similarities and differences between thinkers, eras, traditions, texts, and so forth. In a way, it does not matter that the pre-Qin masters were not writing with Renaissance Italy in mind. My students and I want to think deeper about politics; one way to do that is to stage a kind of Socratic dialogue between great thinkers living in different times and places.

In this chapter, I explain the framework that undergirds my lectures in the history of political thought. Here is a list of questions that I ask of each author we cover in a course:

- What is their biography?
- What real-world problems were they addressing?
- What philosophical problems were they addressing?
- What is their view of human nature?
- What are their political principles?
- How do they justify their views?
- What do we think?

In my lectures, I discuss key passages from the text itself and secondary literature. My students and I parse each word of key passages and fill each box in the grid: this is the work of analysis. Then, we compare how different authors answer the same questions: this is the work of synthesis. Based on my own training and set of concerns, I find this list of questions useful for organizing my teaching and research agenda. You will make your own.

In this chapter, I explain how I write lectures to facilitate a conversation between political thinkers who wrote in different times, places, and languages, and who did not read the same sources or know about each other. In other words, I want to show how asking the same list of questions enables us to stage a conversation between perfect strangers. The first is Han Feizi, one of the key figures in the movement subsequently known as Legalism (*Fajia*); the other is Niccolò Machiavelli, one of the central figures in realist political theory. The chapter offers ideas about how to write lectures that illuminate the history of ideas and, in this instance, introduce students to realist accounts of the ocean flows of politics.

Box 3.1 describes how using images helps students visualize the literature.

BOX 3.1   USE IMAGES

One of the challenges facing a political theory teacher is helping students visualize the action in the text. One reason we read and reread passages in class is so we can make sense of each step of the argument. I want students to read political theory texts like movie scripts that describe people moving, arguing, lifting, drawing blueprints, erasing, congregating, fighting, leaping, and so forth. This is easy enough when reading plays, dialogues, or narratives like Plato's *Republic* or Nietzsche's *Thus Spoke Zarathustra*, but you can also use etymology to find the basic things or actions that underlie much philosophical terminology. If a philosopher describes an event as aleatory, it is helpful to know that aleatory comes from the Latin word for dice.

Political theorists today may also take advantage of the Internet, using images to find pictures of authors, events, and relevant artwork. Khristina H. Haddad and Claudia Mesa Higuera (2021) explain how sharing images from around the time of the Italian Renaissance can help students visualize key philosophical images from *The Prince*. Machiavelli famously advises the prince or would-be prince to know how and when to be cunning like the fox and ferocious like the lion. One can show one's students an image of Titian's *An Allegory of Prudence* (c. 1550–65) and explain that the Latin inscription means "From the past/the present acts prudently/lest it spoil future action." Then, one can discuss with one's students what Titian means by displaying the animals horizontally rather than with humanity's angelic or rational nature dominating its base nature.

One can do the same with the pre-Qin master Han Feizi. While visiting the Hubei Provincial Museum, I saw an exhibit from the Ming dynasty of tasseled crowns with strings of jewels to cover the ruler's face. I teach my students that Han Feizi advised the ruler to conceal his intentions, and these crowns illustrate this point. One can also find images on the Internet of Chinese imperial swords and armor. Using these images, one can ask students to explain how Machiavelli and Han Feizi agreed and disagreed on how they rule over their subjects with fear but (maybe) not hatred.

"In a digital world overflowing with combinations of images and texts, teaching a critical reading of the two combined makes sense" (Haddad and Higuera 2021: 575). Agreed. Teachers can enliven the classroom, and help students visualize complex arguments, by incorporating images into their lectures and discussions.

BIOGRAPHY

If we are going to imagine ourselves in conversation with authors from another time and place, we should be able to visualize their lives, family, education, experience in wartime, occupation, audience, peers, and so forth.

I begin my lectures on Han Feizi by reading his biography in Sima Qian's *Records of the Grand Historian* (Ch'ien 1995: 23–32). We learn that Han Feizi was born into a noble family in the state of Han. He had a stutter but was a skilled writer. Han Feizi studied with the Confucian scholar Xunzi, and one of his fellow students was Li Si, who became the prime minister of the Qin dynasty that unified China.[1] Han Feizi gave advice to the king of Han to strengthen Han's laws and institutions, but instead the king of Han "raised up frivolous, dissolute parasites and placed them above those with merit and substance" (Ch'ien 1995: 47). The king of Qin read some of Han Feizi's writings, wanted to meet him, and to make this happen, invaded Han. The king of Han sent Han Feizi to Qin as an emissary, and the king of Qin was pleased to meet him but did not trust him enough to employ him. Li Si encouraged the king to punish Han Feizi for being an agent of Han, and then Li Si had someone give Han Feizi poison so that he could kill himself. The king of Qin regretted his decision and pardoned Han Feizi, but it was too late: Han Feizi had already died.

Because most of my students have never heard of Han Feizi, I give them a reason to read him: Legalist political theory provides many ideas embraced by the current Chinese leadership, including centralizing power, punishing dissidents, and creating a strong military and economic force to repel foreigners (Schneider 2016).

Introducing students to Machiavelli, I ask them to read aloud Machiavelli's letter to Francesco Vettori written on December 10, 1513 as well as the Dedicatory letter to *The Prince*. I explain that Machiavelli lived at the height of the Italian Renaissance and collaborated with Leonardo da Vinci on a plan to redirect the Arno River to help Florence gain direct access to the sea. Machiavelli was an Italian diplomat who worked with the republican regime of Piero Soderini and tried to build up Florence's militia. Running afoul of the Medici, Machiavelli was tortured and exiled to his farm estate in Sant'Andrea in Percussina. In his letter to Vettori, Machiavelli describes how he wastes his days but spends his evenings dressed in scholarly garb talking with the ancients about politics in his study. "There I am not ashamed to speak with them and to ask them the reason for their actions; and they in their humanity reply to me. And for the space of four hours I feel no boredom, I forget every pain, I do not fear poverty, death does not frighten me. I deliver myself entirely to them." In his conversations with the dead—an apt description of many political theory classes—Machiavelli has written "a little work *De Principatibus* [On Principalities], where I delve as deeply as I can into reflections on this subject, debating what a principality is, of what kinds they are, how they are acquired, how they are maintained, why they are lost" (Machiavelli 1998: 109–10). Machiavelli dedicated *The Prince* to Lorenzo de' Medici, the then-ruler of Florence, but he did not offer Machiavelli a job or apparently read the book.

Han Feizi and Machiavelli are individuals trying to get the ear of powerful people who do not sufficiently appreciate them. Both are, or at least want to be, at the center of the action rather than in the groves of academia. Both wrote books as a second-best option, when what they really wanted to do was advise rulers. Both are realists who think that many scholars do not appreciate that governing often requires getting your hands dirty. Finally, Machiavelli and Han Feizi both have a playful side that delights in the clash of ideas and arms; they "fool around with utmost seriousness" (Marasco 2021: 19).

REAL-WORLD POLITICAL PROBLEMS

Why did you write your book? Virtually every political thinker, across traditions, identifies a real-world problem, often in the opening pages of their book or essay, that calls their project into being. For both Han Feizi and Machiavelli, that problem is disorder in the world.

Han Feizi lived at the end of what scholars call the Warring States period. China in the Zhou dynasty was a feudal regime in which noble families ruled over a largely agrarian population. During the Spring and Autumn period (770–476 bce) and Warring States period (476–221 bce), China changed. Regional aristocracies became bureaucratized territorial states; iron utensils revolutionized agriculture, which led to larger populations and urbanization; new technologies such as the crossbow and mass infantry armies changed warfare; and hereditary aristocracy became supplanted by "men of service" (*shi*) (Pines 2018).

Han Feizi's priority was to strengthen and protect the state of Han. The state needed to become stronger, militarily and economically, if it was to survive an attack from the state of Qin to the west. Han Feizi's "goal was simply to determine which measures were most effective in ensuring the continued survival of the state and furthering the public interests of the ruler and his people" (Han Feizi 2005: 312).

The way that Han Feizi frames the problem, however, transcends the context of Warring States China. Consider the following passage: "if a ruler can get rid of private crookedness and promote the public law, his people will become secure and his state will become well ordered. If he can expel private conduct and enforce the public law, his troops will grow strong while his enemies grow weak" (Han Feizi 2005: 318). In this passage, Han Feizi identifies problems that have bedeviled societies throughout history: individuals look out for themselves and their clan over the community. Selfish or partial behavior leads to physical insecurity, which in turn leads to problems concerning agriculture and industry. Who wants to work, raise a family, or stay in a place when they fear for their very lives? If we read Han Feizi through a Darwinian lens, we may see that he identifies a problem ingrained in human nature: a desire to survive in order to reproduce (Flanagan and Hu 2011).

For much of Chinese history, rulers followed the principle of "Confucianism on the outside, Legalism on the inside" (Crane 2021). Legalism "is China's alternative to 'Confucian compassion': when faced with serious threats to their power or China's social order, rulers in Beijing have often relied on Legalist methods that justify heavy-handed state power and harsh punishments to achieve their ends" (Bell 2020). One reason that the Chinese keep returning to Han Feizi is that he addresses a recurrent problem in human affairs: disorder.

Like the *Han Feizi*, *The Prince* seems to be written with two different contexts in mind: sixteenth-century Italy and posterity. Renaissance Florence faced threats from Venice and Milan in the north, Naples to the south, the papacy in Rome, and France, Spain, and the Holy Roman Empire on the continent. Florence's survival as an independent state hinged on prudent diplomacy and military planning. In the last chapter of *The Prince*, Machiavelli describes the situation of Italy at the time: "more enslaved than the Hebrews, more servile than the Persians, more dispersed than the Athenians, without a head, without order, beaten, despoiled, torn, pillaged, and having endured ruin of every sort" (Machiavelli 1998: 102). One purpose of *The Prince* was to call upon a strong executive to unify Italy; another was to envision a politics not beholden to a Christian ethics that undermines political stability.

Han Feizi and Machiavelli wrote to address the problems confronting states surrounded by powerful enemies. People still read them today because they addressed a recurrent problem in human affairs: disordered states in which people may not safely live, work, and raise a family.

PHILOSOPHICAL PROBLEMS

Political theorists tend to open their books and essays by identifying problems that demand redress. To explain the different kinds of problems, I stand next to the classroom window. Theorists see one kind of problem when they look out the window: these are the political problems. If another author or school of thought had adequately identified a remedy for these problems, then there would be little reason to write other than to amplify their proposals. When scholars turn away from the window and look inside the academy, however, they often think that other scholars have made mistakes. When this happens, theorists identify philosophical problems they wish to address.[2]

For both Han Feizi and Machiavelli, one reason why their states were weak was because of what Bernard Williams calls "political moralism," the notion that politics should be governed by the same moral rules that apply to personal interactions (Williams 2009: 5). In this section, I focus on how Han Feizi and Machiavelli presented their versions of realism as an antidote to, respectively, the teachings of Confucius and Savonarola.

According to Confucius, rulers govern through virtue (*de*).[3] "The Master said, 'One who rules through the power of virtue is analogous to the Pole Star: it simply remains in its place and receives the homage of the myriad lesser stars'" (Kongzi 2005: 5). One purpose of the *Analects* is to teach rulers how to cultivate virtue that will in turn permeate their societies. "Yan Hui asked about running a state. The Master said, 'Follow the calendar of the Xia, travel in the carriages of the Yang, and clothe yourself in the ceremonial caps of the Zhou'" (Kongzi 2005: 45). One theme in the *Analects* is that the moral goodness of the ruler will influence everyone in his realm in subtle but powerful ways. "The virtue of a gentleman is like the wind, and the virtue of a petty person is like the grass—when the wind moves over the grass, the grass is sure to bend" (Kongzi 2005: 37).

Confucius thought that one of the vital tasks of statecraft was to install gentlemen (*junzi*) as rulers or turn rulers into gentlemen. Before Confucius, *junzi* meant "son of the lord" and was a position that one was born into; Confucius changed the meaning of the term to become an ideal kind of ruler that the ruler should strive to become: virtuous, benevolent, and culturally refined. "Master Zeng said, 'The gentleman acquires friends by means of cultural refinement'" (Kongzi 2005: 25). How does one become refined? The *Analects* details what may and may not be done to become a *junzi*. For example: "The Master said, 'A ceremonial cap made of linen is prescribed by the rites, but these days people use silk. This is frugal, and I follow the majority. To bow before ascending the stairs is what is prescribed by the rites, but these days people bow after ascending. This is arrogant, and—though it goes against the majority—I continue to bow before ascending'" (Kongzi 2005: 25). For Confucius, virtuous rulers are an essential condition for a well-ordered society, one in which "people would not steal even if you reward them for it" (Kongzi 2005: 37).

Han Feizi responds that Confucius' plan is based on a faulty assumption about human nature. He calls Confucius "a great sage of the world," but points out that for all his benevolence and righteousness, he only attained 70 followers. "It seems that those who value benevolence are rare while those with the ability to be righteous are difficult to find" (Han Feizi 2005: 341). It is unrealistic to expect many people, much less most, to attain virtue or become gentlemen.

Han Feizi proposes that the "power of position" (*shi*) ought to be the operative notion in statecraft instead of virtue or personal talent (*xian*). The term *shi* originally referred to terrain as in a battle; the goal is to be higher than your opponents (Moody 2008: 107). Han Feizi gives an example of how the power of position works. Duke Ai of Lu was an inferior ruler and lacked Confucius' righteousness. However, because he was the ruler of the state, he was able to force Confucius to comply with his edicts. Confucius "did not yield to the Duke's righteousness, he submitted to the power of the duke's superior position" (Han Feizi 2005: 342).

For Han Feizi, the problem is not simply that Confucius propounds notions that do not apply to human affairs; it is that Confucius' notions cause mischief for rulers and states. Han Feizi takes aim at Confucius' notion that uprightness consists in sons covering up the crimes of their fathers. For Han Feizi, a ruler should never permit, much less praise, the righteousness of people who disobey the laws of the state: "these are the customs of a disordered state." At one point, Han Feizi calls Confucius and his ilk vermin: "They put on a grand appearance and speak in elegant phrases in order to cast doubt upon the laws of the current age and create division in the hearts of the rulers of men" (Han Feizi 2005: 344, 351).

Han Feizi maintains that the rules of statecraft are of a different character than those that Confucians maintain apply to the individual.[4] In ancient times, Han Feizi explains, Cang Jie called things that revolve around the self "private" and things that oppose the private "public" (*gong*). "Now, believing that public and private interests are the same is the kind of disaster that comes from not being discerning" (Han Feizi 2005: 344–5). How is that the case? Han Feizi asks the reader to think through what happens if people follow Confucius' advice. Individuals will cultivate benevolence, righteousness, and practice the arts of culture. They will earn respect and trust and become government ministers. In that case, people will want to sit around all day and read and argue and perfect their rituals. People will soon discover that the way to get ahead is to become literati (*Ru*) rather than farmers or soldiers. To create a state in which people can live in peace and have enough to eat, a ruler has to identify and enforce a set of rules to regulate behavior. Is it proper to describe these rules as moral, immoral, or amoral? That is a question that scholars still debate (Harris 2013; Van Norden 2011: 196–8) and is a perfect topic for students to discuss in class.

Machiavelli, like Han Feizi, thinks that his state and politics in general have been harmed by idealism, the notion that philosophers should set high moral standards to govern the realm of politics. Machiavelli is often identified as the pivotal figure between classical and medieval political philosophy and modern political philosophy (Strauss 1995; Wolin 2016). A remarkable feature of Machiavelli's work is how much remains unstated—that is, how he almost never explicitly discusses Plato, Aristotle, the Bible, or the specifics of the theologies and political philosophies he wishes to subvert. In the opening to the *Discourses*, Machiavelli compares himself to Christopher Columbus in his discovery of "new modes and orders" (Machiavelli 1996: 5). This does not change the fact that Machiavelli formulates his philosophical problem in conversation with other thinkers. Alison McQueen explains the relationship between Machiavelli and Savonarola in *Political Realism in Apocalyptic Times*.

In *The Prince*, one of the problems that Machiavelli was confronting was the theme of apocalypticism. The notion of the apocalypse could be found in the Book of Daniel in the Old Testament, the Book of Revelation in the New Testament, and in the preaching of Machiavelli's contemporary, the Dominican friar Girolamo Savonarola. An apocalypse is "an imminent and cataclysmic end to the known world, along with its attendant 'evils.' It is a rupture in the apparent temporal continuity of history, a revelatory moment around which the past is given meaning and a radically new future is announced" (McQueen

2017: 56). In the late fifteenth and early sixteenth century, prophecy flourished in Italy, and people often interpreted signs—such as the conjunction of Saturn and Jupiter or lightning hitting the Duomo in Florence—as evidence of an impending apocalypse. Savonarola drew upon this tradition when he organized a "bonfire of the vanities" in which the famous Renaissance artist Sandro Botticelli destroyed some of his own paintings. Savonarola framed his problem as preparing Florence for when God "would burst into secular history and build his heavenly kingdom on earth" (McQueen 2017: 63).

Living in Florence at the same time, Machiavelli took a different tack than Savonarola. Rather than call for a kind of religious revival, Machiavelli thought that Florence had to arm itself, a task that he himself performed through creating and leading a citizen militia. Rather than prepare for an imminent apocalypse, Machiavelli maintained that Florence needed to find a way to protect itself from the vicissitudes of fortune. In *The Prince*, Machiavelli admires Savonarola for his lofty ambitions but criticizes him for failing to recognize that establishing a new political order requires force. "Moses, Cyrus, Theseus, and Romulus would not have been able to make their peoples observe their constitutions for long if they had been unarmed, as happened in our times to Brother Girolamo Savonarola. He was ruined in his new orders as soon as the multitude began not to believe in them, and he had no mode for holding firm those who had believed nor for making unbelievers believe" (Machiavelli 1998: 24). In the *Discourses*, Machiavelli continues his critique of Christianity in his day for not being strong enough to unite Italy but strong enough to prevent others from doing so (Machiavelli 1996: 36–9). Machiavelli sees "unarmed prophets" as a problem for those trying to build stable political orders.

McQueen's book complicates the narrative that Machiavelli was a secular realist opposed to Savonarola's Christian apocalypticism. She shows that Machiavelli used apocalyptic tropes in the last chapter of *The Prince* calling for a new prince to free Italy from barbarians. "Machiavelli does not just call for a great founder here. He calls for a redemptive prince, someone to save Italy 'from these barbarous cruelties and insults'—to give form to the matter of a suffering people. The chapter is suffused with the language of salvation" (McQueen 2017: 85). That said, Machiavelli's deployment of apocalyptic imagery serves a secular function: mobilizing people to perform the military actions necessary to expel foreign invaders.

In *The Prince*, Machiavelli frames the philosophical problem as freeing oneself from moralistic or religious frameworks and looking at political affairs as they are and not as they ought to be:

> Since my intent is to write something useful to whoever understands it, it has appeared to me more fitting to go directly to the effectual truth of the thing [*la verità*

effettuale della cosa] than to the imagination of it. And many have imagined repub-
lics and principalities that have never been seen or known to exist in truth; for it is
so far from how one lives to how one should live that he who lets go of what is done
for what should be done learns his ruin rather than his preservation. (Machiavelli
1998: 61)

Thucydides and other ancient authors knew about the seedy side of politics,
where politicians lie and rely on extralegal violence, but they publicly dis-
approved of this fact (Strauss 1995: 10). Machiavelli launches the modern
tradition of realism in *The Prince*. In the *Discourses*, Machiavelli envisioned
republican institutions to empower the common people to rule themselves and
oppose the wealthy and ambitious (the *grandi*), but this side of his thought
has gained less attention and influence than his apparently amoral doctrine of
"reasons of state" (McCormick 2014).

In the previous section, we saw that Han Feizi and Machiavelli were concerned about the fortunes of their state and the problem of disorder in general.
In this section, we have seen them wage a war of ideas against those who try
to moralize politics by demanding that gentleman rulers practice virtue or that
cities prepare for an apocalypse after which all politics will end. Categories
risk simplifying the complexities of complicated figures; Han Feizi never
called himself a Legalist (Pines 2018), nor did Machiavelli disavow all apocalyptic themes. Still, the similarities are great enough to suggest that Han Feizi
and Machiavelli are both realists opposed to idealistic treatments of politics.

HUMAN NATURE

When I was a graduate student at Johns Hopkins University, I received
a Dean's Teaching Fellowship to lead a seminar related to my dissertation.
I thought a course on Kant's reception in contemporary political theory would
have too narrow a focus for an undergraduate course. Instead, I proposed
a seminar on Human Nature and Political Principles. The course resembled
one I took on Defining Humanity with Anthony Pagden and Giulia Sissa at the
Villa Spelman in Florence in the fall of 1999 that covered authors such as John
Locke, Marcel Mauss, Sigmund Freud, and Martin Heidegger. That seminar
opened my eyes to how virtually every major political thinker, regardless of
which academic discipline claims them, addresses the topic of human nature.[5]
To make the discussion as concrete as possible in my lectures, I break the
question of human nature into two parts: (1) How do human beings differ
from other animals? (2) How do human beings differ from one another? In this
section, I explain how Han Feizi and Machiavelli share similar conceptions of
human beings as fundamentally selfish.

One of Leo Strauss's points about Machiavelli is that you cannot understand his novelty unless you understand how he was rebelling against authors and traditions that preceded him. A similar point applies to Han Feizi. Confucius himself said little explicitly about human nature, but his two most influential followers, Mengzi and Xunzi, had a debate on this topic. In my Introduction to Political Theory course, I spend as much time on Mengzi and Xunzi as I do on Han Feizi and Machiavelli, so for space considerations I will merely summarize an interesting debate on whether human nature is good (Mengzi) or evil (Xunzi). Mengzi maintained that "humans all have hearts that are not unfeeling toward others," and as evidence of that, he argued that all human beings would instinctively want to help a child about to fall into a well (Mengzi 2005: 129). People can be bad as adults, but this is because their goodness has been destroyed such as when an ox eats the vegetation off the side of a mountain. Xunzi, on the other hand, maintained that "people's nature is bad. Their goodness is a matter of deliberate effort." According to Xunzi, people are born with "a fondness for profit," "feelings of hate and dislike," and "desires of the eyes and ears." The good news, for Xunzi, is that people may be transformed by teachers, rituals (*li*), and standards of righteousness (*yi*). In a famous metaphor, Xunzi compares human nature to "crooked wood" that must be steamed to become straight (Xunzi 2005: 298). Though Mengzi and Xunzi differed on human nature and how to make it better, both of them shared the Confucian ideal of gentlemen ruling with virtue and rituals (Flanagan and Hu 2011: 297–8).

Han Feizi's position is like Xunzi's in that he thinks that human beings are born with a fondness for profit. He disagrees with Xunzi, however, in that he does not describe human nature as evil, nor does he think that the crooked timber of humanity can be flattened with steaming. Here is one passage in which Han Feizi describes the inherent selfishness of human nature as reflected in the vocations of the physician, carriage maker, and carpenter:

> A physician will often suck men's wounds clean and hold the bad blood in his mouth, not because he is bound to them by any tie of kinship but because he knows there is profit in it. The carriage maker making carriages hopes that men will grow rich and eminent; the carpenter fashioning coffins hopes that men will die prematurely. It is not that the carriage maker is kind-hearted and the carpenter a knave. It is only that if men do not become rich and eminent, the carriages will never sell, and if men do not die, there will be no market for coffins. The carpenter has no feeling of hatred toward others; he merely stands to profit by their death. (Han Feizi 2003: 87)

What about Confucius? He would seem to be an example of somebody who is motivated by respect for the ancients, righteousness (*yi*), humaneness (*ren*), and other noble qualities. Han Feizi acknowledges these kinds of human beings exist but thinks they are rare: "public-spirited people are few while private-minded individuals are numerous." Most people run from danger to safety, with little concern about high-minded ideals. "The natural aspirations of the people are such that they all move toward security and benefit and avoid danger and poverty" (Han Feizi 2003: 87).

Han Feizi disagrees with Xunzi that rulers should even try to make subjects virtuous. Han Feizi thinks that selfishness is so deeply woven into human nature that it will always reemerge. His writing is filled with passages of mistresses planning to kill their rulers, sons figuring out how to take advantage of their parents, ministers trying to fool dukes. Han Feizi advises rulers to think that all people, no matter their appearance, ultimately desire profit rather than virtue. But what if rulers *make* the few naturally good people self-interested? Han Feizi is fine with that; it will be easier for rulers to govern if they can anticipate the behavior of their subjects. "If in a hundred generations there is not a single arrow shaft that is naturally straight, or a single piece of wood that is naturally round, how is it that every generation is able to ride around in chariots and shoot down birds with arrows? It is because they use the Way of straightening and bending" (Han Feizi 2005: 357). Unlike Xunzi, however, Han Feizi's Way is to straighten behavior rather than character.

According to Han Feizi, once rulers properly understand human nature, they may create institutions that run on self-interest, the desire for individuals to acquire pleasure (wealth, security) and avoid pain (torture, death). He explains how:

> Now, there are no more than ten officers in the whole world who are virtuous and honest, and yet the offices within the borders of a single state number in the hundreds. So, if one insists on employing only officers who are virtuous and honest, there will not be enough men to fill the offices of the state. And if there are not enough men to fill the offices of the state, those promoting order will be few while those promoting disorder will be numerous. Therefore, the way of an enlightened ruler is to unify the laws and not seek after wisdom, to establish the proper methods and not yearn for honesty. In this way, the law will not be defeated and the offices will all be free of corruption and treachery. (Han Feizi 2005: 346)

If the political problem is creating order, then this passage explains how one may harness human nature to create institutions that will solve large-scale problems: bureaucracies that do not depend on the goodness or propriety of the people who staff them (Van Norden 2011: 198).

We are now able to answer our two questions about Han Feizi's view of human nature. Human beings differ from other animals because humans are smarter, better with tools, have longer time horizons, and so forth. There is no moral core or faculty that differentiates human beings from tigers or dogs. Human nature is roughly the same for all human beings; rulers govern because they have a higher position (*shi*), just like a worm looks like a dragon when it rides a cloud. Reading Han Feizi through the lens of neo-Darwinism, Owen Flanagan and Jing Hu contend that Han Feizi fails to see the possibility of "genuinely affectionate" and "possibly even virtuous" social relations with other people. On the whole, however, they think that his account of a "universal deep selfish dispositional core" is "passably Darwinian" in ways that Mengzi's and Kant's views of human nature are not (Flanagan and Hu 2011: 298, 309).

What about Machiavelli? When I teach the history of political philosophy, I often draw circles on the board to show how philosophers posit the difference between human nature and between human beings. When teaching *The Republic*, for instance, I diagram Plato's tripartite division of the soul as a circle with three layers marked mind (*nous*), spirit (*thymos*), and desire (*epithymia*). For Plato, animals like pigs have desires; animals like lions have spirit; but only human beings of all the animals possess mind. On the board, I draw a solid line between the top layer and the rest of the circle to denote that the higher and lower parts of human nature reside on different levels of reality. For Plato, the tripartite division of the soul also serves to differentiate three kinds of human beings with different mixes in their souls, which leads me to diagram a small circle of philosophers over a larger circle of auxiliaries over a much larger circle of farmers, artisans, and soldiers. This schema helps generate a shock when we learn that Machiavelli refuses to draw a solid line between human beings and other animals.

There are many passages in *The Prince* where Machiavelli presents his account of human nature. We may cite this one from Chapter 17 on whether it is better to be feared than loved:

> For one can say this generally of men: that they are ungrateful, fickle, pretenders and dissemblers, evaders of danger, eager for gain. While you do them good, they are yours, offering you their blood, property, lives, and children…when the need for them is far away; but, when it is close to you, they revolt. And that prince who has founded himself entirely on their words, stripped of other preparation, is ruined; for friendships that are acquired at a price and not with greatness and nobility of spirit are bought, but they are not owned and when the time comes they cannot be spent. And men have less hesitation to offend one who makes himself loved than one who makes himself feared; for love is held by a chain of obligation, which, because men are wicked, is broken at every opportunity for their own utility, but fear is held by a dread of punishment that never forsakes you. (Machiavelli 1998: 66–7)

Is Machiavelli closer to Xunzi or Han Feizi in this passage? On the one hand, Machiavelli says that "men are wicked," and elsewhere in *The Prince*, he suggests that it would better if a prince could rule according to Aristotelian or Christian principles "when possible" (Machiavelli 1998: 70). Machiavelli seems close to Xunzi who says that human nature is evil but can be made good. On the other, Machiavelli maintains that moralizing is out of place here because human beings are what they are: "ungrateful, fickle, pretenders, and dissemblers, evaders of danger, eager for gain" (Machiavelli 1998: 66). Like Han Feizi, Machiavelli seems to acknowledge that virtue might be possible, that friendships may be acquired through "greatness and nobility of spirit," but he also tells princes to never rely on noble motivations. It is a short step from this position to one where the prince may encourage selfishness if it enables him to anticipate the moves of his ministers and subjects.

Machiavelli is an egalitarian insofar as he refuses to identify a fundamental difference between human beings. This theme is brought to the forefront in Chapter 18, "In What Mode Faith May Be Kept by Princes":

> Men in general judge more by their eyes than by their hands, because seeing is given to everyone, touching to few. Everyone sees how you appear, few touch what you are... So let a prince win and maintain his state: the means will always be judged honorable, and will be praised by everyone. For the vulgar are taken in by the appearance and the outcome of a thing, and in the world there is no one but the vulgar. (Machiavelli 1998: 71)

For Plato, philosophers are distinguished from everyone else by their ability to escape the cave of ignorance and enter the sunlight of knowledge. One of the shocking aspects of *The Prince* is its refusal to acknowledge the existence of philosophers as a class. They are not named in *The Prince*, nor are they given any right to rule. In the political vision of *The Prince*, everyone is vulgar and self-interested. "Truly it is a very natural and ordinary thing to desire to acquire, and always, when men do it who can, they will be praised or not blamed" (Machiavelli 1998: 14). For Machiavelli, as for Han Feizi, rulers should assume that human beings are selfish, and if there appear to be exceptions, they may be ignored or molded to fall in line with everyone else.

So, what differentiates human beings, according to Machiavelli? Again, he rules out the possibility that any human being has more goodness than anybody else: there are no philosophers or saints in Machiavelli's worldview. However, he is willing to admit that some human beings can choose what kind of animals they will emulate in their pursuit of riches, power, and glory:

> Since a prince is compelled of necessity to know well how to use the beast, he should pick the fox and the lion, because the lion does not defend itself from snares and the fox does not defend itself from wolves. So one needs to be a fox to recognize snares and a lion to frighten the wolves. (Machiavelli 1996: 69)

In this intuitive way, Machiavelli explains how a ruler should be strong and aggressive when the times call for it, and smart and sneaky in other circumstances.[6] When drawing Machiavelli's view of human nature on the board,

I put fox on one side of the circle, lion on the other, and a perforated line down the center. All human beings desire to acquire; half of human affairs are controlled by fortune (*fortuna*); human beings have a kind of virtue (*virtù*) that enables them to read the circumstances and decide whether to use brains or brawn to triumph over fortune.

On the question of human nature, we may see similarities between Han Feizi and Machiavelli. Both of them reject moralistic accounts of human nature or politics. For both of them, human beings may be cleverer than other animals, but we are fundamentally driven to acquire power, whether in the form of money, arms, or reputation. For both, human beings are vulgar, and it makes as much as sense to complain about that as to complain about the weather.[7] Machiavelli, Han Feizi, and social scientists who work in the rational choice paradigm share "individualistic and instrumentalist assumptions about human behavior and political action" (Moody 2008: 96).

At this point in class, I pause and ask students: Are Han Feizi and Machiavelli right about human nature? Do carpenters hope that people die so that they may make more money? Do "men forget the death of a father more quickly than the loss of a patrimony" (Machiavelli 1998: 67)? Are there examples of people sacrificing for the greater good, or does all human behavior boil down to self-interest?

POLITICAL PRINCIPLES

The goal of my lectures is to stage a conversation between people living in different times and places, writing in different languages and styles, participating in different traditions, and so forth. One question I pose to authors is about their political principles. I tell students that principles connotes two things. The word principle is from the Latin *principium*, "a beginning, commencement, origin, first part," which in turn comes from the Latin *primus* "first" (Online Etymology Dictionary, 2020b). Principles are the starting point of a political theory. The German word for principles is *Grundsätze*, from the words for "ground" and "sentences." *Grundsätze* are the fundamental sentences in a political theory, the basic rules that political actors ought to follow. I ask students: Where can we find the principles of the United States political system? And students tell me, correctly, that we can find them in the Constitution. When I teach political theory, I tell students that we will ask the authors who should govern and what rules people should follow. And with the answers, my students and I can stage a conversation about the deepest currents of politics between authors who lived in different times and places.

In *Fortune and the Dao: A Comparative Study of Machiavelli, the Daodejing, and the Han Feizi*, Jason P. Blahuta compares how Han Feizi and Machiavelli offer advice to a ruler on exercising prudence, establishing and following laws, and handling ministers (Blahuta 2015: 162–72). In this section, I investigate in more depth how Han Feizi and Machiavelli articulate principles about how political actors should use cruelty. Both Han Feizi and Machiavelli were realists concerning cruelty, which means that they both asserted that political actors must use cruelty well in certain circumstances. One difference is that Machiavelli views cruelty as an extraordinary measure, while Han Feizi suggests that it may be an ordinary measure.

Han Feizi on Cruelty

To understand Han Feizi's position on cruelty, it is worth reviewing what Confucius, Mengzi, and Xunzi said on the topic. Then, we will be in a better position to understand the novelty of Han Feizi's teaching.

Confucius maintains that a ruler governs through virtue (*de*), a kind of moral charisma that pulls the population, as with a magnet, towards humaneness and righteousness (Van Norden 2011: 8). Laozi used to speak of nonaction (*wuwei*), as a kind of governing principle, and Confucius seems to share the view that a ruler should govern more by example than by force:

> The Master said, "If you try to guide the common people with coercive regulations and keep them in line with punishments, the common people will become evasive and will have no sense of shame. If, however, you guide them with Virtue, and keep them in line by means of ritual, the people will have a sense of shame and will rectify themselves." (Kongzi 2005: 5)

Every time you make a law, you bring to people's minds the crime that gets punished. Just as saying "Don't think of a pink elephant!" makes the hearer think of a pink elephant, so does listing crimes and penalties educate people about crimes they may not have even considered. Confucius seems to suggest that a ruler's virtue and example of ritualistic behavior will be sufficient to establish a well-ordered society—though scholars have shown that Confucian political philosophy had a realistic side concerned with establishing and maintaining political order (Amine 2015).

Mengzi shares Confucius' view that in well-ordered society, a ruler will not have to use cruelty, though he thinks that a king will need to be more proactive to ensure that people have what they need, such as security and food, to flourish. Here is Mengzi's advice to King Xuan of Xi: "Simply return to fundamentals. Suppose Your Majesty were to bestow benevolence in governing. This would call all under Heaven who serve others to all want to take their place in Your Majesty's court" (Mengzi 2005: 122). Mengzi places the responsibility for the people's good behavior on the ruler: "an enlightened ruler, in regulating the people's livelihood, must ensure that it is sufficient, on the one hand, to serve one's father and mother, and on the other hand, to nurture wife and children... Only when the people have a regulated livelihood do they rush toward the good, and thus the people follow the ruler easily" (Mengzi 2005: 122–3).

Xunzi, we saw above, maintained that the ruler might need to take a more heavy-handed approach to make his subjects virtuous. His two preferred techniques to do this include rituals (*li*) and standards of righteousness (*yi*). He explains: "Blunt metal must await honing and grinding, and only then does it become sharp. Now since people's nature is bad, they must await teachers and proper models, and only then do they become correct in their behavior. They must obtain ritual and the standards of righteousness, and only then do they become well ordered" (Xunzi 2005: 298–9). The metaphor of steaming wood and grinding metal both suggest a certain amount of coercion, or deliberate effort (*wei*), against recalcitrant subjects.

Han Feizi agrees with Xunzi that rulers should not try to rule by virtue (*de*) alone, and he also takes Xunzi's position that rulers should focus on fashioning compliant subjects rather than creating a nurturing environment. In Han Feizi's conception of realist politics, rulers should focus on acquiring power rather than trying to become moral exemplars or thinking from the perspective of their subjects. "An enlightened ruler works to accumulate power. In a stern household there are no impertinent servants, but a compassionate mother will often have spoiled children" (Han Feizi 2005: 357). A recurrent theme in Confucian political thought is that rulers and subjects must treat each other like family; Han Feizi is willing to concede that point if rulers view themselves as "tiger parents" who, without affection or tolerance for misbehavior, raise hard-working, rule-following children (Herr 2016).

One reason that Han Feizi is called a Legalist is that he holds that "the sage does not work on his Virtue, he works on his laws [*fa*]" (Han Feizi 2005: 357). The translation of the word *fa* into law can be misleading, for *fa* does not mean laws that constrain the behavior of rulers, as the term suggests in much of Western political thought (Samuelson 2017). Rather, *fa* are a ruler's edicts, and they can often be arbitrary, cruel, and effective. Han Feizi approvingly notes the actions of Gongsun Yang when he controlled the state of Qin: "He linked the population together into groups of five and ten households and made all the members of each group collectively responsible for crimes committed by any of them. He ensured that rewards were substantial and reliable and that punishments were heavy and certain. Because of this, the people of Qin were industrious" (Han Feizi 2005: 337). Good laws, according to Han Feizi, are easy to understand, consistently applied, and reward obedience and punish violations (Van Norden 2011: 193–4).

One way that Xunzi and Han Feizi differ is in what they think harsh punishment, or cruelty, accomplishes. For Xunzi, steaming wood in effect makes wood straight: punishments can make people internalize benevolence, righteousness, and other Confucian virtues. For Han Feizi, human nature does not change, and the ruler's task of enforcing laws never ends. Han Feizi maintains fear of punishment, not rituals or standards of righteousness, keeps people in line, and there is no point in talking about inculcating virtue (Moody 2008: 106).

Han Feizi articulates a doctrine of how cruelty may be well used in his doctrine of "performance and title" (*xing ming*). The idea is that a ruler should demand alignment between what ministers say that they will do and what they do. If ministers do not achieve what they lay out in their proposals, then they are ineffective and should be punished. If ministers achieve more than what they were asked to, they should be punished for trying to acquire reputation and power, which in turn could lead to the formation of cliques that threaten the ruler. Here is a famous story from the *Han Feizi* that is worth reading aloud and discussing with students:

> Marquis Zhao of Han once became drunk and fell asleep. The Steward of Caps, seeing that his ruler was cold, placed the Marquis' cloak over him. When Marquis Zhao awoke he was pleased by this, and asked his attendants, "Who covered me with my cloak?" This attendant replied, "It was the Steward of Caps." Consequently, the ruler punished both the Steward of Caps, and the Steward of Cloaks. He punished the Steward of Cloaks because he felt the man had failed to fulfill his appointed task, and he punished the Steward of Caps because he felt the man had overstepped the bounds of his position. It was not that the Marquis did not dislike the cold, but rather that he felt that the harm that comes from ministers encroaching on each other's office is even greater than the harm that comes from being cold. (Han Feizi 2005: 325)

The example in this story is of a ruler punishing ministers who fail at their jobs, including by exceeding their assignment.

Han Feizi maintains that the ruler should use two "handles"—rewards and punishments—to control the ministers and thereby the state (Pines 2018). Han Feizi holds that rulers should reward and venerate ministers. So, Han Feizi does seem to have a place in the ruler's toolkit for kindness and generosity. At the same time, Han Feizi counsels the ruler against permitting any minister to have an independent base from which to launch an attack on the ruler. The force of Han Feizi's argument is that the ruler should use fear as the main mechanism to keep ministers and subjects in line. There are many passages in the *Han Feizi* that advise the ruler to use heavy punishments, or cruelty, to keep people doing their job and not asking questions or challenging the rules. "For strictly regulating the offices and overawing the people, thwarting licentiousness and idleness, and stopping trickery and falsehood, nothing is better than punishments. If punishments are heavy then the noble and the base will not presume to change places" (Han Feizi 2005: 323).

Han Feizi does not seem to relish causing people pain, and as a writer rather than a ruler himself, he probably did not have occasions to take or order the advice he gives in his book. As noted above, Han Feizi's conception of a political order governed by inflexible rulers, overseen by a ruler who does not make exceptions to the laws, provides the basis for a modern bureaucracy. And Han Feizi's political philosophy can articulate a kind of public morality insofar as political stability seems to be a precondition for many of the other kinds of goods that people value.

That said, Han Feizi's reception throughout much of Chinese, and increasingly world, intellectual history is that he counseled rule by cruelty. Sima Tan (d. 110 bce), the first person to use the term Legalism (*Fajia*), said that Legalists are "strict and have little kindness," and advocated "a one-time policy that could not be constantly applied" (Pines 2018). Given that Han Feizi influenced the prime minister and emperor of the Qin dynasty, Chinese administrators and literati have studied his teachings even if they publicly disavow Legalism. But given that the Qin dynasty collapsed quickly and Emperor Wu of the Han dynasty (r. 141–87 bce) embraced Confucianism, the consensus among Chinese and even contemporary Western scholars is that Legalism is too cruel to be sustainable; it is a one-time policy that may be useful for establishing order but not maintaining it (Blahuta 2015).

The ruling political philosophy of China for much of the past two millennia, according to Tongdong Bai, has been a Confucian velvet glove covering an iron Legalist fist (Bai 2011: 11). With my students, we would consider recent Chinese policies that confirm or problematize this thesis.

Machiavelli on Cruelty

Rulers were cruel—from the Latin *crudus* "rough, raw, bloody" (Online Etymology Dictionary, 2020a)—before Machiavelli wrote *The Prince*. According to Leo Strauss, nothing that Machiavelli wrote in *The Prince* would have shocked the classical Greek and Roman authors who knew that cruelty is an important part of politics and governance. What is new about Machiavelli is that he puts in his own words the teachings that the ancients taught covertly through the words of characters in their dialogues (Strauss 1989: 43).

In Chapter 7 of *The Prince*, "Of New Principalities That Are Acquired through Others' Arms and Fortune," Machiavelli describes in detail how Cesare de Borgia used cruelty well to bring order to Romagna. The story begins with Cesare de Borgia entrusting Messer Remirro de Orco to use cruel means to stop robberies and quarrels in Romagna and institute a good government:

> In a short time Remirro reduced [the Romagna] to peace and unity, with the very greatest reputation for himself. Then the duke judged that such excessive authority was not necessary, because he feared that it might become hateful; and he set up a civil court in the middle of the province, with a most excellent president, where each city had its advocate. And because he knew that past rigors had generated some hatred for Remirro, to purge the spirits of that people and to gain them entirely to himself, he wished to show that if any cruelty had been committed, this had not come from him but from the harsh nature of his minister. And having seized this opportunity, he had him placed one morning in the piazza at Cesena in two pieces, with a piece of wood and a bloody knife beside him. The ferocity of this spectacle left the people at once satisfied and stupefied. (Machiavelli 1998: 29–30)

In *Machiavelli and the Orders of Violence*, Yves Winter offers valuable insights on what is new and important about Machiavelli's doctrine of cruelty well used. One is that Machiavelli, in conversation with Roman sources such as Cicero, differentiates force (*forza*) and cruelty (*crudeltà*). Force does not have a normative charge; it refers to the deployment or threat of violence for various political ends. Cruelty "characterizes actions that inflict gratuitous and shocking forms of injury. In contrast to force, cruelty is a decidedly non-euphemistic category. It refers to an essentially offensive, provocative, and often scandalous mode of violence" (Winter 2018: 28–9). Machiavelli is not a moralist who blanketly condemns cruelty; nor is he a cruel person himself who enjoys inflicting pain on others. He is, rather, a scholar of how cruelty works well or poorly as a political tactic. Cesare established peace in Romagna by entrusting Remirro to ruthlessly take power from the oligarchic families that ruled little fiefdoms in the area. And he wisely had Remirro murdered, and his body displayed so that people would no longer seek revenge and keep the cycle of violence going. The missing details in the story, such as whether the knife belonged to Cesare or Remirro, invite the reader to "become participants in the enquiry" (Winter 2018: 50). *The Prince*'s various descriptions of cruelty prompt the reader to think about how cruelty can be used well to establish political order.

One of Winter's other insights is that Machiavelli's doctrine of cruelty is part of his popular realism. Classical realism is often for the benefit of rulers; an apology, as it were, for the cruel acts they needed to maintain power. Machiavelli, on the other hand, purveys what the Italian Marxist Antonio Gramsci called "a pedagogy for the people" (Winter 2018: 16). On Winter's reading of *The Prince*, the *Discourses*, and the *Florentine Histories*, Machiavelli praises rulers who rule for the benefit of the people and who put down the elites. Cruelty is a part of politics; by explaining its mechanisms to the people, Machiavelli paves the way for its intelligent use by radical democrats. "Rendering violence intelligible as event, mechanism, and strategy of a popular politics is one of Machiavelli's signal contributions to political theory. His commitment to popular freedom and anti-oligarchic politics is thus central to his account of violence" (Winter 2018: 20). For Machiavelli, popular realists should not use excessive violence for its own sake; they ought to think about how it may be used as a kind of theater that educates and mobilizes the people and stupefies the elites. Cesare was a civil prince because he had popular support; he was not a democrat per se. But Machiavelli teaches subsequent democrats that cruelty should be an essential part of their governing practice, at least when it comes to dealing with oligarchs.

* * *

We may now compare how Han Feizi and Machiavelli advise rulers on how to use cruelty well.

Both Han Feizi and Machiavelli are realists who think that clear-eyed observers of politics must recognize that cruelty is an ineluctable part of ruling. Confucius says that the ruler is like the North Star around which the stars turn, or the wind that gently blows the grass; Han Feizi agrees with Xunzi that politics requires forcing people to change their behavior in the same way that steaming wood makes it straight; Han Feizi disagrees with Xunzi that rulers may ever hope that subjects become virtuous. Machiavelli thinks that Savonarola was an unarmed prophet whose activities weakened Italy; his model for *The Prince* may have been Cesare de Borgia who knew how to have his underlings do the dirty work of pacifying a region. Compared to Confucius and Savonarola, Han Feizi and Machiavelli are "teachers of evil." For political realists, however, this description ignores that establishing political order contains its own kind of ethics. Leo Strauss was a critic of Machiavelli, but he still acknowledged that Machiavelli was the only non-Jew of his age who protested the cruelty of Ferdinand of Aragon in expelling the Marranos from Spain (Strauss 1989: 43–4). Likewise, Han Feizi tried in his own way to create a political system that would harness individual material interests to advance a public good (Moody 2008: 95). Perhaps because they were writing in a time of political chaos, both recognized that cruelty would be essential to create an order with less cruelty.

One difference between Han Feizi and Machiavelli concerns whether the ruler should commit cruelty or entrust these unsavory tasks to someone else. Han Feizi says that the ruler should not entrust his ministers to be feared by the populace:

> The reason why the tiger can subdue the dog is because he has claws and fangs. But if the tiger loses his claws and fangs and allows the dog to use them, then the tiger

will instead be subdued by the dog. A ruler of men is someone who uses punishments and favor to control his ministers. Now if the ruler of men loses his power to punish and grants favors and allows his ministers to use them, then the ruler will instead be controlled by his ministers. (Han Feizi 2005: 323)

Han Feizi disagrees with Machiavelli, who praises Cesare for having Remirro kill the noble families in the Romagna. We can leave it to students to debate with each other how much Han Feizi and Machiavelli actually disagree.

One disagreement may be whether Han Feizi and Machiavelli think that cruelty must become an ordinary part of politics. Sima Tan, we saw above, said that Legalism collapsed because it relied too much on cruelty; it was useful for establishing but not maintaining political order. According to Jason Blahuta, the *Han Feizi* and *The Prince* offer similar advice for a new ruler, but Han Feizi lacks a book like Machiavelli's *Discourses* that explains how rulers may govern in a time of peace and order (Blahuta 2015: 149). If you are just teaching the *Han Feizi* and *The Prince*, it may be sufficient to pose the question to students: What do you think of Han Feizi's and Machiavelli's doctrines of cruelty? Do you think that rulers should have minions do their dirty work, like Machiavelli, or not, like Han Feizi?

JUSTIFICATION

Leo Strauss once shared a general rule regarding teaching: "Always assume that there is one silent student in your class who is by far superior to you in head and in heart" (Strauss 1989: 322). I take his point to be that you should be humble about your abilities, share your best insights, and prepare students for advanced work in the subject. One of the things that differentiates having an opinion from doing political philosophy is reflecting upon how one justifies one's views. Though I do not treat my undergraduate lectures as graduate seminars, I still dedicate time to teaching about how philosophers justify their political theories, a topic sometimes called metaethics.

Here is how I present this topic to students. When justifying a philosophical doctrine, there are two main ways to do so: to close one's eyes and make a rationalist argument or to open one's eyes and make an empiricist argument. Plato and Kant are idealists who aspire to make political arguments based on pure reason; Han Feizi and Machiavelli are realists who think with their eyes wide open. Among realists, there is a further divide between those who think that political thinkers and actors should study the past to glean lessons, and those who maintain that theorists should focus on the present. Han Feizi asserts that political actors should not concern themselves with the past, and yet his arguments often mention historical figures. Machiavelli advises rulers to study history to prepare themselves for the decisions they will have to make, but his examples notoriously do not always support the point they are supposed to make. Despite their different counsels, both maintain that historical research is necessary and inadequate to justify political principles here and now.

Confucians and Mohists looked back to the ancient sage-kings for guidance on good governance. Han Feizi responded that human beings do not know what happened in the distant past: "if someone wants to examine the Way of Yao and Shun that existed more than three thousand years in the past, how can they possibly be certain about their ideas!" (Han Feizi 2005: 352). Adding to the uncertainty of the past, Confucians and Mohists disagree about the teachings of the founders of their eponymous schools. There are eight factions of Confucians, and three factions of the Mohists, and "the doctrines and practices that each of these factions accept and reject are divergent and conflicting" (Han Feizi 2005: 352). If Han Feizi's main concern is establishing political order, then these ideological factions threaten his plan.

Even if we could have accurate knowledge of the past, Han Feizi continues, political rulers still must act within their environment. The *Analects* report: "The master said, 'The Zhou gazes down upon the two dynasties that preceded it. How brilliant in culture it is! I follow the Zhou'" (Kongzi 2005: 9). Han Feizi thinks we cannot know the ways of the Zhou and trying to emulate their way today makes no sense. Han Feizi explains why in a famous story about a farmer from Song:

> Among the people of Song there was a farmer who had a stump in the middle of his field. One day, a rabbit running across the field crashed into the stump, broke its neck, and died. Seeing this, the man put aside his plow and took up watch next to the stump, hoping that he would get another rabbit like this, and he soon became the laughing-stock of the entire state of Song. Now if one wants to use the government of the former kings to bring order to the people of the current age, this is all just so much stump-watching. (Han Feizi 2005: 340)

The Zhou ruled a relatively small, agrarian population. Rulers during the Warring States period had to address a larger population, the emergence of cities, and new kinds of warfare. For Han Feizi, rulers trying to follow Confucian advice about following the way of the Zhou were as intelligent as the farmer who watched a stump on the off-chance another rabbit would break its neck running into it. For Han Feizi, rulers were wasting their time learning about a past that no longer exists, if it ever did.

On the other hand, Han Feizi does draw lessons from historical episodes (Blahuta 2015: 150–51). In the chapter on the two handles of reward and punishment, Han Feizi discusses the dangers of allowing ministers to dispense favors or administer punishments. Duke Jian permitted Tian Ching to grant titles and stipends and control ministers and was assassinated. Zi Han told the Lord of Song: "Veneration, rewards, boons, and gifts—these are things that the people all enjoy. Let you, my Lord, take care of these things. Death, mutilation, punishments, and penalties—these are things that the people all hate. Let me, your servant, take care of these" (Han Feizi 2005: 324). As a result of empowering Zi Han to punish people, the Lord of Song lost his authority. Machiavelli cites the example of Cesare and Remirro to recommend that princes have ministers do the dirty business of punishing people; Han Feizi draws the exact opposite maxim from looking at the case of the Lord of Song and Zi Han. Han Feizi's relationship to history, then, is ambivalent: he criticizes the Confucian and Mohist obsession with the distant past, but he also thinks that political thinkers can discern patterns in history.

To explain Machiavelli's realism, I contrast it with Plato's idealism. In *The Republic*, Plato arranges a dialogue in which a conversation prompts Socrates to wonder about the meaning of justice. Socrates suggests the following procedure: the meaning of justice in the individual is hard to glean because it is written, in effect, in small letters; it would be "like a godsend" to read these same letters on a larger scale. "If you want," Socrates tells Adeimantus, "first we'll investigate what justice is like in the cities. Then, we'll also go on to consider it in individuals, considering the likeness of the bigger in the *idea* of the littler?" (Plato 2016: 45; original emphasis). Socrates then goes on to discuss a "city in speech" in which there are three different kinds of people in a political regime, which then sheds light on the three different parts of the soul and suggests that justice on the larger and smaller scales is harmony. A remarkable feature of *The Republic* is how few empirical referents there are in the book after the first few pages. The book exemplifies a kind of political philosophy that proceeds by thought experiments rather than empirical investigation.

As Leo Strauss details in *Thoughts on Machiavelli*, Machiavelli waged a kind of spiritual war against Plato and most of classical and medieval political philosophy. As part of this war, he asserted that building cities in speech is a waste of time and the results of these thought experiments do not provide any useful information for how princes ought to acquire and maintain a state. *The Prince* is filled with advice that rulers should study real-world politics for clues on what kind of actions succeed in which kind of circumstances:

> As to the exercise of the mind, a prince should read histories and consider in them the actions of excellent men, should see how they conducted themselves in wars, should examine the causes of their victories and losses, so as to be able to avoid the latter and imitate the former. Above all, he should do as some excellent man has done in the past who found someone to imitate who had been praised and glorified before him, whose exploits and actions he always kept beside himself, as they say Alexander the Great imitated Achilles. (Machiavelli 1998: 60)

Machiavelli served as Florence's diplomat to Cesare de Borgia, and Machiavelli in turn teaches "maxims of public and private gangsterism" (Strauss 1995: 9).

To his defenders, however, Machiavelli was not so much recommending gang-sterism as identifying patterns in real-world politics, that is, doing empirical political science. Machiavelli was correct that political actors should study real history rather than imagined principalities.

In sum, Han Feizi and Machiavelli both use an empiricist methodology to justify their brands of realism. Han Feizi and Machiavelli are "diabolical," in that they are "fallen angels" who know the traditions that they encourage readers to abandon (Strauss 1995: 13). Han Feizi held that Mohism and Confucianism confused people by appealing to a past shrouded in fog, and this confusion led to political factionalism and disorder. Machiavelli thought that philosophers and religious figures wanted people to imagine a "city in speech" or an impending apocalypse rather than calmly learn the right lessons from the facts on the ground. Han Feizi disparaged reading old histories; Machiavelli encouraged rulers to read histories for the same reasons that hunting foxes prepares one for war: you can mentally practice for how you would conduct yourself in different circumstances (Machiavelli 1998: 58–60). The differences between them can be overstated because both authors disparage book learning without worldly experience.

EVALUATION

At the end of each unit, I ask students to share their own responses to the material. In this conclusion, I identify one theme that has emerged from reading Han Feizi and Machiavelli alongside one another: whether politics, the public disputation about the future direction of one's community, is a good thing.

In *The Human Condition*, Hannah Arendt extols the *vita activa*, a life dedicated to politics. Politics requires public debate about matters of common concern. Politics, on her account, does not take place in dark backrooms; it happens in speeches and debates in which individuals disclose themselves to their peers. Politics is a site of contest, of wrestling, of people competing with one another to articulate the aims of the community: "Excellence itself, *arete* as the Greeks, *virtus* as the Romans would have called it, has always been assigned to the public realm where one could excel, could distinguish oneself from all others" (Arendt 2018: 48–9; original emphasis). Using these three criteria—in public, about matters of public concern, agonistic—we may see a clear difference between Han Feizi and Machiavelli in their orientation to politics: Han Feizi is an anti-political thinker, while Machiavelli can be a pro-political thinker.

Han Feizi tells the ruler:

> The character of ministers is not always such that they can love their ruler. Some become ministers only to increase their personal benefit. Now if a ruler of men does

not cover up his true character and conceal the origins of his actions, and instead allows his ministers to have the means to encroach upon their ruler, then the assembled ministers will not find it difficult to become a Zi Zhi or a Tian Chang [ministers who duped their rulers]. (Han Feizi 2005: 326–7)

If ministers know what a ruler wants, then they will be able to tailor their messages to fit what they think the ruler wants to hear. The ruler will have a harder time figuring out the truth if ministers know, for instance, that the ruler only likes to hear good news. Han Feizi's advice, then, is that the ruler should be reclusive and secretive and should not make exceptions to the law. This begs the question: well, what exactly does the ruler do if he is not seen or heard and simply demands that the law be followed? One scholar calls this "the paradox of an entrapped sovereign" (Pines 2018). In Han Feizi's system, the ruler should be neither seen nor heard. If Arendt extols the political actor who is a "doer of great deeds" and a "speaker of great words," then the Han Feizian ruler does not fit the bill (Arendt 2018: 25).

Han Feizi, in the language of contemporary realist theory, is an "ordorealist" (Rossi 2019: 640). That is, he believes that the "first political question" is "the securing of order, protection, safety, trust, and the conditions of cooperation" (Williams 2009: 3). In this respect, Han Feizi's closest analogue in modern European political thought may be Thomas Hobbes, who justified a strong executive state to protect people from a violent state of nature (Martinich 2011; Moody 2008: 109).[8] Ordorealists, as a rule, tend not to favor political debates or contestation: Han Feizi would have likely agreed with Hobbes that human beings are not political animals who only flourish in civic participation. For Han Feizi, nothing good happens by encouraging people to rule themselves or tell the rulers what they think.

According to Arendt, politics requires plurality, the recognition that we are all the same in that each of us is unique in our concerns, thoughts, expressions, and so forth. Politics "would be an unnecessary luxury, a capricious interference with general laws of behavior, if men were endlessly reproducible repetitions of the same model, whose nature or essence was the same for all and as predictable as the nature or essence of any other thing" (Arendt 2018: 8). Han Feizi sees no value in allowing people to form any base independent of the ruler's control: "When relationships are profuse and confederates are numerous, so that cliques and factions flourish both and inside and outside the state, then even if a minister commits a great transgression, he will have ample means to cover it up" (Han Feizi 2005: 318–19). One theme in Legalism is that the only two appropriate careers for people, the only avenues for them to get ahead in life, are farming and soldiering (Pines 2018). Machiavelli lived at the height of the Italian Renaissance and collaborated with Leonardo da

Vinci; Han Feizi would have had no interest in befriending artists, scientists, or republicans.

For Arendt, politics thrives on speech and reasoned debate. Han Feizi thinks that both pose a threat to the stability of a political regime and should be prohibited. A ruler keeps his populace so busy that they have neither the time to speak nor plan a revolution: "An enlightened ruler uses the people's strength and does not listen to their words; he rewards their achievements and completely prohibits useless activities. As a result, the people exhaust every ounce of their strength in obedience to their superiors." The same goes for intellectuals who are vermin who eat from the stockpile of the state and threaten the stability of the regime: "In the state of an enlightened ruler there are no texts written on bamboo strips, the law provides the only education; there are no words of learned masters, the civil officers are the only teachers" (Han Feizi 2005: 347).

In sum, Han Feizi sees no value in what we, at least in the modern West, consider as politics. Han Feizi's regime has no elections, no public debates, no professors teaching students about political theory, no political activism, no civil society, no independent newspapers. The ruler is a recluse, the laws are strictly enforced, people are rewarded or punished based on whether they reach certain metrics in their job. The *Han Feizi* envisions an ordorealism that blends into authoritarianism, totalitarianism, or despotism—basically, a regime that does not tolerate any disagreement or resistance to the ruler's orders. There is a conception of the public good (*gong*), but it is basically synonymous with the security of the ruler. The only reason people have to go along with this plan is that they will be secure and fed—which may be enough for many people.

Machiavelli, on the contrary, envisions a world of endless public debate and contestation, with rulers coming and going, with conflict between aristocrats and plebeians, where rulers must exercise *virtù* to survive and prosper. The Machiavellian ruler must make countless decisions about when to exercise the cunning of the fox or the strength of the lion, be bold or cautious, stingy or generous, and when to be good or not to be good. The Machiavellian ruler can read histories, but the Machiavellian world is an Epicurean-Lucretian one in which things constantly swerve in unexpected directions and the ruler must be prepared to jump at opportunities or dodge dangers. Machiavellian rulers are constantly staging spectacles and conveying messages, in the pursuit of wealth, power, and glory. An undergraduate at Indiana University once told me that all U.S. presidents have had two books in their library: the Bible and *The Prince*. I do not know if this is true, but it is a plausible way to interpret much of U.S. political history. Every four years, elites compete to become the next prince, even though, if they read Machiavelli, they know that the wheel of fortune will eventually bring them low.

Machiavelli is not so much an ordorealist as a "radical realist." A radical realist is like Michelangelo looking at a block of Carrara marble and finding the David within it. A radical realist uses the best social science at hand to attain a clear-eyed view of the political situation, but they may also exercise imagination in shaping reality one way or another (Rossi 2019). Machiavelli's realism does not have a status-quo bias, and *The Prince* offers advice to people trying to disrupt the political regime just as much as it does to the person trying to stabilize it. Alison McQueen describes Machiavelli's political vision as such: "Against an ideal of an eternal stillness, Machiavelli celebrates a Roman ideal of institutionalized antagonism and struggle. The 'tumults between the nobles and the plebs,' for instance, 'were the first cause of keeping Rome free.' Rome negotiates political contingency internally by institutionalizing discord" (McQueen 2017: 102). The idea of *institutionalizing discord* has exercised a profound hold on the Western political imagination, from Montesquieu's notion of the separation of powers, to James Madison's call for ambition to counteract ambition in *Federalist No. 51*, to Bonnie Honig's critique of political theorists who wish to settle political disputes once and for all with their theories (Honig 1993).

If you read Han Feizi, you see one influential account of politics as the effort to suppress disorder, public debate, philosophical disputation, factionalism. If you read Machiavelli, you see another account of politics as the effort to create freedom through competition, elections, spectacles, revolutions. One ought to be wary of attributing too much influence to thinkers in the course of human events, nor should one overlook that history is rich with exceptions to any general rule. Still, one can see, in the prism of these two thinkers, a different orientation to politics in Western and Chinese civilizations. With my students, I would ask them to compare and contrast how Han Feizi and Machiavelli would look at moments in recent Chinese history in which the people demand a say in how they are governed, from the May Fourth Movement to the protests in Tiananmen Square up to the Hong Kong Yellow Umbrella Movement (Wasserstrom 2019). We could also discuss things such as the PATRIOT Act and Wikileaks. Then, together, we would discuss the relative merits of political stability and political freedom.

NOTES

1.   Tongdong Bai tells me that this detail is not confirmed in any other place and that this scholarly lineage may not better help us understand Xunzi or Han Feizi.
2.   Sabina Knight commented on this passage: "One might look out the window, philosophically, out of a love of wisdom, wonder at nature and its workings, yearnings for spiritual inquiry, aesthetic curiosity, desires for 'direct' experience of phenomena, or other leadings, no?" (Knight, personal correspondence with the author, May 1, 2021). She is right. But political theory texts almost always begin

by identifying something threatening the *polis*. It is telling that the word *problem* shares the same root—Latin, *ballein* "to throw"—as the word ballistics.

3. For a taxonomy of contemporary Confucian political theories, see Jin (2021). Teachers have their own reasons for assigning and interpreting passages, but you do not need to spend much time in class justifying your interpretive decisions. Discuss the secondary literature, if at all, after students have had a chance to hear from the primary source directly.

4. Problems arise whenever you translate a text into a different language family. Kongzi, "Master Kong," belonged to a group of literati that called themselves *ru*. The fact that English-speaking scholars discuss Confucius and Confucianism is a result of a long history of translation, arguments, and redescriptions (Standaert 1999). Comparative political theorists often use translations that are imperfect but that are necessary to have a conversation.

5. Hannah Arendt maintains that her famous book is about the human condition, not human nature (Arendt 2018: 9–11). That said, Arendt elaborates the difference between human beings and other animals—namely, that the former can speak and act politically and the latter cannot. This is an instance where scholars may acknowledge the complexity of authors and still find a way to stage conversations over shared themes.

6. Later in my Introduction to Political Philosophy course, I show that the Scottish Enlightenment philosopher David Hume agrees with Machiavelli that human beings are animals but contends that Machiavelli overlooks an important aspect of the animal kingdom: sympathy.

7. According to Xunzi, "If stars fall or trees cry out, the people of the state are filled with fear and say, 'What is this?' I say: It is nothing. These are simply rarely occurring things among the changes in Heaven and earth" (Xunzi 2005: 271–2). Machiavelli would agree with this but would add that savvy rulers, like the Romans reading the birds, sometimes interpret natural phenomena in ways that generate public support for their plans (Machiavelli 1996: 285).

8. One key difference between Han Feizi and Hobbes is that the latter justified the state to each individual, and thus could be viewed as a proto-liberal political thinker (Flathman 2002), while the former exclusively speaks to the ruler about the state: there is no liberal strain in Han Feizi.

REFERENCES

Amine, L. E. (2015), *Classical Confucian Political Thought: A New Interpretation*, Princeton, NJ: Princeton University Press.

Arendt, H. (2018), *The Human Condition* (2nd edition), Chicago, IL: University of Chicago Press.

Bai, T. (2011), "Preliminary Remarks: Han Fei Zi—First Modern Political Philosopher?," *Journal of Chinese Philosophy*, **38** (1), 4–13.

Bell, D. A. (2020), "China's Anti-Corruption Campaign and the Challenges of Political Meritocracy," *American Affairs*, **4** (2), Summer, accessed September 7, 2020 at https://americanaffairsjournal.org/2020/05/chinas-anti-corruption-campaign-and -the-challenges-of-political-meritocracy/.

Blahuta, J. P. (2015), *Fortune and the Dao: A Comparative Study of Machiavelli, the Daodejing, and the Han Feizi*, Lanham, MD: Lexington Books.

Ch'ien, S.-M. (1995), *The Grand Scribe's Records, Vol. 7: The Memoirs of Pre-Han China*, Bloomington, IN: Indiana University Press.

Chin, A. (2007), *The Authentic Confucius: A Life of Thought and Politics*, New York: Scribner.

Crane, S. (2021), "China History and Philosophy Friends," *Twitter*, October 1, accessed October 1, 2021 at https://twitter.com/UselessTree/status/1443737534459154432.

Flanagan, O. and J. Hu (2011), "Han Fei Zi's Philosophical Psychology: Human Nature, Scarcity, and the Neo-Darwinian Consensus," *Journal of Chinese Philosophy*, **38** (2), 293–316.

Flathman, R. E. (2002), *Thomas Hobbes: Skepticism, Individuality, and Chastened Politics*, Lanham, MD: Rowman & Littlefield Publishers.

Gramsci, A. (2000), *The Gramsci Reader: Selected Writings, 1916–1935*, New York: New York University Press.

Haddad, K. H. and C. M. Higuera (2021), "Seeing What is Said: Teaching Niccolò Machiavelli's *The Prince* Through Its Images," *PS: Political Science & Politics*, **54** (3), 575–85.

Han Feizi (2003), *Han Feizi: Basic Writings*, trans. B. Watson, New York: Columbia University Press.

Han Feizi (2005), "Han Feizi," in P. J. Ivanhoe and B. W. Van Norden (eds), *Readings in Classical Chinese Philosophy* (2nd edition), Indianapolis, IN: Hackett Publishing Company, pp. 311–61.

Harris, E. L. (2013), "Han Fei on the Problem of Morality," in P. R. Goldin (ed.), *Dao Companion to the Philosophy of Han Fei*, Dordrecht: Springer, pp. 107–31.

Herr, R. S. (2016), "Confucian Mothering: The Origin of Tiger Mothering?," in M. Foust and S.-H. Tan (eds), *Feminist Encounters with Confucius*, Leiden: Brill, pp. 40–68.

Honig, B. (1993), *Political Theory and the Displacement of Politics*, Ithaca, NY: Cornell University Press.

Jin, Y. (2021), "What Confucianism and for Whom? The Value and Dilemma of Invoking Confucianism in Confucian Political Theories," *The Journal of Value Inquiry*, accessed December 2, 2021 at https://doi.org/10.1007/s10790-021-09858-2.

Kongzi (2005), "The Analects," in P. J. Ivanhoe and B. W. Van Norden (eds), *Readings in Classical Chinese Philosophy* (2nd edition), Indianapolis, IN: Hackett Publishing Company, pp. 1–57.

Machiavelli, N. (1996), *Discourses on Livy*, trans. H. C. Mansfield and N. Tarcov, Chicago, IL: University of Chicago Press.

Machiavelli, N. (1998), *The Prince* (2nd edition), trans. H. C. Mansfield, Chicago, IL: University of Chicago Press.

Marasco, R. (2021), "Machiavelli and the Play-Element in Political Life," *Political Theory*, accessed October 14, 2021 at https://doi.org/10.1177/00905917211046573.

Martinich, A. P. (2011), "The Sovereign in the Political Thought of Hanfeizi and Thomas Hobbes," *Journal of Chinese Philosophy*, **38** (1), 64–72.

McCormick, J. P. (2014), "Machiavelli, Niccolò (1469–1527)," in M. T. Gibbons et al. (eds), *The Encyclopedia of Political Thought*, Oxford: Wiley-Blackwell, pp. 2219–24.

McQueen, A. (2017), *Political Realism in Apocalyptic Times*, New York: Cambridge University Press.

Mengzi (2005), "Mengzi (Mencius)," in P. J. Ivanhoe and B. W. Van Norden (eds), *Readings in Classical Chinese Philosophy* (2nd edition), Indianapolis, IN: Hackett Publishing Company, pp. 115–59.

Meyer, H.-D. (2016), *The Design of the University: German, American, and "World Class,"* New York: Routledge.

Moody, P. R. (2008), "Rational Choice Analysis in Classical Chinese Political Thought: The 'Han Feizi'," *Polity*, **40** (1), 95–119.

Online Etymology Dictionary (2020a), "cruelty (n.)," accessed September 2, 2020 at https://www.etymonline.com/word/cruelty.

Online Etymology Dictionary (2020b), "principle (n.)," accessed August 26, 2020 at https://www.etymonline.com/word/principle.

Pines, Y. (2018), "Legalism in Chinese Philosophy," in E. N. Zalta (ed.), *The Stanford Encyclopedia of Philosophy* (Winter edition), accessed July 21, 2020 at https://plato.stanford.edu/archives/win2018/entries/chinese-legalism/.

Plato (2016), *The Republic of Plato*, trans. A. Bloom, New York: Basic Books.

Rossi, E. (2019), "Being Realistic and Demanding the Impossible," *Constellations*, **26** (4), 638–52.

Samuelson, R. (2017), "A Government of Laws, Not of Men," *Claremont Review of Books*, Fall.

Schneider, D. K. (2016), "China's Legalist Revival," *The National Interest*, April 20.

Standaert, N. (1999), "The Jesuits Did NOT Manufacture 'Confucianism'," *East Asian Science, Technology, and Medicine*, **16**, 115–32.

Strauss, L. (1989), *An Introduction to Political Philosophy: Ten Essays by Leo Strauss*, ed. H. Gildin, Detroit, MI: Wayne State University Press.

Strauss, L. (1995), *Thoughts on Machiavelli*, Chicago, IL: University of Chicago Press.

Van Norden, B. W. (2011), *Introduction to Classical Chinese Philosophy*, Indianapolis, IN: Hackett Publishing Company.

Wasserstrom, J. N. (2019), "May Fourth, the Day That Changed China," *The New York Times*, May 3.

Williams, B. (2009), *In the Beginning Was the Deed: Realism and Moralism in Political Argument* (3rd edition), Princeton, NJ: Princeton University Press.

Winter, Y. (2018), *Machiavelli and the Orders of Violence*, New York: Cambridge University Press.

Wolin, S. S. (2016), *Politics and Vision: Continuity and Innovation in Western Political Thought*, Princeton, NJ: Princeton University Press.

Xunzi (2005), "Xunzi," in P. J. Ivanhoe and B. W. Van Norden (eds), *Readings in Classical Chinese Philosophy* (2nd edition), Indianapolis, IN: Hackett Publishing Company, pp. 255–309.

4. Making assignments, with illustrations from Indian and African American political thought

INTRODUCTION

How is it possible to teach students to think for themselves about a topic such as how to end race and caste oppression? In this chapter, I explain how I create assignments that press students to join a conversation between two authors. Initially, I describe how Nietzsche's discussion of "the three metamorphoses" in *Thus Spoke Zarathustra* prompts me to make assignments to teach students to work hard like a camel, challenge ideas like a lion, and be playful like a child. After an interlude about the pedagogical value of movies in Box 4.1, I show how I create assignments that may be a ten-page research paper, a possible question given to students a week before the exam, or an idea for a term paper or thesis. The assignments construct dialogues between Indian and African American political theorists who think deeply about race and caste. The first dialogue is between Vinayak Damodar Savarkar and Marcus Garvey on solidifying group identity; the second is between B. R. Ambedkar and W. E. B. Du Bois on annihilating caste and transcending the veil that separates races; the third is between Martin Luther King, Jr. and Mohandas Gandhi on civil disobedience and truth force; and the final one is between Saidiya Hartman and Varsha Ayyar on intersectionality. There are other ways to teach this material and make assignments, of course, but I find that this way sets up lively debates that linger in students' minds long after the course ends.

TRAINING STUDENTS TO THINK FOR THEMSELVES

Political theory instructors create assignments to give students grades. As an undergraduate, I chose to attend New College of Florida, in part because the school used narratives rather than letter grades. At the end of each semester, I would receive evaluations of how I did mastering the material, learning to write, becoming a better public speaker, taking intellectual risks, and so forth. Daniel Chambliss, a fellow alumnus, professor of sociology at Hamilton

College, New York, and author of a celebrated article on the training of Olympic swimmers, once told me that New College is a good place for spikers, students who excel at some things but are indifferent at others. That said, New College had only a few hundred students when I attended and many of my classmates went on to earn doctorates and become professors. At most institutions of higher education, many students take political theory courses, at least initially, to fulfill requirements or by accident. Political theory teachers need to make assignments that enable smart, hard-working students to enjoy and succeed in the course. The best way to teach political theory—like sailing, gardening, or swimming—is to have students do the activity itself as soon as possible.

Political theory can help you make sense of your life and the world in which you live. It is like climbing to the top of a mountain and surveying the city in one glance and humanity's place in the cosmos. A teacher cannot think for a student, but they can, like a mountain guide, help students find the path, scramble over rocks, keep going when they want to give up, until they reach the summit with its fresh air and panoramic views (Marx and Engels 1978: xix). When it works well, students will learn to love the activity, and even if they do not want to do it as a vocation, they can still acquire habits of reading and thinking that continue for the rest of their lives.

When thinking about how to design assignments, I often return to a section of *Thus Spoke Zarathustra* entitled "On the Three Metamorphoses" that dramatizes how studying the history of ideas can prepare one to think for oneself (Nietzsche 2011: 16–17). According to Nietzsche, the first step in learning to achieve intellectual autonomy is to become a camel. A camel is a "strong, carrying spirit imbued with reverence" whose "strength demands what is heavy and heaviest" (Nietzsche 2011: 16). For a student of political theory, becoming a camel means studying the past with care. This can involve reading, taking notes on, transcribing into notebooks, and memorizing lines from texts. As a professor, I ask students to identify the dates of authors and texts, the definitions of key terms, or the steps in an argument. My lectures often use lists, and my exams ask students to identify the things on the list. Pedagogically, students must go through a camel phase and that entails understanding a thinker in their own terms. In addition, if you give students a list of possible questions in advance, then students have a clear path to earn a good grade in the course. For grading, I mostly test students' camel-like ability to learn the material of the course.

The next step in a philosophic education is to become a lion that "wants to hunt down its freedom and be master in its own desert" (Nietzsche 2011: 16). "Who is the great dragon whom the spirit no longer wants to call master and god? 'Thou shalt' is the name of the great dragon. But the spirit of the lion says 'I will'" (Nietzsche 2011: 17). Political thinkers battle with one another and bringing students into this conversation means teaching them to say, "I will" when a canonical figure says "thou shalt." In class discussions and assignments, I invite students to identify where they disagree with the authors. I make sure that my courses are filled with authors who discuss the same topics from different perspectives: it is impossible for students to agree with both Marcus Garvey and W. E. B. Du Bois, we will see, about whether Blacks should aspire to integrate with whites. In my courses, students need to decide where they stand on the battlefield of ideas even if they may change their minds over time.

The final step in a political theory education is to become a child who sees the world with fresh eyes: "The child is innocence and forgetting, a new beginning, a game, a wheel rolling out of itself, a first movement, a sacred yes-saying" (Nietzsche 2011: 17). When I first taught this passage at Johns Hopkins University, a student asked why people could not just start as a child. The issue is that human beings are encultured from the earliest moments of their lives. Most human beings grow up speaking the same language as their parents and sharing their political viewpoints. To become a child who can see the world fresh, ironically, requires hard work, a spirit of rebellion, and *neoteny*, the human capacity to remain young and playful (Crossman 2021). Political theory assignments should provide students with a chance to carry the weight of the past like camels, revolt against common sense like lions, and play with ideas like children.

Continuing the theme of playfulness, Box 4.1 discusses the idea of watching movies to explore political theory.

BOX 4.1   WATCH MOVIES

As I was thinking about what to teach in the summer, a colleague recommended that I develop a course in which students can watch movies. The idea makes sense. Students often work or intern in the summer, and they normally take summer school courses to graduate on time. They tend not to be interested in reading intense texts like Kant's *Groundwork for the Metaphysics of Morals* or Nietzsche's *On the Genealogy of Morality*. The challenge was to develop a course that would count as a legitimate political theory course and allow students to enjoy movies together in the summer. I created a course called Political Theory in Popular Culture that revolves around exploring the political ideologies of the Marvel Cinematic Universe (MCU).

The course alternates between two approaches. In the first half of most classes, I give a lecture on a political ideology using Andrew Heywood's (2021) textbook. Like many political theorists, I prefer to use primary sources (Moore 2011), but this textbook has a good structure with themes and facts that students can learn for their midterm and finals, and in my lectures, I can bring in primary sources and put my own spin on the material. In the second half of most classes, students present on the political ideology of an MCU movie or television series. On the syllabus, I assign scholarly and popular articles about the Marvel characters, and when we meet we discuss what political teachings the Marvel properties convey.

Take *Black Panther*. Christopher Lebron argued that despite having a cast of mostly Black actors and actresses, the movie reinforced negative stereotypes of African Americans. Lebron notes that the villain in the movie, Erik Killmonger, is "the black American who has rightly identified white supremacy as the reigning threat to black well-being" and "who will no longer stand for patience and moderation" and who is defeated by an African man (Lebron 2018).

Melvin L. Rogers replied that the movie offers a more complicated narrative. In its portrayal of Killmonger's tough upbringing in Oakland, California and in his desire to use vibranium to right the wrongs of colonial dispossession, the movie invites us to sympathize with Killmonger's pan-Africanism. "If you find yourself rooting for 'team' Killmonger, if your heart aches just a bit at the sight of his death, it may well be because the tragic and the heroic found each other in him" (Rogers 2018).

Over the years, students have written and presented outstanding research papers on political themes in the MCU, including ones dealing with monarchy (Asgard, Wakanda, Atlantis), feminism (Black Widow, Jessica Jones, Gamora), the Second Amendment (*Punisher*, *Iron Man 3*, *Captain America: Civil War*), and liberty and security as applied to vaccine passports (Mutant Registration Act in the *X-Men* movies, the Sokovia Accords in *Captain America: Civil War*).

A political theorist could use this approach for any other aspect of popular culture, including video games, popular music, or young adult literature. Political theorists have a responsibility to hand over a stack of books to the next generation. They can make the tradition relevant by connecting it to things students think about, care about, and do in their free time.

ASSIGNMENT ON FORGING IDENTITY

Compare and contrast Vinayak Damodar Savarkar's conception of Hindutva and Marcus Garvey's conception of the Negro people of the world.

When teaching race and caste, one faces the immediate problem that such categories are dubious from a scientific perspective. Evolutionary biologists have shown that the family tree of humanity is interconnected. All human beings alive today have common ancestors who lived sometime between 5300 and 2200 bce. All human beings share the same forebears at the time of the genetic isotope (Hershberger 2020). Nevertheless, the categories of race and caste profoundly affect how billions of people around the world live, think, feel, and identify themselves. If one is trying to gain a deep understanding of caste, race, and politics today, one ought to read authors who think that such categories serve a useful function. To accomplish this, I find value in teaching Vinayak Damodar Savarkar, an advocate of Hindutva, and Marcus Garvey, a spokesperson for what he called the Negro people of the world.

* * *

On May 27, 2020, the Prime Minister of India, Narendra Modi, tweeted, "I bow to the courageous Veer Savarkar. We remember him for his bravery, motivating several others to join the freedom struggle and emphasis on social reform" (Modi 2020). Who was Savarkar and how does he continue to inspire Modi and the Hindutva moment in India?

Savarkar (1883–1966) was born in Maharashtra, a state on the west coast of India, and, from an early age, became an Indian independence activist. After attending Fergusson College in Pune, he journeyed to England to study law and was arrested for his association with the revolutionary group India House. While being extradited back to India, he jumped out of a window of the ship in Marseilles, earning the moniker Veer, meaning brave. While incarcerated in 1922, Savarkar wrote *Essentials of Hindutva*, a tract that became "the bible of militant and exclusionary Hindu nationalism" (Bakhle 2010: 151), and upon his release from jail, he served as president of the Hindu Mahasabha, a Hindu nationalist political party. In 1948, a member of the Hindu Mahasabha, Nathuram Godse, assassinated Mahatma Gandhi, and though Savarkar was acquitted of being a co-conspirator, he became a *persona non grata* in the first half-century of independence when the Indian National Congress dominated Indian politics. With the rise of the Bharatiya Janata Party and the paramilitary volunteer organization the Rashtriya Swayamsevak Sangh, Savarkar has emerged as arguably the most profound and influential theorist of Hindutva.

In *Essentials of Hindutva*, Savarkar addressed the political problem of how to unite Hindus to oppose British rule on the subcontinent. The philosophical problem of the tract was to give an account of Hindu identity that could include all Hindu castes, the Untouchables, Sikhs, and a few exceptional Europeans and exclude Christians, Jews, Muslims, and Buddhists. Savarkar had to contest the narrative that the British created the nation by welding together a disparate collection of kingdoms and nationalities as well as the story that invading Muslims invented the term Hindu to name the people on the other side of the

Indus river (Sampath 2019: 400, 409). Savarkar envisioned an India ruled by and for Hindus, and the task of this prison writing was to draw a line between insiders and outsiders.

The essay opens by describing the power of words to conjure an identity as well as to describe an already-existing identity. *Hinduism* is a term projected onto Hindus by Protestant Europeans that fails to capture the whole Being of the Hindu race. Though Bal Gangadhar Tilak and others used the word Hindutva before him, Savarkar sees his own role as extracting its meaning that will change the lives of those who understand it:

> Hindutva embraces all the departments of thought and activity of the whole Being of our Hindu race. Therefore, to understand the significance of this term Hindutva, we must first understand the essential meaning of the word Hindu itself and realize how it came to exercise such imperial sway over the hearts of millions of mankind and won a loving allegiance from the bravest and best of them. (Savarkar 1923)[1]

Essentials of Hindutva is a history of a term and a people, but it makes no pretense of being a scholarly work like his earlier book of 1909, *The Indian War of Independence*, about the Indian rebellion of 1857. The essay is a polemic aimed at people like Gandhi, Nehru, and Ambedkar who envision India becoming a secular, constitutional democracy. Savarkar wants to solidify Hindu identity while, perhaps surprisingly, excising orthodox Hindu beliefs about the caste system and cow worship (Sampath 2019: xvi).

Savarkar identifies three things that unite Hindus. The first is common blood or race: *Jati*. The word *Jati* derives from the word *Jan*, to produce, suggesting that all Indians have a common origin. "All Hindus claim to have in their veins the blood of the mighty race incorporated with and descended from the Vedic fathers, the Sindhus" (Savarkar 1923: 31–2). To his credit, Savarkar immediately problematizes this criterion of who is or is not a Hindu. Scientifically, all human beings have "one common blood, the human blood" (Savarkar 1923: 33). Furthermore, it would defeat his purpose if Hindus fragmented according to their genetic lineages, which is why Savarkar eschewed the Aryan thesis to describe the essence of Hindutva. For Savarkar, Indians have enough genetic overlap to suggest that they are a family in a way that foreigners are not: "Some of us were Aryans and some Anaryans; but Ayars and Nayars—we were all Hindus and own a common blood. Some of us are Brahmans and some Namashudras or Panchamas; but Brahmans or Chandalas—we are all Hindus and own a common blood" (Savarkar 1923: 32). As we will see shortly, the criterion of race could include many people who Savarkar does not want to count as Hindus.

The second criterion of being a Hindu is love of fatherland: *Rashtra*. This is a love of the land stretching from the Indus River in the north to the sea below

India to the south, a love that encompasses the soil and water that constitute the natural home of Hindutva:

> A country, a common home is the first important essential of a stable strong nationality; and as of all countries in the world our country can hardly be surpassed by any in its capacity to afford a soil so specially fitted for the growth of a great nation; we Hindus whose very first article of faith is the love we bear to the common Fatherland. (Savarkar 1923: 51)

Like blood, though, this criterion can admit too many people into the Hindu fold for Savarkar. It makes sense that Hindus would love the ancestral home—the food, the smells, the climate, the views—but Savarkar demands one more thing before he will permit somebody to identify as a Hindu.

Savarkar's final criterion is adherence to a common culture or civilization: *Sanskriti*. According to Savarkar, Hindus grow up hearing stories of Hindu gods like Sita and Rama. Indian buildings express the principles of the Vaidik or Avaidik schools of thought. Across India, you find the same common law and rites, the same festivals, and the same habits. The defining feature of *Sanskriti* is language:

> Thought, they say, is inseparable from our common tongue, Sanskrit. Verily it is our mother-tongue—the tongue in which the mothers of our race spoke and which has given birth to all our present tongues. Our gods spoke in Sanskrit, our sages thought in Sanskrit, our poets wrote in Sanskrit. (Savarkar 1923: 35)

Here, it is important to recognize that Savarkar is not saying that Hindus must believe in the existence of the gods, the reality of caste, or continue the rites of their parents. Rather, Savarkar's argument is that "great combinations are the order of the day," and India must create its own version of Pan-Islamism, Pan-Slavism, and Pan-Africanism or the nation will perish. For this reason, Savarkar opposed the caste system: Hindus needed to bring the Untouchables into the Hindutva fold so that Hindus could fight their enemies rather than fight amongst themselves. Savarkar's fundamental demand is that Indians need to unify. The driving force of his conception of Hindutva is that it will make Indians physically strong: "Let this ancient and noble stream of Hindu blood flow from vein to vein, from Attock to Cuttack till at last the Hindu people get fused and welded into an indivisible whole, till our race gets consolidated and strong sharp as steel" (Savarkar 1923: 53).

Unlike Gandhi, who fasted to quell riots between Muslims and Hindus, Savarkar thinks that Hindutva depends on having Muslims as enemies. In one way, Savarkar hates Mohammad of Gazni for crossing the Indus and invading

Sindhusthan; in another, he relishes having an enemy that can galvanize Hindu civilization:

> Nothing can weld peoples into a nation and nations into a state as the pressure of a common foe. Hatred separates as well as unites. Never had Sindhusthan a better chance and a more powerful stimulus to be herself forged into an indivisible whole as on that dire day, when the great iconoclast crossed the Indus. (Savarkar 1923: 19)

Muslims may share the same blood, love the country, and speak the same language as Hindus, but for Savarkar, Muslims cannot simultaneously pray in the direction of Mecca and fit within Hindu civilization (*Sanskriti*) as a whole. Muslims—and Christians and Jews—belong "to a cultural unit altogether different from the Hindu one" (Savarkar 1923: 37). When Modi was the Chief Minister of Gujarat, Hindu mobs in the state rioted and killed 1,000 people, destroyed 20,000 Muslim homes and businesses, and displaced 150,000 people (Sinha and Suppes 2014). Modi honors Savarkar and seemed to put into practice what Savarkar called for in *Essentials of Hindutva*: a conflict of life and death between Hindus and Muslims.

Savarkar did not so much argue for the existence of Hindutva as enchant "a secular nationalism by placing a mythic community into a magical land" (Bakhle 2010: 182). Savarkar asserts that Indians need *a* civilization to become physically strong.[2] Hindutva is Savarkar's term for an identity that will enable Indians to stand up to Muslims, the British, the Chinese, the Russians, and other peoples on the world stage.

* * *

It is good to teach Savarkar so that students may better understand the appeal of ultranationalism in India; it is also beneficial to juxtapose him with Marcus Garvey who was working at roughly the same time to unite Africans and members of the African diaspora. In the 1910s and 1920s, Marcus Garvey was in New York City leading the Universal Negro Improvement Association (UNIA). According to Martin Luther King Jr., Garvey was "the first man, on a mass scale, and level, to give millions of Negroes a sense of dignity and destiny, and make the Negro feel that he was somebody" (Garvey 2005: iii). Savarkar and Garvey differed in their lives, strategies, definitions of race, orientation to religion, and so forth. But one reason to read them in conjunction is to see that people around the world in the early twentieth century, and up to today, feel the need to overlook differences to form collectives that enhance the strength of its members.

Marcus Garvey (1887–1940) was born in Jamaica, traveled to Costa Rica, Panama, and England, and founded the UNIA in Jamaica in 1914. In 1916, he moved to Harlem in New York City and gave speeches and wrote articles, including in his newspaper, *The Negro World*. In 1919, he became president of the Black Star Line to bring African Americans to Liberia. The shipping line lost money, however, and in 1923 Garvey went to jail on the charge of defrauding stockholders. In 1927, President Calvin Coolidge pardoned Garvey and deported him to Jamaica. Garvey moved to London, where he died in 1940. Garvey's contemporary, W. E. B. Du Bois, called him the "the most dangerous enemy of the Negro race in America and in the world" (Du Bois 1987c: 990), and his supporters have had to wrestle with his meeting the Imperial Wizard of the Ku Klux Klan, his sympathies for European fascism, and the political right's fascination with him (Brown and Roig-Franzia 2019).

In 1921, Garvey gave a speech in Liberty Hall, New York City, explaining the political problem confronting Blacks: how to form an identity that would enable them to compete with peoples such the English, French, Irish, Indian, and Japanese:

> This world in which we live is divided up into separate and distinct national groups. It is also divided up into great human groups. Each and every one of these national groups and each and every one of these many race groups is fighting for its own interests; fighting for those things that are dear to it. This conflict of groups and conflict of nations has called for the best in each group and the best in each nation. If you were to take a survey of humanity—if you were to take a survey of the world politically, you will find every little group of humanity striking out in its own domain. (Garvey 2005: 37)

In his lifetime, Garvey faced discrimination from white families in Jamaica as well as the "black whites" of Jamaica (Garvey 2005: 4). He knew that Black identity as such did not exist yet. He also lived during a time of Jim Crow segregation, race riots, and lynching, and partly because of his travels, he felt the situations of Blacks around the world bound them together. His task was to help conjure into being "a new world of black men, not peons, serfs, dogs and slaves, but a nation of sturdy men making their impress upon civilization and causing a new light to dawn upon the human race" (Garvey 2005: 3). But how could he impress upon Blacks around the world that they were one people?

One strategy that Garvey took was to argue that Blacks were essentially a different race than other peoples. In speeches like "Africa for the Africans" (1922), he suggests that "the Negro peoples of the world" (Garvey 2005: 69) share a blood, and a family connection, that make them different than other races:

> Everybody knows that there is absolutely no difference between the native African and the American and West Indian Negroes, in that we are descendants from one common family stock. It is only a matter of accident that we have been divided and kept apart for over three hundred years, but it is felt that when the time has come

for us to get back together, we shall do so in the spirit of brotherly love. (Garvey 2005: 72)

Throughout his writings, one finds reference to "our blood" or "Negro blood." Is this a sustainable position given miscegenation? Garvey replies that "100 percent Negroes and even 1 percent Negroes will stand together as one mighty whole" (Garvey 2005: 122).

A second strategy that Garvey used to consolidate Black identity—for instance, in his 1923 speech, "Who and What Is a Negro?"—was to place Blacks at the center of the march of history. Referring to contemporary anthropologists who argued that Moroccans, Algerians, and Senegalese were not Negroes, Garvey replied: "the white world has always tried to rob and discredit us of our history" and that "every student of history, of impartial mind, knows that the Negro once ruled the world, when white men were savages and barbarians living in caves" (Garvey 2005: 120). Looked at charitably, Garvey was trying to remind his audience in Harlem, as well as Europeans and Americans, that Africans and the African diaspora have a history and philosophy worth learning (Garvey 2020b).

Garvey's most promising strategy to consolidate Black identity was to give it a forward-looking orientation, like when Garvey said, "the new Negro desires nationhood" (Garvey 2005: 84). Garvey thinks that Blacks are not already a self-conscious race but can become one to achieve their ideal of self-determination. For Garvey, "what matters is whether a group expresses an aspiration for self-rule, not whether its members retain a pervasive culture or other characteristics generally preserved by a state" (Jagmohan 2020). Garvey conveyed this message with his words, but also with spectacles such as parades, conventions, and rituals that fused Black people together as a force to fight for their own interests (Getachew 2021). Blacks are not held together solely by blood or historical traumas but by a desire to govern and protect themselves.

One of the controversies surrounding Garvey was his meeting with the Acting Imperial Wizard of the Ku Klux Klan on June 25, 1922. Garvey maintained that people tended to congregate into groups, and those groups had the right to exercise sovereignty in their country. "You cannot blame any group of men, whether they are Chinese, Japanese, Anglo-Saxons or Frenchmen, for standing up for their interests or for organizing in their interest" (Garvey 2005: 76). According to Garvey, the Ku Klux Klan were the de facto leaders of the white race and therefore of the United States. Garvey envisioned Liberia as being the anchor state for the global population of Blacks. Garvey did not think that it was feasible or desirable for all Blacks in America to go to Liberia, but he did think that it was essential that Blacks around the world have a country that they could appeal to for help. If a French person were unjustly arrested in another country, diplomats could intervene on their behalf. Garvey envisioned a Black country serving as a shield for Black people around the world. What Garvey could not envision was Black people assimilating and becoming, for example, a president, governor, or mayor in the United States (Garvey 2005: 9).

Garvey believed that strong Black men would be needed to galvanize Black people into a nation. The state reflects the character of the man who leads it, whether it is a Nero, Alexander, Washington, Lincoln, or Roosevelt Black. Garvey asserted that the "government should be absolute, and the head should be thoroughly responsible for himself and the acts of his subordinates" (Garvey 2020a). Michael Dawson notes that Garvey envisions a Black man following Machiavelli's advice in *The Prince* about how to establish new modes and orders. Garvey's Black prince must see the world clearly, act boldly, realize that the success of an endeavor justifies it in the eyes of the world, and face fortune bravely. "The Black Prince must be a singular and exceptional leader—one who will stand firm and with a clear eye in 'a world without charity'" (Dawson 2021: 273). Responding to the charge that Garveyism was fascistic in its veneration of a strong leader, Adom Getachew argues that Garvey manifested the movement's desire for "reverential self-regard" (Getachew 2021: 1207). Black nationalists did not blindly follow Garvey but decided that he gave voice to their aspirations for dignity, power, and self-rule.

At the International Convention of the Negroes of the World in 1920, Marcus Garvey made a point that Malcolm X would later take up: "in consideration of the fact that as a race we are now deprived of those things that are morally and legally ours, we believe it right that all such things should be acquired and held by whatsoever means possible" (Garvey 2005: 18). W. E. B. Du Bois charged Garvey with threatening the district attorney, intimidating witnesses, and possibly having a former associate killed in regard to his trial (Du Bois 1987a). For Garvey, Blacks are deluding themselves if they think they can get what they deserve by trying to soften the hearts of white people:

> Power is the only argument that satisfies man. It is the naval and political power of Great Britain that keeps her mistress of the seas. It is the commercial and financial power of the United States of America that makes her the greatest banker in the world. Hence it is advisable for the Negro to get power of every kind. POWER in education, science, industry, politics and highest government. That kind of power that will stand out signally, so that other races and nations can see, and if they will not see, then FEEL. Man is not satisfied or moved by prayers or petitions, but every man is moved by that power of authority which forces him to do even against his will. (Garvey cited in Dawson 2021: 275)

* * *

One reason to teach Savarkar and Garvey alongside one another is to learn about ultranationalist movements in the early twentieth century. Another is to understand the appeal of militant group identities. Savarkar opposed British rule in India; Garvey confronted white supremacy in the United States; both were trying to liberate their groups from racial oppression. Savarkar led the Hindu Mahasabha; Garvey led the Universal Negro Improvement Association; both were eclipsed in the twentieth century by the more centrist Indian National Congress and the National Association for the Advancement of Colored People (NAACP). Savarkar and Garvey appealed to race and blood but recognized that "nature is constantly trying to overthrow the artificial barriers you raise between race and race" (Savarkar 1923: 33). Instead of grounding their arguments on science or history, both emphasized the benefits that would accrue to the groups if they solidified now and in the future. For Savarkar, Hindutva promised a Hindu nationalist identity free of Muslim and English accretions; for Garvey, the Negros of the world could step confidently on the world stage if they had strong Black leaders. Savarkar and Garvey also exemplify the dangers of ultranationalism, including its propensity to brutality, masculinity, violence, and intolerance (Gilroy 2000; Madhav and Jafri 2021).

ASSIGNMENT ON ENDS

Compare and contrast Ambedkar's conception of annihilating caste and Du Bois's idea of the veil.

In this section, I explain what educators gain when they teach, and make assignments about, Indian and African American thinkers who envisioned an egalitarian future in which caste and race would no longer matter. If Savarkar and Garvey may be placed on the political right, we may place B. R. Ambedkar and W. E. B. Du Bois on the political left because of their commitment to the ideal of equality. Ambedkar was a leader of the Dalits (formerly Untouchables); Du Bois founded the NAACP; and Du Bois and Ambedkar were part of a generation of political thinkers envisioning a new form of global struggle against race and caste oppression (Cabrera 2020; Getachew 2020; Purkayastha 2019; Valdez 2019). Teaching Ambedkar and Du Bois alongside one another presses students to consider the ideal and challenges of transcending caste and race.

* * *

When teaching Ambedkar, I begin by sharing a story of visiting the Tata Institute of Social Sciences in Mumbai in 2017 and seeing on the side of the library a massive poster of B. R. Ambedkar listing his accomplishments and publications. Quietly leaving the conference I was attending, I went to the Dr. Ambedkar memorial lecture and heard Sukhadeo Thorat, a professor from Jawaharlal Nehru University in New Delhi, give a talk—subsequently published (Thorat 2019)—to a packed auditorium on Ambedkar's vision of how to safeguard minorities in a democracy. What I learned from my week in Mumbai was that Ambedkar is a national hero for Dalits and Indians who want the country to leave behind the legacy of caste.

Bhimrao Ramji Ambedkar was born in 1891 into a Mahar (Dalit) caste whose family had long served in the army of the British East India company. When he was six years old, he moved with his family to Mumbai and eventually attended Elphinstone High School and then Bombay University. In 1913, he traveled overseas to Columbia University, where he studied with the American philosopher John Dewey, whose pragmatism and faith in democracy left a permanent residue in his thinking (Stroud 2017b). Ambedkar moved to London where he earned a doctoral degree in economics at the London School of Economics and studied law at Gray's Inn. When he returned to India, he led campaigns for Untouchables to drink from communal wells and enter Hindu temples, and in 1927 he famously burned the Hindu lawbook, the *Manusmriti*. In 1936, he prepared a talk on "Annihilation of Caste" that he never delivered but that he subsequently published—and which became required reading for all students at the Tata Institute for Social Sciences. In 1947, Prime Minister Nehru invited him to serve as law minister, and then he became the lead writer of India's Constitution. In 1956, the last year of his life, Ambedkar led a mass conversion of Dalits to Buddhism and prepared his magnum opus: *The Buddha and His Dhamma* (Stroud 2017a).

For Ambedkar, caste is an artificial construct that has real consequences for people. In a paper he wrote in 1916 for an anthropology seminar at Columbia University, Ambedkar explains that there is no biological basis for caste. Human beings "of pure race exist nowhere" and there "has been a mixture of all races in all parts of the world" (Ambedkar 2004a: 236). Indians combine genetic elements from Aryans, Dravidians, Mongolians, and Scythians. Indians do not especially care about the color of skin or whether someone's family or tribe was originally racially Aryan or Dravidian. Ambedkar maintains that when Western scholars apply the category of race, this says more about them than the situation in India. All Indians can interbreed with one another, of course, so the category of race does not apply. That said, caste infuses the life of all Indians: "Caste in India means an artificial chopping off of the population into fixed and definite units, each one prevented from fusing into one another through the custom of endogamy" (Ambedkar 2004b: 245). In this essay, "Castes in India," Ambedkar floats a thesis about the genesis of caste. Originally, the priestly class, the Brahmins, decided to procreate only with one another, and then other groups tried to replicate this high-status group, until most people in the caste system—including those technically outside of it, the Untouchables—only reproduce with those in the same caste. Though the

Constitution prohibits discrimination based on caste, and few Indians today vocally defend the caste system, the practice of endogamy persists, which means that caste persists (Akbar 2017).

Annihilation of Caste describes the violence, the indignities, the hardships caused by the caste system:

> Under the rule of the Peshwas in the Maratha country, the Untouchable was not allowed to use the public streets if a Hindu was coming along, lest he should pollute the Hindu by his shadow. The Untouchable was required to have a black thread either on his wrist or around his neck, as a sign or a mark to prevent the Hindus from getting themselves polluted by his touch by mistake. In Poona, the capital of the Peshwa, the Untouchable was required to carry, strung from his waist, a broom to sweep away from behind himself the dust he trod on, lest a Hindu walking on the same dust should be polluted. (Ambedkar 2014: 213–14)

Caste discrimination takes forms other than demanding that Dalits sweep the dust behind them. One form of casteism is when cow vigilantes attack Dalits for skinning an animal that Hindus consider sacred. When I was at the Ambedkar memorial lecture, I saw a display about young Dalit men recently tied to a car and beaten by a crowd of Hindus.

How is it possible to convince upper-caste Hindus to abolish a system that benefits them? Ambedkar's argument in *Annihilation of Caste* is that caste hurts everyone in society, even the most privileged. In a well-ordered society, the most qualified people will get and perform the jobs that use their talents. People who have leadership abilities will lead, people with martial abilities will become soldiers, people with an interest in business will go into entrepreneurship, and so forth. In a caste society, however, people are slotted into careers based on their lineage and name. The government, military, and economy are all weaker because of it:

> Social and individual efficiency requires us to develop the capacity of an individual to the point of competency to choose and to make their own career. This principle is violated in the caste system, insofar as it involves an attempt to appoint tasks to individuals in advance—selected not on the basis of trained original capacities, but on that of the social status of the parents. (Ambedkar 2014: 234)

Ambedkar's followers often point to his prestigious degrees as evidence that Dalits are as capable of learning and leading people as any other caste.

In addition to the moral and social efficiency arguments against caste, Ambedkar argued that caste makes Hindus weaker as a fighting force. According to Ambedkar, inbreeding within castes has weakened the genetic stock and turned Hindus "into a race of pygmies and dwarfs." Even if we bracket this argument about physical degeneration and regeneration, Ambedkar's point is that caste separates Hindus and renders them unable to assist each other the way that other groups do. The Hindus "are not merely an assortment of castes, but are so many warring groups, each living for itself and for its selfish ideal." According to Ambedkar, what makes Sikhs and Muslims better soldiers than Hindus is not physical strength, diet, or drill, but rather the feeling in each group that members will come to the rescue of each other (Ambedkar 2014: 240–41, 246, 255).

Mohandas Gandhi, a leader of the Indian National Congress, argued that it was possible to abolish caste without necessarily discarding the notion of traditional family occupations (*varna*). Gandhi opposed the practice of untouchability and wanted the Untouchables to be called Harijan, "children of God." At the same time, in his 1936 response to Ambedkar, Gandhi maintained that village life, the basis of Indian civilization, required people to fill their inherited roles:

> Caste has nothing to do with religion. It is a custom whose origin I do not know, and do not need to know for the satisfaction of my spiritual hunger. But I do know that it is harmful both to spiritual and national growth. Varna and ashrama are institutions which have nothing to do with castes. The law of varnas teaches us that we have each one of us to earn our bread by following the ancestral calling. (McDermott 2014: 428)

According to Gandhi, each human being has a duty to perform their ancestral calling, whether that means being a spiritual teacher, a soldier, a merchant, a servant, or a scavenger. In the face of Ambedkar's critique, Gandhi thinks that Hindus may reform themselves by considering all *varnas* "good, lawful and absolutely equal in status" (Ambedkar 2014: 326). Ambedkar responds that this reform does not touch upon the root of the problem. Priests have a high status in Hinduism, and if occupations are passed on from parents to children, then there will be a strong incentive for Brahmins to marry Brahmins, members of the Kshatriyas to marry other members of the military caste, and so forth.

Ambedkar disagreed with Savarkar's plan to annihilate caste by bringing Dalits into Hindutva. Ambedkar dismissed Savarkar's etymology of the word Hindu as mythology: "The name Hindu is itself a foreign name. It was given by the Mahomedans to the natives for the purpose of distinguishing themselves. It does not occur in any Sanskrit work prior to the Mahomedan invasion" (Ambedkar 2014: 241–2). Ambedkar could not conceive how Hindu society could survive in any recognizable form if it discarded caste or *varna*. "Religion compels the Hindus to treat isolation and segregation of castes as a virtue… If Hindus wish to break caste, their religion will come in the way" (Ambedkar 2014: 281). Kalyan Kumar Das provides evidence to confirm Ambedkar's worry in an essay discussing the memoir of a Dalit, Bhanwar Meghwanshi's *I Could Not Be Hindu*, who was attracted to Hindutva's message of inclusivity but then discovered a replication of the caste system within the Rashtriya Swayamsevak Sangh (RSS). Das observes that Hindutva may welcome Dalits on the political level, but it has not yet welcomed them on the social level, as individuals worthy of dignity and not just voters or foot soldiers (Das forthcoming). In *Annihilation of Caste*, Ambedkar leaves open the possibility that Hindus may renounce Brahminism and articulate a worldview consonant with liberty, equality, and fraternity. Hindus are making such efforts (Parikh 2021), but Ambedkar himself could not imagine how it would work (Ambedkar 2014: 310–11).

Ambedkar's vision is to annihilate caste and replace it with democracy. Quoting his teacher John Dewey, Ambedkar says: "Democracy is not merely a form of government. It is primarily a mode of associated living, of conjoint communicated experience. It is essentially an attitude of respect and reverence towards fellow men" (Ambedkar 2014: 260). In a democratic society, people treat everyone else with respect, and they allow each person to shine through their own unique talents and hard work. In a modern society, there will be prestigious occupations, but individuals qua individuals should be able to compete for them: occupations should not be the property of any one caste. The day after Ambedkar burned the *Manusmriti*, Ambedkar gave a speech before a group of women advising them to abandon every aspect of the caste system that holds that Brahmin men, women, and children deserve respect, while Dalits face insults everywhere. Even something as quotidian as clothing must reflect the new situation:

> The way you wear your saris is a sign of your being untouchable, you must wipe out that sign. You must begin the practice of wearing your saris in the same fashion that upper-caste women do, it will not cost you anything. In the same way, your habit of wearing heavy necklaces round your necks and bracelets and bangles of *kathil* on your arms up to the elbow, mark you out as being untouchable. There is no need for more than one necklace. (Pawar and Moon 2015: 122)

When I was in Mumbai, female students would alternate between wearing saris and jeans on different days. Based on passages like this one, Ambedkar seems to think that traditional clothing is just another way for Hindu society to perpetuate caste. Just as Ambedkar made a point to wear suits, the force of his argument is that all young Indians should only wear modern Western clothing.

Ambedkar recognized that dismantling caste in the long term meant recognizing its existence in the short term. As architect of the Constitution of India, Ambedkar wrote Article 15 with two provisions somewhat at odds with each other. On the one hand, "the State shall not discriminate against any citizen on grounds only of religion, race, caste, sex, [or] place of birth"; on the other, "nothing in this article…shall prevent the State from making any special provision for the advancement of any socially and educationally backward classes of citizens or for the Scheduled Castes and the Scheduled Tribes." The goal is to reach a society where everyone can compete on their own merits, but one cannot simply ignore the benefits that have accrued to upper-caste Hindus over millennia. The reservation system, much like the United States policy of affirmative action, aims to ensure that the Scheduled Castes (Dalits), the Scheduled Tribes, and Other Backward Classes (including Shudras, the servant caste) get a chance to hold elevated positions within the basic structure of society. Martha Nussbaum observes that "the very programs that Ambedkar promoted to end caste have in some ways backfired, entrenching caste identities and promoting a type of identity politics that he abhorred." By making admission to the Indian Institutes of Information Technology (IIITs) or the job market hinge on one's caste, the reservation system led to "caste-based parties and a politics of competitive bean-counting" seemingly at odds with Ambedkar's democratic egalitarian vision (Nussbaum 2016: 303, 317). By relying on justice to remedy the low status of Dalits, Ambedkar took a risk that the caste system would become even more solidified as Dalits fought to protect their reservations.

To complicate matters further, Ambedkar did not want to annihilate caste if that meant that Dalits would simply be welcomed into the Hindu fold. In 1935, Ambedkar famously declared that though he was born a Hindu, he would not die a Hindu. Ambedkar considered converting to Christianity or Islam but decided that Buddhism offered Dalits the best opportunity to draw upon Indian traditions to assert their own worth. "The principles of equality, compassion, fraternity and brotherhood which are essential for the welfare of humanity are found only in Buddhism." In the last year of his life, Ambedkar convinced hundreds of thousands of Dalits to convert to Buddhism. Though Ambedkar did not want the Dalits to retain their identities as Dalits, he entertained the idea that the group could redescribe the features that separated them from Hindus. At the conversion ceremony on October 15, 1956, he pointed to a surviving member of the Nag people and said: "we are descendants of him" (Stroud 2017a: 327, 333, 331). Ambedkar explored ways to reconstruct the Dalit identity even after the temporary measures of the reservation system.

In his career, Ambedkar never wavered that Dalits and their allies needed to destroy the caste system, but he equivocated on what would replace it: a society in which all individuals deserved respect but rose or fell in professions based on their talent and work ethic; a social arrangement in which disadvantaged groups had positions reserved for them, at least for the time being; and an order in which the Dalits became Buddhists who fit uneasily within a Hindu society.[3]

* * *

In *The Souls of Black Folk*, W. E. B. Du Bois used the image of the veil to describe the divide between whites and Blacks and envisioned a time when human beings could meet each other as souls above it. But Du Bois grappled with the complexities of race in ways that prompt students to think about whether this category describes a natural essence, a contingent social formation, or a distinct civilization worth preserving. Like Ambedkar, Du Bois wanted to annihilate white supremacy, but his alternatives changed over his lifetime and sometimes even within a single text.

William Edward Burghardt Du Bois (1868–1963) was born and raised in New England, taught high school, and went to Fisk University in Tennessee, became the first African American to earn a doctorate from Harvard University, and taught for many years at Atlanta University. In 1909, Du Bois helped found the NAACP, and as editor of its monthly magazine, *The Crisis*, Du Bois exercised a profound influence on African American political thought and politics. Du Bois's texts span history (1896's *The Suppression of the African Slave Trade to the United States of America, 1638–1870*), sociology (1899's *The Philadelphia Negro: A Social Study*), political theory (1903's *The Souls of Black Folk*), and autobiography (1940's *Dusk of Dawn*).

In "The Conservation of Races" (1897), Du Bois suggests that Blacks constitute a different race than whites and calls for social equilibrium between them. The text makes several claims that do not square easily with each other. The opening mentions the idea that "out of one blood God created all nations" (Du Bois 1987c: 815) but then asserts that there are physical, psychic, and spiritual differences between races:[4]

> What, then, is a race? It is a vast family of human beings, generally of common blood and language, always of common history, traditions and impulses, who are both voluntarily and involuntarily striving together for the accomplishment of certain more or less vividly conceived ideals of life. (Du Bois 1987c: 817)

A race does involve biological differences, and at one point in the essay Du Bois refers to "the black-blooded people of America" (Du Bois 1987c: 819). But what really binds a race together is a shared history, laws, religion, habits of thought, and ideals of life. The English stand for liberty and commerce, the Germans for science and philosophy, the Romance nations for literature and art, and the world awaits "the development of Negro genius" (Du Bois 1987c: 820). Du Bois argues that the dispute about whether Blacks exist as a race is merely academic and that Blacks deserve a chance to make their own contribution to world history: "We believe it the duty of the Americans of Negro descent, as a body, to maintain their race identity until this mission of the Negro people is accomplished, and the ideal of human brotherhood has become a practical possibility" (Du Bois 1987c: 825). Du Bois calls for Blacks to create their own colleges, newspapers, businesses, and research centers. Much like Booker T. Washington, the founder of the Tuskegee Institute, Du Bois maintains that peaceful segregation offers Black people the best opportunity to develop their own economic, political, and cultural power to resist white supremacy (Jagmohan 2021).

In *Dusk of Dawn*, Du Bois offers a more pragmatic, rather than metaphysical, account of race (Taylor 2021). Du Bois himself had Alsatian and Dutch ancestors, and his travels throughout his world weakened his belief that there were solid borders between races. "In Europe my friendships and close contact with white folks made my own ideas waver. The eternal walls between races did not seem so stern and exclusive. I began to emphasize the cultural aspects of race" (Du Bois 1987c: 628). Du Bois's time at Fisk University in Tennessee solidified the notion that people who share a history and memories, joyful and sad, do have a bond. The "physical bond is least and the badge of color relatively unimportant save as a badge; the real essence of this kinship is its social heritage of slavery; the discrimination and insult; and this heritage binds together not simply the children of Africa, but extends through yellow Asia and into the South Seas" (Du Bois 1987c: 640). For Du Bois, the situation in America between whites and Blacks is a local manifestation of a global conflict between the white world and the colored races, a category that can encompass any group contending with white supremacy and the legacy of imperialism and colonialism.

In *The Souls of Black Folk*, Du Bois describes the pain caused by the veil that separates white and black people. The book opens with a scene from his youth in New England where children were exchanging cards in school: "The exchange was merry, till one girl, a tall newcomer, refused my card—refused it peremptorily, with a glance. Then it dawned upon me with a certain suddenness that I was different from the others; or like, mayhap, in heart and life and longing, but shut out from their world by a vast veil" (Du Bois 1987b: 364). Once the veil dropped, or Du Bois became aware that he belonged to a different race in the eyes of white people, he affected a pose of indifference to white people. But then he became aware that race meant that he might be excluded from certain professions—including law, medicine, and academia—and cultural pursuits such as classical music that reflected the tastes of Europeans and white Americans. "Alas, with the years all this fine contempt began to fade; the worlds I longed for, and all their dazzling opportunities, were theirs, not mine" (Du Bois 1987b: 364). As the book proceeds, Du Bois tells the stories of how racism has damaged the lives of Josie, the young woman he met as a schoolteacher in Tennessee, Alexander Crummell, the founder of the American Negro Academy, and John, the young Black man who faced insults and setbacks while the young white man from the same village faced glittering life prospects. Du Bois imagines what John felt when he returned to the South after experiencing relative freedom in college: "If he could only live up in the free air where birds sang and setting suns had no touch of blood!" (Du Bois 1987b: 527).

Why should white people, who presumably benefit from racism, try to lower the veil separating their souls from Black souls? Du Bois's argument is that white people lose out in myriad ways from a system that keeps another race in an abject condition. From a concern with safety, white people should try to ameliorate the poverty that leads to crime and insurrection: "no secure civilization can be built in the South with the Negro as an ignorant, turbulent proletariat." From an economic perspective, whites lose out when the "powers of body and mind" of Blacks are "wasted, dispersed, or forgotten" (Du Bois 1987b: 435, 365). Bracketing the moral question, Du Bois's point is that white people will be safer and richer if Black people enter the workforce as skilled laborers and professionals, property owners, and educated voters. It is in white people's self-interest to advance the cause of Reconstruction after the Civil War to bring African Americans into the schools, the workforce, and the electorate.

Du Bois maintains that racism hurts white workers as well as Black workers. In *Black Reconstruction in America, 1860–1880* (1935), Du Bois argues that white southern agricultural interests and northern industrialists realized during Reconstruction that it would be in their economic interest to have the white working class identify as white, rather than as members of a multiracial working class. In an essay on "The Negro and Radical Thought" (1921), Du Bois argues that combating the injustices of wage slavery requires forming alliances across races: "We have to convince the working classes of the world that black men, brown men, and yellow men are human beings and suffer the same discrimination that white workers suffer. We have in addition to this to espouse the cause of the white workers" (Du Bois 1987c: 1188).

Focusing on safety, money, and distributive justice is insufficient, for Du Bois: it is also important to explain that Black people may make their own unique contributions to civilization, humanity's finest spiritual, intellectual, artistic achievements. "Herein the longing of black men must have respect: the rich and bitter depth of their experience, the unknown treasures of their inner life, the strange rendings of nature they have seen, may give the world new points of view and make their loving, living, and doing precious to all human hearts" (Du Bois 1987b: 438). For Du Bois, the best and brightest African Americans—what he calls "the talented tenth"—may take their place with the best representatives of any other race. Blacks may learn from all other peoples, and they may make their own unique contributions to world knowledge, literature, art: "I sit with Shakespeare and he winces not" (Du Bois 1987b: 438). Du Bois invites his readers to imagine Black Shakespeares, and one can even read his novels—including *The Quest of the Silver Fleece* (1911) and *Dark Princess: A Romance* (1928)—as efforts to achieve that goal. As a scholar and artist, Du Bois explains, "I dwell above the Veil" (Du Bois 1987c: 438), and his call anticipates many of the finest cultural products of the twentieth century, including Ralph Ellison's *Invisible Man* (1952) and Zora Neale Huston's *Their Eyes Were Watching God* (1937).

Du Bois's vision is to achieve a world in which there is no veil separating Blacks, whites, or the members of any other race. A veil separated him and a classmate as a child, and he would spend his entire life trying to raise people above the arbitrary divisions of skin color and hair texture that make humans strangers to one another. One of the sources of Du Bois's veil imagery is 2 Corinthians 3:14–16: "when one turns to the Lord, the veil is removed. Now the Lord is the Spirit, and where the Spirit of the Lord is, there is freedom. And all of us, with unveiled faces, seeing the glory of the Lord as though reflected in a mirror, are being transformed into the same image from one degree of glory to another." For Du Bois, freedom lies in our ability to rise above the color line, above the veil, and meet each other as universal, sovereign spirits (Mariotti 2009). In "On the Passing of the First-Born," Du Bois offers a heart-rending account of his son who died as a child but whose brief life provided a glimpse of how human beings could relate to one another without racial prejudice: "He knew no color-line, poor dear—and the Veil, though it shadowed him, had not yet darkened half his sun. He loved the white matron, he loved his black nurse; and in his little world walked souls alone, uncolored and unclothed. I—yea, all men—are larger and purer by the infinite breath of that one little life" (Du Bois 1987c: 509). Du Bois envisions a world in which artists, scholars, businesspeople, athletes and so forth will be judged solely by their character and talent. The Sorrow Songs, or spirituals, breathe a hope that "sometime, somewhere, men will judge men by their souls and not by their skins" (Du Bois 1987c: 544).

Du Bois's vision of pure souls rising above raced bodies, then, put him at odds with Marcus Garvey. Garvey believed in the forcible separation of races, according to Du Bois, which made him indistinguishable from white supremacists. "Every man who apologizes for or defends Marcus Garvey from this day forth writes himself down as unworthy of the countenance of the decent Americans. As for Garvey himself, this open ally of the Ku Klux Klan should be locked up or sent home" (Du Bois 1987c: 992). For Du Bois, the goal is to end racism, not perpetuate it in the name of essential racial differences.

Du Bois realized, however, that eliminating racism in the United States required facing the consequences of slavery and how blacks were not yet ready to compete as equals with whites. Du Bois supported the Freedmen's Bureau, in the aftermath of the Civil War, to bring to bear the power of the federal government to help African Americans acquire land, become educated, vote, have access to fair courts, and be safe. Du Bois praises the Freedmen's Bureau for putting 30 000 black teachers in the South, wiping out illiteracy for most black people, and establishing the Tuskegee Institute for black students. It does not "require any fine-spun theories of racial differences to prove the necessity of such group training after the brains of the race have been knocked out by two hundred and fifty years of assiduous education in submission, carelessness, and stealing" (Du Bois 1987c: 478). If America is going to actualize its founding principle that all human beings are created equal, then it must consider reparations to close the wealth gap that perpetuates inequality (Balfour 2003; Coates 2014).

Throughout his writings, Du Bois maintained that Black people *are* different than white people, that Black souls are not the same as white souls, and that erasing the veil would constitute its own kind of harm. In his early work, *The Souls of Black Folk*, he says that he would "not bleach his Negro soul in a flood of white Americanism, for he knows that Negro blood has a message for the world" (Du Bois 1987b: 365). And in his late autobiography, *Dusk of Dawn*, he describes what he saw on his trip to the African bush: "African life with its isolation has deeper knowledge of human souls. The village life, the forest ways, the teeming markets, bring in intimate human knowledge that the West misses, sinking the individual in the social" (Du Bois 1987c: 648). I will leave it to Du Bois scholars to explain the relationship between Du Bois's early and late work on the question of racial identities.[5]

Through his writings, example, leadership, and connections to different movements in the United States and around the world, Du Bois "has achieved remarkable centrality in African American political thought (and beyond)" (Taylor 2021: 235). Du Bois envisioned a world in which Black people would be judged by their talent and character, not by the color of their skin. He called for black people to work with their white allies, inside and outside government, to redress the legacy of slavery and economic inequality. And he cherished African and African American culture and thought that Black people had their own contribution to make to world civilization. Du Bois's image of the veil helps his readers envision how to negotiate the divide that separates Blacks and whites.

* * *

Though Ambedkar and Du Bois envision a post-caste and post-race future, they think that reservations and reparations are necessary to address the legacy of oppression at least in the short term. And both worry about what will be lost if their minority group dissolves into the majority one. When making assignments about Ambedkar and Du Bois, I would invite students to consider possible responses the authors would make to a real-world attempt to remedy racism or casteism and whether the students agree with the responses or not.

ASSIGNMENT ON MEANS

Compare and contrast Mohandas Gandhi's conception of satyagraha *and Martin Luther King's conception of civil disobedience.*

In the spring of 2020, a white Minneapolis police officer knelt on the neck of a Black man named George Floyd, and the event and the video footage of the murder shocked the country. Watching the video, I cried and wanted to harm the officer who asphyxiated a man who could not defend himself. Shortly afterwards, I taught a course at Fordham University in the Bronx and several of my students were attending protests in New York City, some of which turned violent. Two students in the course were New York City police officers responsible for keeping peace in the city. The police officers were both Black and Latinx and fathers to young children. Both thought that the white police officer had crossed the line of professionalism as well as of ethics. They were both struggling with their mental health as they had to do crowd control on hot days. Some of the people arrested at demonstrations were carrying gasoline, hammers, hooks, and ropes (*The New York Times* 2020). My goal as a professor is to help students think more deeply about political things, including what marching accomplishes and whether it is sometimes appropriate to use violence. In this context, I created an assignment that could draw upon the history of political thought to help students think about the means to end race and caste oppression. The third assignment, then, invites students to think with Mohandas Karamchand Gandhi and Martin Luther King, Jr. about how to balance justice and love, an effort to redress wrongs and heal the injuries of the past so that people can become civic friends with those they once hated.

* * *

Mohandas Karamchand Gandhi, also known as Mahatma ("great-souled"), was born in Gujarat, on the west coast of India, in 1869. Gandhi studied law in London, and then moved to South Africa where he led a campaign of passive resistance on behalf of Indian civil rights. In 1909, he wrote *Hind Swaraj*, in which he laid out what it would take for India to become spiritually, as well as physically, independent from British rule. In 1915, he returned to India and assumed a leadership position in the Indian National Congress. Gandhi adopted the term *satyagraha* ("truth force") to signal that Indians needed to be brave and energetic in repelling oppression without physical violence. Gandhi led Indians on the Dandi Salt March, on which they collected salt without paying the British tax, and Gandhi fasted, almost to the point of death, on behalf of the anticolonial Quit India campaign, to stop separate electorates for Dalits, and to quell rioting between Muslims and Hindus. Gandhi's thought changed over time, a point that he defended on principle: "The truth that we see is relative, many-sided, plural and it is the whole truth for a given time" (Gandhi 2008: 55). Gandhi was consistent, however, that violence begets more violence, and that Indians needed a new kind of protest movement to achieve freedom without harming the British or each other.

Gandhi's notion of *swaraj* means "freedom from the English yoke" (Gandhi 2008: 153). *Swaraj* means that the British may no longer rule unwilling subjects in India, and that Indian voters will elect their leaders. Like Du Bois, Gandhi situates the Indian struggle in a global one of colored peoples resisting white supremacy: "My ambition is much higher than independence. Through the deliverance of India, I seek to deliver the so-called weaker races of the earth from the crushing heels of Western exploitation in which England is the greatest partner" (Gandhi 2008: 153). Gandhi still wishes to be friendly with the English people, and even entertains the idea of joining a world commonwealth in which India and England are equal members, but the days of British rule in India are over.

Home rule (*swaraj*) also means that Indians will no longer retain modern English habits.[6] Gandhi explained in 1947:

> The foreign power will be withdrawn before long, but for me real freedom will come only when we free ourselves of the domination of Western education. Western culture and Western way[s] of living which have been ingrained in us, because this culture has made our living expensive and artificial, both for men and for women. Emancipation from this culture would mean real freedom for us. (Gandhi 2008: 149)

Gandhi's full conception of *swaraj* included demands such as speaking Hindi rather than English, replacing Western medicine with Ayurveda, lawyers giving up their profession and taking up the handloom, wearing home-spun clothes rather than Western garb, and viewing villages, rather than cities, as the heart of Indian civilization. Jawaharlal Nehru, Gandhi's protégé and the first prime minister of India, laid the foundation for a modern, industrial India at odds with Gandhi's vision of republican village life (Dasgupta 2017). Gandhi's experiments with self-sufficient *ashrams* rarely took root in India or other parts of the world.

Supporters of Hindutva argue that India achieved independence from England because of the militancy of people like Sri Aurobindo (Klausen 2014). Gandhi, however, maintained that nonviolence (*ahimsa*) and truth force (*satyagraha*) can enact personal and institutional change without bloodshed. Gandhi's view of human nature is that human beings may transcend their violent animal impulses and live on a higher plateau of nonviolence:

> I learn that the law of the beast is not the law of Man; that Man has by painful striving to surmount and survive the animal in him and from the tragedy of *himsa* which is being acted around him he has to learn the supreme lesson of *ahimsa* for himself.

> Man must, therefore, if he is to realize his dignity and his own mission, cease to take
> part in the destruction and refuse to prey upon his weaker fellow creatures. (Gandhi
> 2008: 53; original emphasis)

Gandhi's thinking about *ahimsa* was informed by the Russian pacificist Leo
Tolstoy, the American transcendentalist Henri David Thoreau, and the suf-
fragettes, at least until they resorted to violence (Livingston 2018). He was
also influenced by the Indian traditions of Jainism, which practices nonharm
towards all living beings (Gandhi 2008: xxx), and yogic texts and practices
(Godrej 2017).

Gandhi was a political leader who recognized that India's freedom required
expelling the British. Gandhi used the term *satyagraha* to describe the politi-
cization of *ahimsa*, the use of noncooperation, fasting, marching, boycotting,
and so forth to awaken the British to the injustice of their occupation of India
(Godrej 2006; Mantena 2012: 459). "*Satyagraha* is pure soul-force. Truth is the
very substance of the soul. That is why this force is called *satyagraha*. The soul
is informed with knowledge. In it burns the flame of love. If someone gives us
pain through ignorance, we shall win him through love" (Gandhi 2008: 316;
original emphasis). *Satyagraha* eschews physically moving or harming other
people. It is a spiritual force that works in public and in the household and may
be used by people of all sexes and ages. *Satyagraha* is "Gandhi's neologism
for his novel account of sacrificial political action" (Livingston 2018: 514–15).

Gandhian *satyagraha* combines strong moral convictions with a realistic
understanding of how power works (Mantena 2012). The state requires the
active cooperation of the populace to function; by refusing to work, pay taxes,
or serve in the police or military, the people can pressure the state to listen to
their demands:

> You are our sovereign, our Government, only so long as we consider ourselves
> your subjects. When we are not subjects, you are not the sovereign either. So long
> as it is your endeavor to control us with justice and love, we will let you do so. But
> if you wish to strike at us from behind, we cannot permit it. Whatever you do in
> other matters, you will have to ask our opinion about the laws that concern us. If
> you make laws to keep us suppressed in a wrongful manner and without taking us
> into confidence, these laws will merely adorn the statute-books. We will never obey
> them. (Gandhi 2008: 313)

In 1930, Gandhi and his companions started off from his *ashram* in Ahmedabad
to the Arabian Sea town of Dandi to harvest salt in defiance of British law. The
Salt Satyagraha resulted in 80,000 arrests, and the subsequent Gandhi–Irwin
Pact resulted in minor adjustments to the British monopoly over the salt trade.
When Gandhi picked up his first lump of salt-rich mud, he announced: "I am
shaking the foundations of the British Empire"; and Winston Churchill later

admitted that the Salt March had "inflicted such humiliation and defiance as has not been known since the British first trod the soil of India" (Andrews 2019). *Satyagraha* is an energetic, nonviolent way to force people to do things that they otherwise wouldn't do.

Satyagraha is also an ethical action meant to awaken the conscience of spectators. Gandhi invites his readers to think about the great religious figures to appreciate how hard one must work, and the sacrifices one must make, to prepare oneself to refuse an order of the state:

> Christ, before he went out to serve the world, spent forty days in the wilderness, preparing himself for his mission. Buddha too spent many years in such preparation. Had Christ and Buddha not undergone this preparation, they would not have been what they were. Similarly, if we want to put this body in the service of truth and humanity, we must first raise our soul by developing virtues like celibacy, nonviolence and truth. Then alone may we say that we are fit to render real service to the country. (Gandhi 2008: 315)

For *satyagraha* to succeed, one must mentally and physically train for the sacrifices one must make, but the spectators of the act must also have a conscience to stir: one cannot "fast against a tyrant" (Mantena 2012: 468). Gandhi is not asking fellow *satyagrahi* to sacrifice themselves for a losing cause. Nonviolence works politically when rulers, or their supporters, call on the state to stop crushing dissidents. The purpose of nonviolent resistance is to "draw out and exhibit the force of the soul within us for a period long enough to appeal to the sympathetic chord in the governors or law-makers" (Gandhi 2008: 310).

For Gandhi, the purpose of *satyagraha* is to achieve a political victory, but to do so in a way that establishes good will between people who used to be at odds with one another. In 1918, he wrote instructions for *satyagrahis* that articulate principles of successful nonviolent resistance. Here are a few of Gandhi's principles that illustrate his conviction that how one fights oppression determines the kind of peace that results:

> Rudeness has no place in *satyagraha*. Perfect courtesy must be shown even to those who may look upon as their enemies.
> We are opposing the intoxication of power, that is, the blind application of law, and not authority as such. The difference must never be lost sight of. It is, therefore, our duty to help the officers in their other work.
> We must not try to be clever. We must always be frank and straightforward.
> At no time and under no circumstances is the use of arms permitted in *satyagraha*. It should never be forgotten that in this struggle the highest type of nonviolence is to be maintained. *Satyagraha* means fighting oppression through voluntary suffering. There can be no question here of making anyone else suffer. (Gandhi 2008: 330–31; original emphasis)

For Gandhi, there is no sharp divide between means and ends. Gandhi differs from modern political thinkers such as Marx, Mill, Weber, and Lenin precisely because he tied ethics and politics together in a way that never permitted the instrumental use of other people (Mehta 2017). That said, Gandhi was a far-sighted political thinker who wanted *satyagrahi* to change the behavior of other people in such a way that they could become friends again. "We may not make people pure by compulsion. Much less may we compel them by violence to respect our opinion. It is utterly against the spirit of democracy we want to cultivate" (Gandhi 2008: 339).

Gandhi and Savarkar disagreed on the kind of bravery that would be required to end British rule on the subcontinent. For Savarkar, we saw above, Indians needed to eat meat, acquire guns, and embrace a kind of fascistic politics to repel the British. For Gandhi, *satyagrahi* needed to purify themselves by following truth at any cost, loving their opponents, and preparing themselves to suffer at the hands of the government or other people. In a speech on March 7, 1919, Gandhi said:

> Satyagraha was a harmless, but unfailing remedy. It presupposes a superior sort of courage in those who adopted it—not the courage of the fighter. The soldier was undoubtedly ever ready to die, but he also wanted to kill the enemy. A satyagrahi was ever ready to endure suffering and ever lays down his life to demonstrate to the world the integrity of his purpose and the justice of his demands. (Gandhi cited in Mehta 2017)

Savarkar has a point: Western powers colonized other parts of the world through violence, and countries around the world achieved independence through armed struggle. It is hard to imagine a politics that does not involve coercion, resistance, or *himsa* (harm). At the same time, Gandhi is right that one can display more bravery in taking a punch than throwing one. I once taught a veteran who felt ashamed of how easy it was for the U.S. military to locate and kill enemy combatants in Afghanistan using drones and missiles. Bracketing the morality of *satyagraha*, sacrificing one's life for a cause can earn you the respect of your attackers.

Satyagraha requires reconciliation with Bahujans, Gandhi's term for the Untouchables or Dalits. "As long as the curse of untouchability pollutes the mind of the Hindu, so long is he himself an untouchable in the eyes of the world, and an untouchable cannot win non-violent swaraj" (Gandhi 2008: 162). Gandhi's argument reflects a kind of political realism. Gandhi agrees with Ambedkar and Savarkar that caste pits Indians against Indians and adds that it makes India look barbaric in the eyes of the English. We saw above that Ambedkar thought that Gandhi's appeal to traditional occupations (*varna*) replicated the oppressive features of caste. We may also appreciate that Gandhi was trying to forge a coalition among Hindus, including Bahujans, to repel the British.

Satyagraha also requires reconciliation with Muslims. Gandhi himself ground his view of *ahimsa* and *satyagraha* on his religion: "I am unable to account for my life without belief in the all-embracing living Light" (Gandhi 2008: 158), and his political thinking is a "creative appropriation of Vedanta nondualism and yogic practice" (Livingston 2018: 521). That said, Gandhi called Hindus and Muslims the two eyes of India, and his political arguments were generally secular to win the support of people in different religious traditions (Chakrabarty 2013: 67). "Without Hindu–Muslim, i.e., communal unity, we shall always remain crippled. And how can a crippled India win swaraj?" (Gandhi 2008: 162). Gandhi could agree with Savarkar that there has been violence between Hindus and Muslims in India's past, but if the goal is to achieve a democracy where people treat each other with respect, then it is necessary to envision a pacific future: "My whole soul rebels against the idea that Hinduism and Islam represent two antagonistic cultures and doctrines" (Gandhi 2008: 210).

Gandhi was living in a time of enmity between Indians and English, caste Hindus and Dalits, and Hindus and Dalits and Muslims. *Satyagraha* was a kind of political spirituality that worked against political oppression but with an eye towards turning foes into friends. Gandhi's position had an internal tension: he believed in *ahimsa*, but he also recognized that cooperating with violent forces could be necessary to advance *satyagraha*, like when he organized an ambulance corps for the British in World War I. Gandhi was not a Jain or a pacificist, though he sympathized with both positions. Gandhi believed that how you act towards somebody influences on a subtle level how they act towards you: "When men become obstinate, it is a difficult thing. If I pull one way, my Moslem brother will pull another. If I put on superior airs, he will return the compliment. If I bow to him gently, he will do it much more so" (Gandhi 2008: 187). Gandhi's great insight is that that how you fight oppression shapes the kind of peace that results.

* * *

Martin Luther King Jr. famously adopted and adapted Gandhi's idea of *satyagraha* for the American civil rights movement. Unlike Gandhi, King evoked Christian ideas and rhetoric and proceeded in an American context where he wanted to support and intensify the federal government's desegregation efforts. Where they agreed is that short-term political victories can come at the cost of long-term enmity; both appreciated how means and ends are merely human conventions for describing two parts of the same process. In this section, as throughout the chapter, I could offer much more detail about fascinating people who made complex arguments, but my purpose is not primarily to teach the history of ideas. It is to press students to think, in this case, about how anger and violence can backfire if the goal is to form a healthy democratic order in which people respect and care for each other as citizens. In an era in which people often associate angry venting on social media with political action, Gandhi and King's words and examples have lost none of their urgency.

* * *

Martin Luther King Jr. was born in Atlanta, Georgia in 1929, enrolled in Morehouse College as an undergraduate, then earned a doctorate in systematic theology at Boston University. In the early 1960s, King was a visiting professor at Morehouse College and taught a senior seminar in social and political philosophy with readings by Plato, Aristotle, Machiavelli, Hobbes, Kant, and Hegel. One exam question asked students to "compare Machiavelli and Kant on the question of moral principles" (Weinberg 2018). One way to understand King's ambition was to answer this question for himself, to explain how political actors could fuse idealism and realism to transform institutions and society. From 1955 to his assassination in 1968, King served as a leader of the civil rights movement, including as head of the Southern Christian Leadership Conference and organizer of the 1963 March on Washington. In 1965, he won the Nobel Peace Prize for protesting racial inequality through nonviolent resistance. In his last years, he opposed the Vietnam War and was planning a Poor People's Campaign. In *Prophet of Discontent: Martin Luther King Jr. and the Critique of Racial Capitalism*, Jared A. Loggins and Andrew J. Douglas note that people have sanitized King's legacy and made him a spokesperson for an order in which Black elites have opportunities and the rest of the black population lives in poverty and disrepair. King's vision of a "beloved community" involved struggle against racial capitalism, imperialism, and police violence. King did not advocate nonviolent means because his reforms were modest or he was scared of getting hurt; he did so because "he knew that racialized groups would have to continue to engage one another in the wake of any bloodletting" (Loggins and Douglas 2021: 70).

King maintains that race is an inextricable part of American history, from the arrival of the first slaves in Jamestown in 1619, through the Civil War, Reconstruction, and Jim Crow, and up to the 1954 Supreme Court decision of *Brown* v. *Board of Education* (King 2003: 6–7). King recalls his sudden estrangement from his peers and environment when people treated him differently because of his skin color: "The first time that I was seated behind a curtain in a dining car I felt as if the curtain had been dropped on my selfhood" (King 2003: 37). King describes how it feels to hear the message that

Black lives do not matter from teachers, police, legislators, presidents, whites, and blacks:

> Only a Negro can understand the social leprosy that segregation inflicts upon him. The suppressed fears and resentments, and the expressed anxieties and sensitivities make each day of life a turmoil. Every confrontation with the restrictions imposed is another emotional battle in a never-ending war. He is shackled in his waking moments to tiptoe stance, never quite knowing what to expect next and in his sub-conscious he wrestles with this added demon. (King 2003: 121)

The purpose of the civil rights movement is not simply to eliminate legal seg-regation but to create a community in which people do not feel shame at the color of their skin.

King maintains that there is no biological basis for distinguishing races. In "The Ethical Demand for Integration" (1962), King explains:

> Integration seems almost inevitably desirable and practical because basically we are all one. Paul's declaration that God "hath made of one blood" all nations of the world is more anthropological fact than religious poetry. The physical differences between the races are insignificant when compared to the physical identities. The world's foremost anthropologists all agree that there is no basic difference in the racial groups of our world. Most deny the actual existence of what we have known as "race." There are four major blood types and all four are found in every racial group. There are no superior and inferior races. (King 2003: 121)

In the dispute between Du Bois and Garvey in the early twentieth century, King is on the side of Du Bois. People of different races may have different hair texture and skin pigmentation, but humans can reproduce across races as well as exchange blood, organs, and so forth. Like his peer Thurgood Marshall, founder of the NAACP Legal Defense and Educational Fund, King was committed to using the force of law to ensure that Black people were not disadvantaged when it came to voting, housing, or education (Moak 2021).

King envisioned a world in which people would eradicate race as a marker of social significance. In his famous speech at the March on Washington in 1963, he said, "I have a dream my four little children will one day live in a nation where they will not be judged by the color of their skin but by the content of their character" (King 2003: 219). According to King, Christianity teaches that "God loves all his children and that the important thing about a man is 'not his specificity but his fundamentum,' not the texture of his hair or the color of his skin but the quality of his soul" (King 2003: 6). Again, like Du Bois in *The Souls of Black Folk*, King envisions human beings transcending the veil that separates their physical bodies and seeing each other as reflections of God's glory. The goal is to eliminate the category of race that prevents human beings as seeing each other as belonging to the great human family.

Of course, ignoring race right now can mean that the legacies of racism will persist for even longer. In an interview in the socialist magazine *Jacobin*, Brandon M. Terry and Tommie Shelby note that King wanted to radically reorganize how the country does schooling, municipal funding, mass transit, education, housing, welfare bureaucracies, and so forth. King wanted to destroy America's racial caste system, but to do that, "you're going to have to take race into the forefront of your considerations" (Denvir 2018). Terry and Shelby warn that the conservative invocation of King's dream of a color-blind society overlooks the race-conscious work necessary to achieve that end.

Violence would not help bring about a just society, King maintained. Black people would lose a police or military confrontation with white people. More importantly, King thought that violence would beget more violence and defeat the whole purpose of creating a community in which people supported each other, cheered for each other, shared their wealth, looked out for one another, and appreciated each person's unique talents:

> Violence brings only temporary victories; violence, by creating many more social problems than it solves, never brings permanent peace. I am convinced that if we succumb to the temptation to use violence in our struggle for freedom, unborn generations will be the recipients of a long and desolate night of bitterness, and our chief legacy to them will be a never-ending reign of chaos. A voice, echoing through the corridors of time, says to every intemperate Peter, "Put up thy sword." History is cluttered with the wreckage of nations that failed to follow Christ's command. (King 2003: 495)

In a 1957 article in *Christian Century* on "Nonviolence and Racial Justice," King identified lessons that the civil rights movement had learned from Gandhi's example in India. Nonviolence is not a method for cowards; it demands that its practitioners exhibit "dynamically aggressive spirituality" (King 2003: 7). The purpose of nonviolence is not to humiliate the opponent but to awaken a sense of shame within them. One must constantly take stock of the motives for which one is acting; the goal is reconciliation, not revenge. Nonviolence is "directed against forces of evil rather than against persons who are caught in those forces" (King 2003: 8). It is tempting to lash out at the perpetrators of injustice, but, in a way, it is too simple to attack police officers as if they were responsible for the system of racism. They too are trapped in an unjust system, a point made powerfully by the HBO television series *The Wire*. Nonviolence seeks to stop physical violence but also the desire to harm others: the goal is to replace hate with love. Finally, "the method of nonviolence is based on the conviction that the universe is on the side of justice" (King 2003: 9). For King, Gandhi and Hebraic-Christian teaching converge on the sacredness of each individual life and the conviction that justice will prevail in the end (King 2003: 7–8).

In a sermon on "A Tough Mind and a Tender Heart" published in *The Strength to Love*, King explains how civil rights activists must, in the words of Matthew 10:16, be as wise as serpents and innocent as doves. On the one hand, people need a sharp mind that can pierce through clichés, common sense, prejudices and think for themselves. A courageous thinker refuses to accept segregation because it has been around for a long time. To be a serpent means to find a way to make people desegregate who may not want to do it. On the other hand, King enjoins his audience to keep a tender heart, to move people without injuring them. The nonviolent movement must use the tools at its disposal, but it must also care about the well-being of the people who currently oppose it. "We must work passionately and unrelentingly for full stature as citizens," King preaches, "but may it never be said, my friends, that to gain it we used the inferior methods of falsehood, malice, hate, and violence" (King 2003: 496).

One of the analogues to Gandhi's notion of *ahimsa*, in King, is love. King distinguishes three kinds of love. *Eros* used to mean yearning for the divine; now it tends to mean romantic love. *Philia* is a kind of reciprocal love between friends. *Agape* is the love of God for humans and among humans. "When we love on the *agape* level we love men not because we like them, not because their attitudes and ways appeal to us, but because God loves them" (King 2003: 8–9). For King, the challenge of nonviolence is to love people who may hate us, not because we like them or agree with them, but because they too bear the stamp of the creator. But *agape* by itself can be a kind of softmindedness; politics sometimes requires protecting people we love.

That is why King said that the civil rights movement needed both love and justice. Civil rights protestors were supposed to turn the other cheek when they were struck, but King maintained that a just society required the legislature to write, the president to sign, and the courts and police to enforce civil rights law:

> Morality cannot be legislated, but behavior can be regulated. Judicial decrees may not change the heart, but they can restrain the heartless. The law cannot make an employer love an employee, but it can prevent him from refusing to hire me because of the color of my skin. The habits, if not the hearts, of people have been and are being altered everyday by legislative acts, judicial decisions and executive orders. Let us not be misled by those who argue that segregation cannot be ended by the force of law. (King 2003: 124)

Over time, as King scholars have shown, he wanted the civil rights movement to rely less on shaming white people to do the right thing and more on disruption and compulsion (Krishnamurthy 2022; Livingston 2019, 2020; Loggins and Douglas 2021; Pineda 2021).

King explained the interconnection between ends and means, justice and love in a 1962 speech on "The Ethical Demands for Integration." King thinks that the enforcement of laws can bring about desegregation, the placing of blacks and whites in physical proximity in neighborhoods, schools, the workforce, and sports teams. That is why the true end of the civil rights struggle is integration, a fusing together of different races into one supportive community:

> Integration is the positive acceptance of desegregation and the welcomed participation of Negroes into the total range of human activities. Integration is genuine intergroup, interpersonal doing. Desegregation then, rightly, is only a short-range goal. Integration is the ultimate goal of our national community. (King 2003: 118)

Justice involves laws and force. There are, of course, certain times when the rules of justice make possible commerce, job opportunities, and protection from blatant discrimination. Though the boundary of where to draw the line between justice and love is often subjection to renegotiation—as with efforts to raise questions about the justice of the online dating market (Bedi 2015)—it is hard to imagine a free society not leaving room for people to make their own choices about who to befriend or choose as an intimate partner. If a historically disadvantaged group fights for its freedom in such a way as to breed ill will, then love and friendship may suffer. To be clear, the fault for injustice lies with the perpetrators, not the victims, but King wants the civil rights movement to model to their oppressors how they want to be treated. If civil rights activists act in a friendly and respectful manner, then they will be more likely to be treated in kind. "The nonviolent resister does not seek to humiliate or defeat the opponent but to win his friendship and understanding" (King 2003: 12).

In sum, King wants the civil rights movement to achieve peace with whites rather than a victory of Blacks over whites. "True peace is not merely the absence of some negative force—tension, confusion or war; it is the presence of some positive force—justice, good will and brotherhood" (King 2003: 6). Civil rights activists must think about how their means colors their ends; if you want peace, then you must act peacefully with those who may deserve worse.

* * *

Though Gandhi and King lived decades before the spring of 2020, both would have counseled against protesting police brutality with violence. Violence begets more violence and alienates people who may already agree with you. Gandhi's notion of *satyagraha* and King's conception of civil disobedience both press us to act nonviolently, and with dignity, to create a feeling of community with those doing wrong. To my students, I would ask: Does nonviolence work?

ASSIGNMENT ON INTERSECTIONALITY

Compare and contrast Varsha Ayyar on urban Dalit women and Saidiya Hartman on riotous black girls.

So far, the three assignments have constructed dialogues between male authors addressing the problems of racism and casteism, but there are, of course, other kinds of oppression. To help students think about intersectionality, I stage a conversation between Varsha Ayyar, investigating the situation of Dalit women in Mumbai in the early twenty-first century, and Saidiya Hartman, reconstructing the lives of "riotous black girls" in Philadelphia in the early twentieth century. In this section, we see how people can be oppressed in several ways but also resist in different ways. I also like to end courses, or units, with living authors to show that political theory is an ongoing practice to which students may contribute.

* * *

At a Deleuze conference in Mumbai in 2017, I met a professor at the Tata Institute of Social Sciences named Varsha Ayyar. Over dinner one night, she described the challenges she faced as a Dalit woman in Mumbai, India, and academia (Ayyar 2017). In 2013, she published part of her dissertation as "Caste and Gender in a Mumbai Resettlement Site," which opens one's eyes to how intersectional oppression works in India today. The article is based on fieldwork she did in a Mumbai resettlement site, Lallubhai, between 2003 and 2012 and shows how the combination of wealth, caste, and gender create hierarchies, construction of "others," and new forms of inclusion and exclusion (Ayyar 2013: 54).

Capitalism oppresses everyone who lives in a Mumbai slum. Mumbai is becoming a global city, and it has hired McKinsey consultants to make the city better for business. One recommendation was to tear down shanties and replace them with apartment complexes that lack open spaces, public transportation, clean water, a functioning sewage system, and so forth. Everyone in the slums she spoke with expressed dissatisfaction and discontent with their living conditions, but a crude Marxist category of "proletariat" would hide the hierarchies within the slums.

Caste further divides people within slums. In her study, Ayyar describes how people rarely became friends with members of other castes, and there was often conflict because the caste Hindus would make the Dalits and Muslims pay for their religious festivals. "In spite of sharing common struggles against the inadequate infrastructure and pathetic living conditions, there were hardly any signs of the residents coming together" (Ayyar 2013: 48). Even if they were poor, upper-caste Hindus still insisted on kicking those beneath them on the social ladder.

Women faced additional difficulties. Men could cross the train tracks to get to work, but it was dangerous, so most women had to walk a longer route to get to their jobs. Many women in the apartment buildings were responsible for getting clean water for their families, but this meant that they had to spend much of their time and energy fighting with other women over scarce resources. "The 'everyday life' of this resettlement was marked by day-to-day conflicts and fights largely referred to as '*kirkir*, *bachabach* or as *bhandan*.' Women were entangled in such conflicts because they dealt with problems of water shortage, garbage collection, etc." (Ayyar 2013: 47; original emphasis). Women in the slums also face sexual harassment when they are alone in public.

In sum, for Ayyar, most people in the slums experience misery, but this is especially the case for Dalit women who experience "discrimination, humiliation and exclusion in such a distressed neighborhood that endlessly produces a multitude of hierarchies both vertical and horizontal" (Ayyar 2013: 54).

Urmila Pawar and Meenakshi Moon's *We Also Made History: Women in the Ambedkarite Movement* describes how Ambedkar himself encouraged Dalit women to resist multiple forms of oppression. In this respect, Varsha Ayyar is a contemporary representative of the Ambedkarite movement. That said, Ayyar makes one major contribution to Dalit feminism. According to Arundhati Roy in her introduction to *Annihilation of Caste*, Gandhi and Ambedkar disagreed on where the future of India lay. For Gandhi, Indians ought to cherish village life; for Ambedkar, the village was "a sink of localism, a den of ignorance, narrow-mindedness and communalism," which is why he encouraged Dalits to move to cities. It is hard to punish Dalits for polluting the village well when each Dalit family uses plumbing in an apartment building (Ambedkar 2014: 49). What Ayyar shows, however, is that caste and sexism persist even in modern cities, that simply moving Dalits from the villages may not solve or ameliorate the problem of caste. Ayyar could also note that the Bharatiya Janata Party (BJP) has placed a high number of women in the Lok Sabha, the Indian Parliament, but that Dalits, and Dalit women in particular, still suffer from caste-based violence (Patil 2021).

Ayyar's research poses a challenge to Indians and Americans alike. The idea of desegregation is that bringing different kinds of people together will advance justice and friendship. Ayyar shows, however, that physical proximity does not necessarily make people like or respect each other. Her work leaves us with the disquieting feeling that there is no easy solution to freeing Dalit women from multiple forms of oppression.

* * *

Saidiya Hartman's *Wayward Lives, Beautiful Experiments* tells the story of young Black women at the turn of the twentieth century fashioning new lives for themselves. The book is grounded in historical documents such as the journals of rent collectors, trial transcripts, slum photographs, reports of vice investigators, social workers, and parole officers, and W. E. B. Du Bois's 1899 monograph, *The Philadelphia Negro*. Hartman faces a dilemma that the women in the time and place under consideration wrote little, and those who wrote about them were not especially sympathetic. "They have been credited with nothing; they remain surplus women of no significance." Hartman tells their story even if she must imagine what people were thinking and doing when the historical record is silent. "I have pressed at the limits of the case file and the document, speculated about what might have been, imagined the things whispered in dark bedrooms, and amplified moments of withholding, escape and possibility, moments when the vision and dreams of the wayward seemed possible" (Hartman 2019: xiv–xv). Some critics say that Hartman writes historical fiction, but Hartman counters that the women in her book were real and deserve to have their stories told.

The book contends that young Black women at the turn of the century were oppressed but "tirelessly imagined other ways to live" (Hartman 2019: xv). Hartman's book details how the women were excluded from the economy, poor, segregated, dispossessed, and disappointed after their migration from the South to the North. But the purpose of the book is not to make the readers angry or sad; it is to inspire them by the portrayal of "young black women as sexual modernists, free lovers, radicals, and anarchists" (Hartman 2019: xv).

One section of the book—"An Atlas of the Wayward"—corrects the moralistic judgment of Du Bois in *The Philadelphia Negro*. Du Bois writes that he overhears one young Black woman looking into a store window and telling her friend, "That's the kind of shoes I'd buy my fellow." Du Bois thinks that this statement reflects the sorry state of African American affairs. For Du Bois, like his mentors at the time Alexander Crummell and Booker T. Washington, African Americans needed to focus on working, studying, raising families, attending church, and building political power, not worrying about fashion. "Du Bois blamed the lax morals, promiscuity, children born out of wedlock, and the disregard of marriage for the social crisis or revolution of black intimate life that was taking place in the slum" (Hartman 2019: 90). Much like the 1965 Moynihan Report—officially titled, *The Negro Family: The Case for National Action*—Du Bois, in effect, blamed Black people for their poverty, ignorance, and dissoluteness. In this case, he inferred that the women looking at the shoes were likely prostitutes supporting a man who did not work. But Hartman thinks that the women who looked at the shoes were really imagining a world in which they could be free. The women "desired a beautiful pair of shoes that lured them into a world so much better, so much bigger than ugly tenements and the press of poverty. They looked long and hard at all the objects on display in the shop window, expectant and dreaming of a way out" (Hartman 2019: 83).

The Philadelphia Negro is a pioneering work in sociology, and without that monograph, Hartman would have even less archival material with which to reconstruct the lives of young Black women. Du Bois and Hartman both draw back the veil that prevents many people from seeing the life conditions of racial and sexual minorities. But Hartman contests Du Bois's harsh judgment of these young Black women and his expectation that they conform to white bourgeois sexual norms. In her reconstruction of turn-of-the-century Black life, she "refused the mug shots and the family albums of black elites who fashioned their lives in accordance with Victorian norms, those best described by W. E. B. Du Bois as strivers, as the talented tenth, as whites of Negro blood" (Hartman 2019: 17). Du Bois thought that public displays of sexual desire would set back the cause of African Americans; Hartman thinks that Du Bois is a prude whose judgment harms people who do not conform to white Protestant expectations of proper behavior.

Hartman wants the reader to see, and appreciate, young Black women who either did not appear in Du Bois's book or who have been disparaged by Black respectability politics up to the present. "Young women with serial lovers, husbands in the plural, and women lovers too. Young women who outfitted themselves like Ada Overton Walker and Florence Mills, young women who preferred to dress like men" (Hartman 2019: 17). Hartman in no way defends how black women have been treated in American history, but she also thinks that they were not merely victims of slavery, rape, and abuse. "Colored girls, too, were hungry for the carnal world, driven by the fierce and insistent presence of their own desire, wild and reckless" (Hartman 2019: 120).

Critics have wondered if the book ought to be called history or whether it accurately portrays the desires of young black women at the turn of the century (Gordon-Reed 2020; Okeowo 2020). Regardless, I find persuasive Hartman's point that "riotous black girls, troublesome women, and queer radicals" have their own conceptions of the good that ought to have space to flourish in a democratic society. My primary goal as an educator is not to teach history but to place more voices in my students' heads.

* * *

In this chapter, I have shared insights about how to make assignments to invite students to think. Professors cannot think for their students, but they can teach a wide array of authors that will lodge in students' minds and speak up when students are grappling with the problems of, in this instance, racism and casteism. It is important to assign authors who plumb the ocean flows of politics, who are at the center and the periphery of the canon, and who disagree with each other. It is important to contextualize authors, and present their views accurately, but political theorists teach the history of ideas to help people here and now make sense of politics and make informed choices about how to act. Near the end of a semester, I brainstorm with students about authors we could have discussed if we had more time. A good political theory course continues after students turn in the last assignment for the semester.

NOTES

1.   There is not a scholarly edition of *Essentials of Hindutva*. The edition I am using does not even identify a publisher or a place of publication. People can find the passages I cite by searching pdfs on the Internet. See, for example, the one cited in this chapter at http://savarkar.org/en/encyc/2017/5/23/2_12_12_04_essentials _of_hindutva.v001.pdf_1.pdf.
2.   When I visited Tsinghua University in Beijing in December 2017, my former student and host Yuanjia Xia told me that the university from its inception had emphasized Chinese students becoming physically stronger. In my visits to other Indian and Chinese universities, I have seen students exercising in groups. Many Americans exercise and care about physical fitness, of course, but there may be a more conscious political component to it in other parts of the world. In London in 1906, Savarkar supposedly told the vegetarian Gandhi that Indians would need to eat animal protein to be strong enough to fend off the British (*The Economist* 2014).
3.   I am surprised that Ambedkar could not envision an India that sustains like-mindedness and fellow feeling between Muslims and Hindus—a category that includes, in the final analysis, Dalits. "In the absence of common historical antecedents, the Hindu view that Hindus and Musalmans [Muslims] form one nation falls to the ground. To maintain it is to keep up a hallucination. There is no such longing between the Hindus and Musalmans to belong together as there is among the Musalmans of India" (Ambedkar 2004a: 467).
4.   At the end of the essay, Du Bois suggests that he still believes in the thesis of human brotherhood and looks forward to the day when individuals will be judged by "culture, ability, and moral worth, whether they be found under white or black skins" (Du Bois 1987c: 825).
5.   Contemporary critics of racial essentialism include Robert Gooding Williams, Eddie S. Glaude Jr., and Shelby Steele. I thank Jared Loggins for telling me about their work.
6.   For a satirical account of how post-independence Indians adopted British habits, including the cocktail hour, see Rushdie (2006).

REFERENCES

Akbar, P. (2017), "How India Deludes Itself that Caste Discrimination Is Dead," *Aeon*, April 20, accessed March 28, 2021 at https://aeon.co/essays/how-india-deludes -itself-that-caste-discrimination-is-dead.

Ambedkar, B. R. (2004a), *The Essential Writings of B.R. Ambedkar*, ed. V. Rodrigues, New Delhi: Oxford University Press.

Ambedkar, B. R. (2004b), "Castes in India, their Origin, Mechanism and Development," in V. Rodrigues (ed.), *The Essential Writings of B. R. Ambedkar*, New Delhi: Oxford University Press, pp. 239–62.

Ambedkar, B. R. (2014), *Annihilation of Caste: The Annotated Critical Edition*, London: Verso.

Andrews, E. (2019), "When Gandhi's Salt March Rattled British Colonial Rule," *HISTORY*, October 2, accessed April 3, 2021 at https://www.history.com/news/gandhi-salt-march-india-british-colonial-rule.

Ayyar, V. (2013), "Caste and Gender in a Mumbai Resettlement Site," *Economic and Political Weekly*, **48** (18), 44–55.

Ayyar, V. (2017), "Caste-Gender Matrix and the Promise and Practice of Academia," *Economic and Political Weekly*, **52** (50), 7–8.

Bakhle, J. (2010), "Country First? Vinayak Damodar Savarkar (1883–1966) and the Writing of *Essentials of Hindutva*," *Public Culture*, **22** (1), 149–86.

Balfour, L. (2003), "Unreconstructed Democracy: W. E. B. Du Bois and the Case for Reparations," *The American Political Science Review*, **97** (1), 33–44.

Bedi, S. (2015), "Sexual Racism: Intimacy as a Matter of Justice," *The Journal of Politics*, **77** (4), 998–1011.

Brown, D. L. and M. Roig-Franzia (2019), "'Railroaded': Roger Stone Seeks Trump Pardon for Black Nationalist Marcus Garvey," *The Washington Post*, February 8.

Cabrera, L. (2020), *The Humble Cosmopolitan: Rights, Diversity, and Trans-State Democracy*, New York: Oxford University Press.

Chakrabarty, B. (2013), *Confluence of Thought: Mahatma Gandhi and Martin Luther King, Jr.*, New York: Oxford University Press.

Coates, T.-N. (2014), "The Case for Reparations," *The Atlantic*, June.

Crossman, S. (2021), "Play Is Cathartic, Allowing People to Sit with Their Shadows," *Aeon*, February 4, accessed March 23, 2021 at https://aeon.co/essays/play-is-cathartic-allowing-people-to-sit-with-their-shadows.

Das, K. K. (forthcoming), "Caste as Hindutva's Limit: Reading a Dalit Autobiography Amidst Hindutva's Majoritarian Claims," in A. S. Purkayastha (ed.), *Majoritarian Reasoning: Hindutva Nationalism and Modern India*, New Delhi: SAGE.

Dasgupta, S. (2017), "Gandhi's Failure: Anticolonial Movements and Postcolonial Futures," *Perspectives on Politics*, **15** (3), 647–62.

Dawson, M. (2021), "Marcus Garvey: The Black Prince?," in M. L. Rogers and J. Turner (eds), *African American Political Thought: A Collected History*, Chicago, IL: University of Chicago Press, pp. 260–89.

Denvir, D. (2018), "The Political Philosophy of Martin Luther King Jr: An Interview with Brandon M. Terry/Tommie Shelby," *Jacobin*, April 4.

Du Bois, W. E. B. (1987a), "A Lunatic or a Traitor," in W. E. B. Du Bois, *W.E.B. Du Bois: Writings: The Suppression of the African Slave-Trade/The Souls of Black Folk/Dusk of Dawn/Essays*, ed. N. Huggins, New York: Library of America, pp. 990–92.

Du Bois, W. E. B. (1987b), "The Souls of Black Folk," in W. E. B. Du Bois, *W.E.B. Du Bois: Writings: The Suppression of the African Slave-Trade/The Souls of Black Folk/Dusk of Dawn/Essays*, ed. N. Huggins, New York: Library of America, pp. 357–547.

Du Bois, W. E. B. (1987c), *W.E.B. Du Bois: Writings: The Suppression of the African Slave-Trade/The Souls of Black Folk/Dusk of Dawn/Essays*, ed. N. Huggins, New York: Library of America.

Gandhi, M. (2008), *The Essential Writings*, ed. J. M. Brown, New York: Oxford University Press.

Gandhi, M. (2014), *Sources of Indian Traditions: Modern India, Pakistan, and Bangladesh*, New York: Columbia University Press.

Garvey, M. (2005), *Selected Writings and Speeches of Marcus Garvey*, ed. B. Blaisdell, Mineola, NY: Dover Publications.

Garvey, M. (2020a), "Governing the Ideal State," *Keyamsha*, accessed March 3, 2021 at https://keyamsha.com/2020/03/15/governing-the-ideal-state-by-marcus-garvey/.

Garvey, M. (2020b), *Message to the People: The Course of African Philosophy*, Mineola, NY: Dover Publications.

Getachew, A. (2020), *Worldmaking After Empire: The Rise and Fall of Self-Determination*, Princeton, NJ: Princeton University Press.

Getachew, A. (2021), "A 'Common Spectacle' of the Race: Garveyism's Visual Politics of Founding," *American Political Science Review*, **115** (4), 1197–209.

Gilroy, P. (2000), "Black Fascism," *Transition*, **81/82**, 70–91.

Godrej, F. (2006), "Nonviolence and Gandhi's Truth: A Method for Moral and Political Arbitration," *The Review of Politics*, **68** (2), 287–317.

Godrej, F. (2017), "Gandhi, Foucault, and the Politics of Self-Care," *Theory & Event*, **20** (4), 894–922.

Gordon-Reed, A. (2020), "Rebellious History," *New York Review of Books*, **67** (16), 4–8, October 22.

Hartman, S. (2019), *Wayward Lives, Beautiful Experiments: Intimate Histories of Riotous Black Girls, Troublesome Women and Queer Radicals*, New York: W. W. Norton & Company.

Hershberger, S. (2020), "Humans Are All More Closely Related Than We Commonly Think," *Scientific American*, October 5.

Heywood, A. (2021), *Political Ideologies: An Introduction* (7th edition), London: Red Globe Press.

Jagmohan, D. (2020), "Between Race and Nation: Marcus Garvey and the Politics of Self-Determination," *Political Theory*, **48** (3), 271–302.

Jagmohan, D. (2021), "Booker T. Washington and the Politics of Deception," in M. L. Rogers and J. Turner (eds), *African American Political Thought: A Collected History*, Chicago, IL: University of Chicago Press, pp. 167–91.

King, M. L. (2003), *A Testament of Hope: The Essential Writings and Speeches* (2nd edition), ed. J. M. Washington, San Francisco, CA: HarperSanFrancisco.

Klausen, J. C. (2014), "Economies of Violence: The 'Bhagayadgītā' and the Fostering of Life in Gandhi's and Ghose's Anticolonial Theories," *The American Political Science Review*, **108** (1), 182–95.

Krishnamurthy, M. (2022), "Martin Luther King Jr. on Democratic Propaganda, Shame, and Moral Transformation," *Political Theory*, **50** (2), 305–36.

Lebron, C. (2018), "*Black Panther* is Not the Movie We Deserve", *Boston Review*, February 16.

Livingston, A. (2018), "Fidelity to Truth: Gandhi and the Genealogy of Civil Disobedience," *Political Theory*, **46** (4), 511–36.

Livingston, A. (2019), "Power for the Powerless: Martin Luther King, Jr.'s Late Theory of Civil Disobedience," *The Journal of Politics*, **82** (2), 700–713.

Livingston, A. (2020), "'Tough Love': The Political Theology of Civil Disobedience," *Perspectives on Politics*, **18** (3), 851–66.

Loggins, J. A. and A. J. Douglas (2021), *Prophet of Discontent: Martin Luther King Jr. and the Critique of Racial Capitalism*, Athens, GA: University of Georgia Press.

Madhav, N. and A. Jafri (2021), "Why India is Witnessing Spike in Attacks on Christians, Churches," *Al Jazeera*, December 2, accessed December 3, 2021 at https://www.aljazeera.com/news/2021/12/2/india-christians-church-hindu-groups-bjp-conversion.

Mantena, K. (2012), "Another Realism: The Politics of Gandhian Nonviolence," *American Political Science Review*, **106** (2), 455–70.

Mariotti, S. (2009), "On the Passing of the First-Born Son: Emerson's 'Focal Distancing,' Du Bois' 'Second Sight,' and Disruptive Particularity," *Political Theory*, **37** (3), 351–74.

Marx, K. and F. Engels (1978), *The Marx–Engels Reader* (2nd edition), ed. R. C. Tucker, New York: W. W. Norton & Company.

McDermott, R. F., L. Gordon, A. T. Embree, F. Pritchett and D. Dalton (eds.) (2015), *Sources of Indian Traditions: Modern India, Pakistan, and Bangladesh*, Third, New York: Columbia University Press.

Mehta, U. (2017), "On Satyagraha," *Uprising 13/13* [Columbia University blog], November 28, accessed April 4, 2021 at http://blogs.law.columbia.edu/uprising1313/uday-singh-mehta-on-satyagraha/?cn-reloaded=1.

Moak, D. (2021), "Thurgood Marshall: The Legacy and Limits of Equality Under the Law," in M. L. Rogers and J. Turner (eds), *African American Political Thought: A Collected History*, Chicago, IL: University of Chicago Press, pp. 386–412.

Modi, T. (2020), "On his Jayanti, I bow to the courageous Veer Savarkar," *Twitter*, accessed March 23, 2021 at https://twitter.com/narendramodi/status/1265850817690492936.

Moore, M. J. (2011), "How (and What) Political Theorists Teach: Results of a National Survey," *Journal of Political Science Education*, **7** (1), 95–128.

Nietzsche, F. (2011), *Nietzsche: Thus Spoke Zarathustra*, eds A. Del Caro and R. Pipplin, New York: Cambridge University Press.

Nussbaum, M. C. (2016), "Ambedkar's Constitution: Promoting Inclusion, Opposing Majority Tyranny," in A. Huq and T. Ginsburg (eds), *Assessing Constitutional Performance*, New York: Cambridge University Press, pp. 295–336.

Okeowo, A. (2020), "How Saidiya Hartman Retells the History of Black Life," *The New Yorker*, October 26.

Parikh, A. (2021), "Dewey's Counsel to Arjuna: A Deweyan Critique of the Ethics of the Bhagavad Gītā," accessed December 3, 2021 at https://drive.google.com/file/d/1PptfSn5okYv3cqPXK2LpR_18Y0B7D16b/view.

Patil, S. (2021), "Law of One's Own? On Dalit Women's Arduous Struggles for Social Justice," *Economic and Political Weekly*, **56** (13), 7–8.

Pawar, U. and M. Moon (2015), *We Also Made History: Women in the Ambedkarite Movement*, New Delhi: Zubaan Books.

Pineda, E. (2021), "Martin Luther King, Jr. and the Politics of Disobedient Civility," in W. Scheuerman (ed.), *Cambridge Companion to Civil Disobedience*, New York: Cambridge University Press, pp. 56–79.

Purkayastha, A. S. (2019), "W. E. B. Du Bois, B. R. Ambedkar and the History of Afro–Dalit Solidarity," *Sanglap: Journal of Literary and Cultural Inquiry*, **6** (1), 20–36.

Rogers, M. L. (2018), "The Many Dimensions of *Black Panther*," *Dissent Magazine*, February 27, accessed November 1, 2021 at https://www.dissentmagazine.org/online_articles/marvel-black-panther-review-race-empire-tragic-heroes.

Rushdie, S. (2006), *Midnight's Children* (25th Anniversary edition), New York: Random House.

Sampath, V. (2019), *Savarkar: Echoes from a Forgotten Past, 1883–1924*, Haryana, India: India Viking.

Savarkar, V. D. (1923), *Essentials of Hindutva*, accessed June 2, 2022 at http://savarkar.org/en/encyc/2017/5/23/2_12_12_04_essentials_of_hindutva.v001.pdf_1.pdf.

Sinha, S. and M. Suppes (2014), "Timeline of the Riots in Modi's Gujarat," *The New York Times*, April 6.

Stroud, S. R. (2017a), "The Rhetoric of Conversion as Emancipatory Strategy in India: Bhimrao Ambedkar, Pragmatism, and the Turn to Buddhism," *Rhetorica*, **35** (3), 314–45.

Stroud, S. R. (2017b), "What Did Bhimrao Ambedkar Learn from John Dewey's Democracy and Education?," *Pluralist*, **12** (2), 78–103.

Taylor, P. C. (2021), "W. E. B. Du Bois: Afro-modernism, Expressivism, and the Curse of Centrality," in M. L. Rogers and J. Turner (eds), *African American Political Thought: A Collected History*, Chicago, IL: University of Chicago Press, pp. 235–59.

The Economist (2014), "The Man Who Thought Gandhi a Sissy; Savarkar, Modi's Mentor," **413** (8918), 56, December 20.

The New York Times (2020), "N.Y.C. Protests Turn Violent," May 31.

Thorat, S. (2019), "Ambedkar's Proposal to Safeguard Minorities Against Communal Majority in Democracy," *Journal of Social Inclusion Studies*, **5** (2), 113–28.

Valdez, I. (2019), *Transnational Cosmopolitanism: Kant, Du Bois, and Justice as a Political Craft*, New York: Cambridge University Press.

Weinberg, J. (2018), "Martin Luther King, Jr.'s Social Philosophy Course," *Daily Nous*, January 16, accessed April 4, 2021 at https://dailynous.com/2018/01/16/martin-luther-king-jr-s-social-philosophy-course/.

PART II

Teaching political theory today

5. Teaching Greek political thought, with a focus on Sextus Empiricus

INTRODUCTION

Political theorists are responsible for carrying on a tradition that begins in the Golden Age of Athens in the fifth-century bce. If you are the only political theorist in a department, you likely teach a course that introduces students to Plato, Aristotle, and Thucydides. If you work at a school with many political theorists and do not need to teach the ancient Greeks, you are still responsible for knowing how subsequent European political thinkers such as Montaigne, Hume, and Kant are in a conversation with their predecessors. Liberal political theorists such as Michael Oakeshott owe implicit or explicit debts to skepticism, and studying the classic texts can facilitate conversations with early Chinese philosophers such as Zhuangzi, a theme I elaborate in Chapter 6. In this chapter, I explain my thought process for teaching Greek political thought, with a focus on how teaching Sextus Empiricus contributes to contemporary democratic, liberal, and pluralist political theory.

WHY TEACH GREEK POLITICAL THOUGHT?

Western political thought, I tell students, runs on a Greek operating system. Political philosophers, political scientists, and anybody who talks about politics in English often uses words—such as politics, ethics, and democracy—whose origins go back to ancient Greece. Much of our political vocabulary originates in ancient Rome, but Roman authors such as Cicero adopted much of their political terminology from their Greek teachers (Lane 2018). Many English words originate from German, and we should be attentive to differences between freedom (*Freiheit*), which has an Indo-European origin and tends to emphasize participating in collective governance, and liberty, which originates from the Greek word *eleutheria* and tends to emphasize the right of the individual to remain separate from the group (Fischer 2004: 4–8). The great philosopher of the Prussian Enlightenment, Immanuel Kant, wrote his earliest work in Latin and, in his mature work, "the Latin referencing is systematic and essential" (Foucault 2008: 96). The point is not to reduce all political thinking to rearranging Greek concepts, but rather to explain that much of our political thinking involves using terms and images that originate from ancient Greece. If things had played out differently, English speakers could have used the Arabic imagery of riding a horse (*siyasat*) to describe ruling; instead, we use the word "govern" (Gk. *kybernan*), which comes from the Greek word to steer a ship (Lewis 1991: 11). Many political debates in the West are about who ought to hold the steering wheel of collective affairs—a conversation that does not happen in the same way in Buddhism (Moore 2016).

When teaching Greek political thought, I cover canonical authors such as Homer, Aeschylus, Thucydides, Xenophon, Plato, and Aristotle. I learned much of the history of political philosophy by reading authors and texts mentioned in the work of Hannah Arendt, Gilles Deleuze, Jürgen Habermas, Martha Nussbaum, John Rawls, Leo Strauss, and Sheldon Wolin. German scholars such as Kant, Hegel, and Heidegger have largely shaped how academic political theorists read the Greek classics, and they tended to exclude African, Chinese, and Indian thinkers from the history of philosophy (Van Norden 2017). Political theorists today ought to learn from the Greeks as well as profound thinkers in other parts of the world.

In his 1957 *Journal of Politics* article, "What is Political Philosophy?," Leo Strauss explains why political theorists ought to start with and periodically return to the ancient Greeks:

> Classical political philosophy…belongs to the fertile moment when all political traditions were shaken, and there was not yet in existence a tradition of political philosophy. In all later epochs, the philosophers' study of political things was mediated by a tradition of political philosophy which acted like a screen between the philosopher and political things, regardless of whether the individual philosopher cherished or rejected that tradition. From this it follows that the classical philosophers saw the political things with a freshness and directness which has never been equaled. (Strauss 1957: 356–7)

If political scientists use terms such as democracy, oligarchy, politics, or justice, then they are using the language of Greek political thought. One way that political theorists add value to political science is to remind their colleagues of the meaning and history of their key concepts. The Greek philosophers explored the deepest levels of politics—the ocean flows, the guiding metaphor of this book—and theorists can teach others how to avail themselves of ancient wisdom. If you are going to call somebody a tyrant, for instance, then you ought to read the classical text dedicated to tyranny: Xenophon's *Hiero* (Strauss 2000). Political theorists can teach students and colleagues how to think more deeply, and speak more clearly, about concepts that originate in ancient Greece.

Box 5.1 discusses the benefits of giving students the opportunity to debate with each other.

BOX 5.1 STAGE DEBATES

One way that political theory teachers can make the material come alive is to provide opportunities for students to argue about public affairs in the quasi-public space of the classroom. A political theory class can give students a taste of what Hannah Arendt called the *vita activa*, a way of life in which one attains glory by saying great words and doing great deeds. Some of my most vivid teaching memories over the years are when students were arguing with great passion about Emma Goldman's critique of patriotism, John Rawls's argument that the rich do not deserve all their wealth, and W. E. B. Du Bois's argument that the Black community should invest its resources in the Talented Tenth.

In an article on "The Use of Debates in Political Science Courses," Claire Abernathy and Jennifer Forestal describe the advantages of having debates in political science courses. Students build political knowledge, hone civic skills including doing research and considering objections to their position, cultivate democratic values of tolerance and civic responsibility, and develop feelings of political efficacy. Abernathy and Forestal consider the relative advantages of professors moderating debates with a heavy or light touch and having the students consider two or more sides of an issue, and conclude that students "benefit from varied in-class debate experiences" (Abernathy and Forestal 2019: 343).

Rather than formal debates, I provide students with opportunities to present and argue together about an issue. For instance, in my course on higher education policy, I pose questions to students—about, for instance, whether college athletes should get paid, or whether students should be required to take philosophy courses at Jesuit universities—and ask them to weigh multiple answers to the question in a group presentation. This way, students can discuss political issues without having to participate in a confrontational debate that may be off-putting for some of them (Sokoloff 2020: Chapter 3, "Against the Socratic Method").

AN OUTLINE OF GREEK POLITICAL THOUGHT

In my lectures on Greek political thought, I focus on the question of what human beings can know and who should rule, or the link between epistemology and political theory. I rarely teach Homer but often allude to the discussion of Homer in Nietzsche's *On the Genealogy of Morality* and "Homer's Contest."

According to Nietzsche, Plato's theory of Ideas made people less appreciative of the real world with its smells, colors, and textures. Plato encouraged people to disparage the senses and enter the realm of pure thinking; Homer, on the contrary, rendered the natural world with "extraordinary artistic precision." "Plato *versus* Homer: that is the complete, genuine antagonism—on the one hand, the sincerest 'advocate of the beyond', the great slanderer of life, on the other hand, its involuntary idolater, a *golden* nature" (Nietzsche 2017: 178, 25; original emphasis). Plato called for rule by philosopher-kings and therefore dethroned warriors like Achilles and Odysseus. In his poetry, Homer "contemplated with deep *relish*" the "murderous greed" of petty wars, the "tiger-like triumph over the corpse of the slain enemy," and the "continual renewal of those Trojan battle-scenes and atrocities" (Nietzsche 2017: 172; original emphasis). In my lectures, Homer sings about a simpler world in which people have a more direct relationship with nature and the physically strong rule with "naïve barbarism" (Nietzsche 2017: 172).

Often, the first reading I assign in a course is Plato's *Apology*, one of his early dialogues that gives us the closest view we can get of the figure of Socrates. In the *Apology*, Socrates appears before a jury of Athenians and defends his way of life against the charges that he is impious and corrupts the young. In his defense, Socrates gives an account of what it means to be a philosopher. The Oracle of Delphi told Socrates' friend Chaerephon that there was nobody wiser than Socrates. To test this thesis, Socrates started conversations with politicians, poets, and craftspeople, and in each case, he found that his interlocutors knew less than they thought that they knew. From this exercise, Socrates drew the following conclusion:

> real wisdom is the property of God, and this oracle is his way of telling us that human wisdom has little or no value. It seems to me that he is not referring literally to Socrates, but has merely taken my name as an example, as if he would say to us, The wisest of you men is he who has realized, like Socrates, that in respect of wisdom he is really worthless. (Cohen 2018: 25)

For Socrates, a philosopher is someone who searches for the truth with an awareness that they (likely) will not attain it. In *What Would Socrates Do?*, Joel Schlosser explains that the *Apology* is a critique of Athenian democracy for its guilty verdict in Socrates' trial, but the text also shows how the Socratic practice of searching (*zeteticism*) expresses an egalitarian sentiment that everyone can and ought to question existing arrangements. "Socrates' philosophy seeks to disturb the complacency of his fellow citizens and non-citizens by demanding their judgment and subjecting these judgments to scrutiny." Socrates thus "challenges and develops the capacities of the very people upon whom the Athenian democracy depended while also expanding the participants in these deliberations beyond conventional boundaries" (Schlosser 2014: 154). For Socrates, a worthwhile life is spent searching for the truth, with the awareness that this activity likely has no terminus. Socrates was not a democrat, but his example shows that all human beings can and probably should think about what makes a satisfactory human life and just political order.

Plato's *Republic* is perhaps the most important text in classical political philosophy, and for nearly every year I've been a professor I have taught students the Allegory of the Cave. The Bloom translation of *The Republic* has a useful diagram that shows how four ascending objects of knowledge (images, things, mathematical objects, forms) align with four ascending kinds of knowledge (imagination, trust, thought, intellection) with a divide between the visible (*to horaton*) and the intelligible (*to noeten*) realms (Plato 2016: 464). Plato's theory is that there is a hierarchy of kinds of knowledge, and those who possess the highest forms of knowledge have more claim to rule. Philosophers, on Plato's account, are like the navigators who come out at night to pilot the ship by the stars; the other sailors on the boat do not know what they do, but the stargazers are the ones who know the right destination. I teach the Allegory of the Cave with an awareness that Walter Lippmann uses a passage from *The Republic* as an epigraph to *Public Opinion*, an agenda-setting work for modern political science and the study of public opinion, political psychology, and political behavior (Tampio 2017). I teach classical political philosophy through the lens of Nietzsche's view that Plato's metaphysics and belief in the right of the smart to rule persists even among political scientists who have never read Plato: "Our faith in science is still based on a *metaphysical faith*— even we knowers of today, we godless anti-metaphysicians, still take *our* fire from the blaze set alight by a faith thousands of years old, that faith of the Christians, which was also Plato's faith, that God is truth, that truth is *divine*" (Nietzsche 2017: 115; original emphasis).

Aristotle's *Politics* is the *locus classicus* of a tradition that holds that politics is an ennobling activity. In *Politics*, Aristotle defines the human as "a political animal" and as "the only animal who has the gift of speech." "It is a characteristic of man that he alone has any sense of good and evil, of just and the unjust, and the like, and the association of living beings who have this sense makes a family and a state" (Cohen 2018: 97). According to Aristotle, human beings must use the standard of knowledge that is appropriate for the activity under consideration, and political affairs often require a context-specific kind of knowledge (*phronesis*) rather than pure wisdom (*sophia*). In my words, Aristotle differentiates street knowledge and book knowledge, and he maintains that political decisions about taxes, warfare, citizenship, and so forth require practical knowledge rather than theoretical knowledge. Experts may have their thoughts, but they need to dialogue with those affected to see if a policy works. Aristotle maintains that a life dedicated to contemplation is the highest form of human life, but he still thinks that participating in politics enables one to exercise capacities that would otherwise lay dormant. Though not a partisan of democracy, which for Aristotle means rule by the poor and uneducated, Aristotle thinks that the most realistic good regime is the *politeia*, an order that gives a sizable portion of the population an opportunity to participate in self-governance. I read and teach Aristotle's *Politics* through the lens of Hannah Arendt's *The Human Condition*, originally published in 1958, a book famous in twentieth-century political theory for extoling the *vita activa*, "an autonomous and authentically human way of life" (Arendt 2018: 13). There is a rich scholarly literature on the relationship between Aristotle and Arendt, and the ways in which she retained, modified, and discarded Aristotelianism under the influence of her mentors Martin Heidegger and Karl Jaspers (Dew 2020). For my introduction to political philosophy class, it is sufficient to present Aristotle as using the inductive method to argue that human beings find fulfillment (*eudaimonia*) in participating in politics. I can also make this point by teaching Pericles' Funeral Oration in Thucydides' *History of the Peloponnesian War* that commends Athens for allowing people to advance in public life because of their capacity, not because of their wealth (Cohen 2018: 12).

In *Natural Right and History*, Leo Strauss provides a heuristic to make sense of much classical Greek political philosophy. He does this in his discussion of the word *politeia* and how it captures more than a society's written constitution. "The character, or tone, of a society depends on what the society regards as most respectable or most worthy of admiration... That is to say, every society regards a specific human type (or a specific mixture of human types) as authoritative" (Strauss 1999: 137). I teach the classics with an emphasis on what kind of person earns the most respect in each thinker's ideal social order. Homer is a timocrat who envisions warriors such as Odysseus and Achilles as deserving to rule. Socrates is a searcher whose political activities mostly involve pressing rulers to recognize their intellectual blind spots. Plato is an aristocrat who thinks that a philosophic elite can know the blueprint for how society ought to be structured. And Aristotle and Thucydides offer qualified praise for seasoned politicians exercising practical wisdom for the good of the city.

I believe that my coverage of classical Greek political thought will be familiar to most academic political theorists. In the rest of the chapter, I will explain how and why I teach Sextus Empiricus to undergraduates.

WHY SEXTUS EMPIRICUS?

For years, the only book of Greek antiquity that I would teach in Introduction to Political Philosophy was Plato's *Republic*.[1] The book is fun to teach. You can have students read passages from the dialogue aloud and have lively conversations about the difference between athletes and warriors, the political consequences of early childhood education, whether rulers should drink alcohol, and whether most people are capable of leaving the cave of ignorance. Over time, however, I have grown to resent the metaphysics and politics of Plato's *Republic*. I have learned from Friedrich Nietzsche, Henri Bergson, and Gilles Deleuze that humans invent words, concepts, ideas, and forms to survive in an infinitely complex world in which we could not move fast enough if we had to perceive the singularity of each thing. Platonic Ideas are metaphors that have "been poetically and rhetorically intensified, transferred, and embellished, and which, after long usage, seem to a people to be fixed, canonical, and binding" (Nietzsche 1990: 84). Ideas are useful fabrications; we could not communicate with one another if we did not place unique entities into boxes that conceal their differences. But it is an intellectual mistake to believe in the ontological reality of Ideas—there is no Idea of chairs, there are just lots of assemblages that we call chairs—and we perpetrate injustices when we denigrate real things for not resembling our made-up projection of Ideas. Think of how much harm has been done to people who do not match up to ideals of beauty or intelligence. Furthermore, I agree with the American pragmatist philosopher John Dewey that Plato's metaphysics supports a hierarchical political order in which intellectual elites rule over physical brutes. Plato "never got any conception of the indefinite plurality of activities which may characterize an individual and a social group, and consequently limited his view to a limited number of classes of capacities and of social arrangements" (Dewey 2008: 94). In other words, Plato gave a philosophic defense of a Greek political order in which a few people used their minds for a living while the majority worked with their hands. For Dewey, if we recognize that individuals have a singular collection of talents, interests, intelligences, and so forth, then we can begin to create a democratic society that values everyone's contribution and worth.

Who can political theorists teach from ancient Greece as a foil to Plato? Plato uses vivid imagery; thinks deeply about education, politics, aesthetics, epistemology, and metaphysics as well as the interconnection between all of them; and exercised a huge influence on the subsequent history of philosophy. It would be wonderful if modern scholars had access to a rich archive of ancient Greek democratic theory; instead, much of what we have explains and justifies oligarchic rule (Simonton 2017). Given their materialism and influence on early modern philosophy, Epicurus and Lucretius could be good foils for Platonic idealism (Greenblatt 2012), but these days, I think the best person to stage a debate with Plato is the Greek skeptic Sextus Empiricus.

Most of what we know about Sextus may be gleaned from his texts. He lived in the second half of the second century and the first quarter of the third century ce; served as the head of a skeptical school in a cosmopolitan city such as Rome, Athens, or Alexandria; wrote in Greek and thus was probably Greek; and worked as a physician. Much of his extant work is critiques of dogmatic philosophies that are of interest mostly to scholars of skepticism and historians of philosophy. Book I of *Outlines of Pyrrhonism*, however, is a perfect text to teach undergraduates. In this short text—fewer than 100 pages in the Hackett edition—Sextus explains the goal of skepticism, its argumentative strategies, how it influences the way people talk, and the distinction between skepticism and other philosophies.

Historians have traced the influence of skepticism through nearly the entire history of philosophy. Richard Popkin has shown that the Dominican friar Savonarola commissioned a translation of Sextus as a resource to combat pagan dogmatic philosophies in the fifteenth century, and early modern philosophers such as Michel de Montaigne, Descartes, and Blaise Pascal, thought with and against the skeptical tradition (Popkin 2003). John Christian Laursen has traced the "politics of skepticism" in Sextus Empiricus, Montaigne, David Hume, Immanuel Kant, and Michael Oakeshott (Laursen 1992, 2005). More recently, Brian C. Ribeiro has written on the Pyrrhonism of Sextus, Montaigne, and Hume (Ribeiro 2021), and Peter S. Fosl explores the difference between Pyrrhonian and Academic skepticism through a close reading of Hume's philosophy (Fosl 2019). I recall one of my professors at Johns Hopkins University, Giulia Sissa in the classics department, prefacing a question at a seminar by saying that the history of philosophy was a sort of back and forth between skeptics and philosophers responding to them. I was fortunate to read *Outlines of Pyrrhonism* in a seminar on "Scepticism, Ethics, and Metaethics" with Richard E. Flathman as a graduate student at Johns Hopkins.

In addition to providing a concise introduction to skepticism, *Outlines of Pyrrhonism* is hilarious. The text presents a world where people are unsure whether grass is green or black, whether it is right or wrong to tattoo babies, whether scorpions are always dangerous, and whether cannibalism and incest are evil. It is a fun exercise to assign students to groups to explain one of the Ten Modes, discussed below, and then report what they find to the rest of the class. Like Plato's *Republic*, the language is clear and vivid, but rather than give students confidence that philosophers can learn the Ideas and rule over others, *Outlines of Pyrrhonism* undermines the conceit of those who claim to be wise and leads the way to an egalitarian disposition. An ancient charge against skepticism is that it leads to *apraxia*, a state of inactivity produced by skeptical doubt and suspension of judgment (Ribeiro 2021: 20). In reply, skeptics may note that people act under conditions of uncertainty all the time. The question is whether people are going to go through the world filled with arrogance or humility about their knowledge and whether they may coerce other people to agree.

ARGUMENT FROM DIFFERENCES IN ANIMALS

Skepticism, according to Sextus, is "an ability to place in antithesis, in any manner whatever, appearances and judgements, and thus—because of the equality of force in the objects and arguments opposed—to come first of all to a suspension of judgment (*epoche*) and then to mental tranquility (*ataraxia*)" (Sextus Empiricus 1985: 32–3). Sextus identifies Ten Modes (*tropoi*) that enable skeptics to juxtapose arguments to induce a suspension of judgment. Sextus supposedly learned the Modes from Aenesidemus, and scholars also have access to the Modes in the work of Philo of Alexandria and Diogenes Laertius (Annas and Barnes 1985). Classicists and philosophers debate how original a thinker Sextus was. As a political theorist primarily interested in the history of ideas as a resource for contemporary political thinking, I think Book I of the *Outlines of Pyrrhonism* is filled with brilliant argumentative strategies to undermine any claim to knowledge of things in themselves rather than how they appear to us right now. Reading Sextus teaches students to question anybody who speaks with too much confidence about how things are or ought to be.

The first kind of argument is to consider the difference between human beings and other animals. Humans perceive the world in a certain way. Other animals perceive it another way. How can we say that the human way is any closer to reality? Dogs, turtles, fish, octopi, insects, and other animals have senses that may grasp things that the human senses cannot, and we would be arrogant to say that our sense perception is more accurate than theirs. "As for acting ourselves as judges between our own sense-impressions and those of the other animals, that is out of the question, because we ourselves are a party to the disagreement" (Sextus Empiricus 1985: 49).

Take eyesight. If a human being has bloodshot eyes, then the world gains a reddish tint. There are dogs whose eyes are always bloodshot and thus likely see the world with this reddish tint. There is no way that human beings can know for sure that the world does or does not have a reddish tint. One could object that eye color does not necessarily change how one sees the world: as far as we can tell, blue-eyed humans do not see the world differently than brown-eyed humans (Annas and Barnes 1985: 42). However, Sextus' argument does not require us to believe that animals *do* see the world differently than humans; it is enough for his purposes that he prompts us to wonder if they *may* see the world differently.

Sensory organs determine what animals can perceive of the natural world, and differences between sense organs suggest that animals perceive the world differently:

- *Touch:* "One could hardly postulate a similarity of sensibility between hard-shelled animals, fleshy animals, thorny animals, and feathered or scaly ones."
- *Hearing:* "As for perceptions conveyed through the sense of hearing, one could hardly say that they are the same in those animals which have a very narrow auditory passage as they are in those which have a very wide one, or the same in animals with hairy ears as in those with smooth ears."
- *Taste:* "since the organs of taste of animals differ from each other…it would follow that they also receive different ideas of the taste of things."
- *Health:* "Perfume seems very agreeable to men, but intolerable to beetles and bees. Olive-oil is beneficial to men, but it kills wasps and bees if sprinkled on them. Sea-water is unpleasant for men to drink, even poisonous, but for fish most pleasant—and drinkable." (Sextus Empiricus 1985: 47–9)

In one passage that is wonderful to read and discuss with students, Sextus argues that dogs possess virtually all of the qualities that human beings do. Dogs have the power to choose what food to eat or not eat. Dogs can do the syllogistic reasoning that allows them to run by the paths that do not have the scent of their prey. Dogs have courage and loyalty and other qualities we would like in a friend. "We say that [a dog] is brave from the way he defends us, and intelligent too, as Homer also testified when he represented Odysseus as going unrecognized by all the members of his household and as being recognized only by his dog Argus, who was not deceived by the changes that had come over the body of the man" (Sextus Empiricus 1985: 51). One could update Sextus' argument with points from A. S. Barwich's recent book on the neuroscience of smell. Dogs possess more olfactory receptors in their noses than humans: "the dog's [smelling] apparatus seems miles beyond ours." On the other hand, dogs lack a retronasal pathway, created by the bony transverse lamina in their noses, and cannot experience flavors in the same way that humans can (Barwich 2020: 156, 86–7). Do dogs have a better sense of smell than humans because of their olfactory receptors or a worse sense of smell because they lack a nasopharyngeal space? We simply cannot say with confidence what the world smells like.

ARGUMENT BASED ON CIRCUMSTANCES

Sextus distinguishes Modes based on whether they deal with the diverse perspectives of perceiving subjects or the changing nature of the objects under consideration. It appears to me that every Mode involves both the subject and the object: internal and external factors combine to ensure we never quite grasp reality. In the fourth Mode, Sextus draws attention to the fact that our perceptions of the world change based on the circumstances in which we find ourselves.

Take the following binaries:

- *Asleep or awake:* "Whether one is in a sleeping or waking state…makes a difference in the sense-impressions, since our manner of perception while awake differs from the perception we have in sleep, and our manner of perception in sleep is not like our waking perception."
- *Youth or old age:* "Old men, for example, may think the air is cold, but the same air seems mild to those who are in the prime of life. The same color appears dim to older persons but full to those in their prime. And a sound, likewise the same, seems faint to the former but quite audible to the latter."
- *Drunk or sober:* "Drunkenness or soberness is another cause [of the difference in our sense-impressions], since what we think shameful when sober does not seem shameful to us when we are drunk." (Sextus Empiricus 1985: 61)

Given that we perceive the world differently if we are asleep or awake, in youth or old age, drunk or sober, Sextus asks us to suspend judgment about the real nature of the objects we are scrutinizing.

The tempting reply is that one of these positions is the natural baseline or the one from which scientific research proceeds. Most people hold that awake, sober adults should conduct experiments rather than people in other circumstances. Skeptics tend to go along with everyone else and would agree with this position for all practical purposes. Sextus was a doctor and presumably tried to cure his patients based on empirical findings. But as a philosophical matter, skeptics argue that there is no reason to assume that dreams do not capture important parts of experience that may elude the awake, a point made famous by Sigmund Freud in *The Interpretation of Dreams*. Just as we cannot say for sure whether humans or dogs more accurately perceive colors, so too we cannot say that the sober are more attuned to reality than the inebriated: "it is possible that the external objects actually are in reality such as they appear to those who are said to be in unnatural state" (Sextus Empiricus 1985: 59).

In this discussion of the fourth Mode, Sextus discusses the problem of finding a criterion to distinguish the circumstance in which we may trust our judgments as true. "A proof cannot be sound without the pre-existence of a true criterion, and a criterion cannot be true either without prior confirmation of the proof. And so both the criterion and the proof fall into circular argument, in which both are found to be untrustworthy" (Sextus Empiricus 1985: 62–3).

On the day I am writing this paragraph, the philosopher of science Maarten Boudry has published an article saying that "objective standards of right and wrong are our main defenses against bad ideas. If we lose those standards, then anything goes" (Boudry 2021). Citing Allan Bloom, student of Leo Strauss and author of *The Closing of the American Mind*, Boudry attacks postmodernists and current college students for their relativism, but Sextus makes arguments for relativism that are about 1800 years old. Sextus' arguments in the *Outlines* are silly and serious at the same time: you cannot tell whether the world is really spinning when you are drunk or that you just don't notice it when you are sober. But Boudry is correct that relativism contains certain ethical and political implications, which Sextus discusses in the tenth Mode on "disciplines, customs, laws, mythical beliefs, and dogmatic notions" (Sextus Empiricus 1985: 69).

ARGUMENT FROM CUSTOMS

What is the right way for people to act as individuals (ethics) or collectives (politics)? If by "right," you mean "our culturally influenced intuitions about the right thing to do in various situations," then skeptics can use the language of right and wrong (Rorty 1994: 117). If by right you meant that there are certain ethical and political truths that are always true, like right angles always equal 90 degrees, then no, the skeptics doubt that right and wrong exist in nature. If the first nine Modes use innocuous examples to help us see the limits of our knowledge, in the tenth Mode, Sextus uses the skeptical strategy of juxtaposing arguments of equal strength (*isostheneia*) to reveal that our moral and political beliefs might be just as contingent as our beliefs in whether the grass is green (daylight) or black (nighttime), the tower is square (seen close up) or round (seen from afar), the sand is sharp (felt individually) or soft (when felt in a pile), and so forth.

Here are a few of the juxtapositions that Sextus makes to show that ethical and political judgments are as relative as any other:

- *Customs:* "Some of the Ethiopians tattoo their babies, while we do not. And Persians that the use of bright-colored, dragging garments is seemly, while we think it is unbecoming. And the Indians have intercourse with their women in public, whereas most other peoples hold this to be shameful."
- *Laws:* "With the Romans, he who relinquishes claim to the property inherited from his father is not obliged to pay his father's debts, but with the Rhodians one must pay them in any event. And among the Tauri of Scythia, there was a law that strangers should be sacrificed to Artemis, while with us the ritual killing of humans is forbidden."

- *Discipline, or ways of life:* "We set the discipline of Diogenes in opposition to that of Aristippus, or that of the Laconians to that of the Italians."
- *Myths:* "We say that in one version Zeus is spoken of as the father of gods and men, while in another version it is Oceanus."
- *Physical dogmas:* "Some declare that there is only one element, while others assume that they are infinite in number."
- *Moral dogmas:* "some believe the soul to be mortal, others immortal" and "some men declare that human affairs are directed by divine providence, while others claim providence has no hand in them." (Sextus Empiricus 1985: 70)

What is amazing about the discussion of the tenth Mode is how relevant and controversial many of its claims are. Take incest: "Whereas intercourse with our mothers is prohibited by our laws, with the Persians it is a custom to marry thus if one possibly can. Among the Egyptians men marry their sisters, a practice which with us is prohibited by law" (Sextus Empiricus 1985: 71). In a *Political Theory* article entitled, "Stumbling toward a Democratic Theory of Incest," John Seery enacts his own dichotomy between two sets of dogmatists on the topic of incest. On the one hand, poststructuralists like Michel Foucault and Judith Butler hold that the incest taboo "is itself symptomatic of ever-looming homoerotic panic-titillation tending nervously toward ever-reenacted heteronormative resolution" (Seery 2013: 15). On the other, liberals like John Rawls and Martha Nussbaum sidestep the poststructuralist line of problematization and insist that their concerns about incest are based on public health requirements and the fact that father–daughter incest violates the liberal prohibition on harming nonconsenting individuals. One remarkable feature of Seery's article is its admission of uncertainty: "I'm not sure what exactly *to do*" (Seery 2013: 16; original emphasis). The nonliberal critics of the incest taboo "seem so emphatic and confident in their theorizing about incest, and yet I remain so confused and quizzical" (Seery 2013: 16). To be clear, Seery does not condone incest, nor does he even suggest that incest may be ethical or legalized. But his skepticism about the wrongness of incest leads him to note that "when one looks at the many incest statutes currently on the books across various jurisdictions, one sees an incomprehensible and pernicious mess" (Seery 2013: 25). Skeptics can find incest disgusting, dangerous, harmful, and so forth, but they are wary of saying that its wrongness is woven into the fabric of the universe. Seery's worry about incest statutes, I take it, is that legislators pile on punishments because they believe that incest is evil.

At this point in the class, I would ask my students: What are other examples of diverse moral standards around the world? Does Sextus Empiricus make a valid point that we cannot speak too confidently about, say, human rights? If students take additional classes with me, we will likely read Martha Nussbaum, whose human capabilities theory challenges the relativist view about what opportunities women around the world want and deserve. But Sextus would welcome this counterpoint: Pyrrhonian skeptics keep an open mind—in fact, they search for arguments that show they might be wrong.

SKEPTICAL LANGUAGE

One of the challenges of teaching skepticism is to correctly present the Pyrrhonian perspective that skeptics make no claim to know the truth even about whether their own skepticism is warranted. I have used the word "likely" several times in this chapter to suggest, for instance, that animals likely see the world differently than humans, but Sextus would warn us that using a term like "likely" or "probably" suggests that a perspective is closer to the truth, which suggests that we can know what the truth is. In Book I of the *Outlines of Pyrrhonism*, Sextus floats ideas about an appropriate skeptical terminology. Skeptics may say how something appears to them, but there is "no more likelihood that this is true than that is true" (*ouden mallon*); skeptics may use the word "believe" (*peithesthai*), but it does not mean an active grabbing of the truth, but rather "a matter of simple yielding, without attachment" (Sextus Empiricus 1985: 9, 95–6). If you are going to infuse skepticism into one's political theory, you must use the right language, but what is that language?

In "Apology for Raymond Sebond," written between 1575 and 1580, Michel de Montaigne introduced Sextus to a modern European reading public. For the moment, I bracket the question of whether Montaigne's famous essay used skeptical arguments to defend Christianity just because it is the culture in which he lived or as a gift of God not accountable to human reason (Ribeiro 2021: 29–30). Regardless, Montaigne explains the challenge awaiting a skeptical political theorist:

> Our way of speaking has its weaknesses and faults, like all the rest. Most of the occasions for the troubles of the world are grammatical... I see the Pyrrhonian philosophers who cannot explain their general conception in any kind of discourse; for they would need a new language. Ours is wholly formed of affirmative propositions, which are entirely inimical to them. (Montaigne 2003: 89)

What would "a new language" look like that does not use the words know, believe, understand, and so forth? If Western political thought runs on a Greek operating system, as noted above, then how can we avoid the language of epistemology, from the Greek word *pistis*, "trust" (Plato 2016: 486)? One way is to fold phrases like "perhaps," "it is possible," "it admits of being," into one's language. It is less important that one use certain words than that one carry oneself with modesty, reserve, and caution and, just, in general, be open-minded (Ribeiro 2021: 146).

THE POLITICAL IMPLICATIONS OF SKEPTICISM

I tell students that it would be wonderful if modern scholars had access to more classical skeptical texts on political themes. There is no skeptical analogue to Plato's *Republic* or Aristotle's *Politics*, at least in our possession. Yet, *Outlines of Pyrrhonism* has political implications, including that Sextus denies anyone the title of sage- or philosopher-king. And subsequent political thinkers such as the Scottish Enlightenment philosopher David Hume formulated their thought in dialogue with the skeptical tradition, including its Pyrrhonian and Academic branches that differ on points such as whether skeptics may use the language of probability (Fosl 2019). Here, I identify two passages from Sextus that may generate thought about the political implications of skepticism.

The first passage addresses the objection that skeptics do not know how to avoid walking into ditches or to fight against injustice. Sextus' reply is that skeptics do act in the world, but they are guided by nature and custom rather than by knowledge of the truth:

> Now, we cannot be entirely inactive when it comes to the observances of everyday life. Therefore, while living undogmatically, we pay due regard to appearances. This observance of the requirements of daily life seems to be fourfold, with the following particular heads: the guidance of nature, the compulsion of the feelings, the tradition of laws and customs, and the instruction of the arts. (Sextus Empiricus 1985: 40)

I explain the skeptical criteria to my students this way. Think of the body. When stimuli hit our senses and our organs, we feel perceptions. We feel the warm sun and see colors. These fall under the guidance of nature. Even though skeptics can provide arguments that grass is not green, they tend to have the same impressions as other people and use ordinary language to describe them. Yes, grass is green. Humans also feel hunger and thirst. These are impressions, but they tend to come from inside the body. The compulsion of feelings are impulses we feel that do not have a direct link to something that is happening outside of us. The first two criteria, then, come from outside and inside the human body.

The other two criteria concern things outside of our body. The tradition of laws and customs include all that we convey by the term culture or society. "It is by virtue of the traditions of laws and customs that in everyday life we accept piety as good and impiety as evil" (Sextus Empiricus 1985: 40). Sextus is not a relativist if that means somebody who believes that truth depends on time or place. Rather, Sextus is what Richard Rorty called an ironist, "someone sufficiently historicist and nominalist to have abandoned the idea that those central beliefs and desires refer back to something beyond the reach of time and chance" (Rorty 1989: xv). To be more precise, a skeptic suspects that most of our moral and political norms are contingent on time and place, but they do not foreclose the possibility that maybe somebody will discover the truth of their beliefs and desires. Still, Rorty conveys the sense in which a skeptic does not hold onto their beliefs too tightly.[2] Finally, a skeptic feels a compulsion to live, and to feed their family, and they seek instruction in the arts to make a living and get along in society. Guided by their bodies and their surroundings, skeptics make their way through the world like everybody else.

So, does this mean that a skeptic is like a leaf in the wind, incapable of resisting their urges and influences? No. The four criteria conflict with one another, and the skeptic must exercise some sort of choice. Natural feelings and social norms do not always align, as when one waits for the host to sit before eating dinner even when one is famished. Traditions of laws and customs can clash, as when one is traveling to another country and trying to figure out when to adopt local customs and when to retain those from home. Skeptics are wary of philosophies that identify a rational pilot steering our bodies or of moral vocabularies that posit things like souls or will that nobody can see with a naked eye. But that does not mean that skeptics deny that there are feelings and customs that lead people to create such notions. Sextus helped launch the skeptical tradition: there is still work to do to flesh out how skeptics can explain thinking, choosing, and acting that steers clear of dogmatism.

A second passage from Sextus about politics is from the text known as *Against the Ethicists*. It concerns how the skeptic responds to a dastardly command from a tyrant:

> If compelled by a tyrant to perform some forbidden act, he will choose one thing, perhaps (*tuchon*), and avoid the other by the preconceptions which accords with his ancestral customs and habits; and in fact he will bear the harsh situation more easily compared with the dogmatist because he does not, like the latter, have any further opinion over and above these conditions [the hardship itself]. (Laursen 2004: 207–8; original emphasis)

This passage seems like a smoking gun for accusers of skepticism. Sextus admits that skeptics may go along with the tyrant and bear the situation more easily than dogmatists troubled by acquiescence to injustice. According to Martha Nussbaum, this passage shows that skeptics do not have a moral compass and are unwilling to risk their lives for a just cause that they know is true. "Is 'perchance' (*tuchon*) enough for us?" (Nussbaum 1996: 314; original emphasis). The skeptical tradition, on Nussbaum's account, is "profoundly selfish, indeed solipsistic" and the precursor to postmodern theorists who play with truth rather than dig their heels in and fight for justice (Nussbaum 2000: 171).

Skeptics do not have to allow their critics to define their political stance. John Christian Laursen defends Sextus and the skeptical tradition on two grounds. History is filled with dogmatists who became tyrants; and skeptics such as Pierre Bayle and David Hume buttressed the liberal conviction that the state should not enforce moral or religious orthodoxies. Empirically, Nussbaum is on shaky ground that there is a tight fit between moral certitude and a willingness to disobey a tyrant. Furthermore, skeptics may resist tyrants on grounds other than the certitude of their moral convictions. They may have a visceral hatred for the cruelty of a tyrant, or local customs may celebrate tyrannicides. The skeptic may disobey the tyrant "because it is a habit or a tradition in his family or his city to do so," and it is even possible that the skeptic will kill the tyrant more easily than a dogmatist because the skeptic does not agonize about the horrors of death or hell (Laursen 2004: 210–11). There is no reason to believe that because skeptics suspend judgment about truth that they are any more lethargic, conformist, or careless than dogmatists. Laursen points to the example of the South African freedom fighter, Nelson Mandela: "Nelson Mandela's public image was of calm perseverance, not of eating his heart out in frustration and rage at injustice" (Laursen 2016: 16). If one cares about stopping a tyrant, it matters what people do, not whether they speak about truth.

To illustrate the contemporary relevance of skepticism, I dedicate a class to Michael Oakeshott (1901–90), a British political philosopher who advocated the politics of skepticism as a counterweight to the politics of faith. The politics of faith is the belief that political actors can redesign society on a grand scale by following an already-made blueprint. The politics of skepticism advocates a slower pace of political reform and highlights what can be lost if people act recklessly. Unlike their peers filled with confidence in their blueprints, what skeptics refrain from doing is claiming to know a truth that will authorize them to turn society upside down, to revolutionize it. Oakeshott expresses this point in many memorable ways, including this passage from his essay "On Being Conservative":

> To be conservative…is to prefer the familiar to the unknown, to prefer the tried to the untried, fact to mystery, the actual to the possible, the limited to the unbounded, the near to the distant, the sufficient to the superabundant, the convenient to the perfect, present laughter to utopian bliss. (Oakeshott 1991: 408)

With my students, I would ask them to explain what Oakeshott means and apply his insights to the present. Oakeshott opposed the creation of the British welfare state after World War II; what are recent examples of large-scale political reforms, about, say, education or health care, about which Oakeshott would raise concerns? What are examples of people preserving political traditions and practices that may not seem rational, but that people cherish?

As a political theorist, I am less concerned about my students properly understanding Greek antiquity than with helping them appreciate skepticism's contribution to political thinking. One way or another—calling on students in class, breakout rooms in an online class, an in-class writing assignment, an exam question—I ask students to consider how a skeptic would reply to a politician making grand plans, say, to reform education, health care, or transportation. And then I ask them what they think of Sextus.

LEARNING OBJECTIVES

I am wary of any attempt to standardize teaching or learning. That said, I can see the value of instructors writing learning objectives to clarify their hopes for the course and to give students pointers if people ask why they took a course. Here, then, are a few learning objectives for a course or unit on Greek political thought:

- Students learn the key names, dates, books, ideas, and arguments of classical Greek political thought.
- Students learn about the relationship between epistemology and politics.
- Students learn how Plato's theory of the Ideas and Aristotle's teleology justify rule by elites.
- Students learn Sextus Empiricus' Ten Modes to suspend judgment and how to apply them to current political claims and plans.
- Students learn how to think about politics, that is, to look at political things from multiple points of view.

A final word on why I care about teaching the Greek skeptics. In *The Divide: How Fanatical Certitude is Destroying Democracy*, Taylor Dotson describes how an obsession with truth is harming contemporary democratic life. In many contemporary political debates, progressive technocrats clash with conservative populists. Technocrats think that policymakers should follow "the science." When pressed, technocrats will admit that science is an ongoing process of inquiry, of patiently accumulating facts and adjusting or even discarding theories, but in practice, many technocrats assume that all smart people agree on the one right policy and anybody who disagrees is not just wrong but stupid. Conservative populists claim to speak on behalf of the disrespected masses, but they too appeal to their own form of dogma in common sense. Democracy as a way of life, Dotson explains, requires people to be less confident of their own position and more receptive to hearing from other people. Democratic citizens "must be capable of recognizing their own ignorance in the face of an almost overwhelmingly complex world" (Dotson 2021: 96). Dotson is not anti-science; on the contrary, he thinks that scientists need to pursue truth but also acknowledge the limits of their knowledge, admit their biases, and recognize that reasonable people can disagree about how to frame or address a problem. A healthy democratic life requires more than widespread intellectual humility. But teaching students how to raise skeptical objections to dogmatism is one small way that I can help the next generation be more open-minded than the present one.

NOTES

1. David Lay Williams and John Christian Laursen have recommended that I teach *The Laws*.
2. Cynicism is a more aggressive form of skepticism that does not go along with laws and customs so easily. Both skepticism and cynicism recover a Socratic impulse to question common sense and scientific dogmatism. For an account of Diogenes and the cynical tradition, see Chaloupka (2001: 3–14).

REFERENCES

Abernathy, C. and J. Forestal (2019), "The Use of Debates in Political Science Courses," *Journal of Political Science Education*, **17** (3), 343–55.

Annas, J. and J. Barnes (1985), *The Modes of Scepticism*, Cambridge, UK: Cambridge University Press.

Arendt, H. (2018), *The Human Condition* (2nd edition), Chicago, IL: University of Chicago Press.

Barwich, A. S. (2020), *Smellosophy: What the Nose Tells the Mind*, Cambridge, MA: Harvard University Press.

Boudry, M. (2021), "Why Relativism is the Worst Idea Ever," *APA Online* [blog], July 29, accessed July 29, 2021 at https://blog.apaonline.org/2021/07/29/why-relativism-is-the-worst-idea-ever/.

Chaloupka, W. (2001), *Everybody Knows: Cynicism in America*, Minneapolis, MN: University of Minnesota Press.

Cohen, M. (ed.) (2018), *Princeton Readings in Political Thought: Essential Texts from Plato to Populism* (2nd edition), Princeton, NJ: Princeton University Press.

Dew, R. (2020), "Arendt Reading Aristotle," in R. Dew, *Hannah Arendt: Between Ideologies*, Cham, Switzerland: Springer Nature/Palgrave Macmillan, pp. 35–51.

Dewey, J. (2008), *The Middle Works of John Dewey, 1899–1924, Volume 9: 1916: Democracy and Education*, ed. J. A. Boydston, Carbondale, IL: Southern Illinois University Press.

Dotson, T. (2021), *The Divide: How Fanatical Certitude is Destroying Democracy*, Cambridge, MA: MIT Press.

Fischer, D. H. (2004), *Liberty and Freedom: A Visual History of America's Founding Ideas*, New York: Oxford University Press.

Fosl, P. S. (2019), *Hume's Scepticism: Pyrrhonian and Academic*, Edinburgh: Edinburgh University Press.

Foucault, M. (2008), *Introduction to Kant's Anthropology*, Los Angeles, CA: Semiotext.

Greenblatt, S. (2012), *The Swerve: How the World Became Modern*, New York: W.W. Norton & Company.

Lane, M. (2018), "Ancient Political Philosophy," in E. N. Zalta (ed.), *The Stanford Encyclopedia of Philosophy*, (Winter), accessed July 26, 2021 at https://plato.stanford.edu/archives/win2018/entries/ancient-political/.

Laursen, J. C. (1992), *The Politics of Skepticism in the Ancients, Montaigne, Hume, and Kant*, Leiden: Brill.

Laursen, J. C. (2004), "Yes, Skeptics Can Live Their Skepticism and Cope with Tyranny as Well as Anyone," in J. R. Mai Neto and R. H. Popkin (eds), *Skepticism in Renaissance and Post-Renaissance Thought*, Amherst, NY: Humanity Books, pp. 201–23.

Laursen, J. C. (2005), "Oakeshott's Skepticism and the Skeptical Traditions," *European Journal of Political Theory*, **4** (1), 37–55.

Laursen, J. C. (2016), "The Moral Life of the Ancient Skeptics: Living in Accordance with Nature and Freedom from Disturbance," *Bolletino Della Società Filosofica Italiana*, **219**, 5–22.

Lewis, B. (1991), *The Political Language of Islam*, Chicago, IL: University of Chicago Press.

Montaigne, M. de (2003), *Apology for Raymond Sebond*, Indianapolis, IN: Hackett Publishing Company.

Moore, M. J. (2016), *Buddhism and Political Theory*, New York: Oxford University Press.

Nietzsche, F. (1990), *Philosophy & Truth: Selections from Nietzsche's Notebooks of the Early 1870's*, ed. and trans. D. Breazeale, Atlantic Highlands, NJ: Humanities Press.

Nietzsche, F. (2017), *Nietzsche: On the Genealogy of Morality and Other Writings* (3rd edition), ed. K. Ansell-Pearson, trans. C. Diethe, New York: Cambridge University Press.

Nussbaum, M. C. (1996), *The Therapy of Desire*, Princeton, NJ: Princeton University Press.

Nussbaum, M. C. (2000), "Equilibrium: Scepticism and Immersion in Political Deliberation," *Acta Philosophica Fennica*, **66**, 171–97.

Oakeshott, M. (1991), *Rationalism in Politics and Other Essays*, Indianapolis, IN: Liberty Fund.

Plato (2016), *The Republic of Plato*, trans. A. Bloom, New York: Basic Books.

Popkin, R. H. (2003), *The History of Scepticism: From Savonarola to Bayle*, New York: Oxford University Press.

Ribeiro, B. C. (2021), *Sextus, Montaigne, Hume: Pyrrhonizers*, Leiden: Brill.

Rorty, R. (1989), *Contingency, Irony, and Solidarity*, New York: Cambridge University Press.

Rorty, R. (1994), "Human Rights, Rationality, and Sentimentality," in S. Shute and S. Hurley (eds), *On Human Rights*, New York: Basic Books, pp. 111–34.

Schlosser, J. A. (2014), *What Would Socrates Do? Self-Examination, Civic Engagement, and the Politics of Philosophy*, Cambridge, UK: Cambridge University Press.

Seery, J. (2013), "Stumbling toward a Democratic Theory of Incest," *Political Theory*, **41** (1), 5–32.

Sextus Empiricus (1985), *Selections from the Major Writings on Scepticism, Man, & God* (2nd edition), ed. P. P. Hallie, trans. S. G. Etheridge, Indianapolis, IN: Hackett Publishing Company.

Simonton, M. (2017), *Classical Greek Oligarchy: A Political History*, Princeton, NJ: Princeton University Press.

Sokoloff, W. W. (2020), *Political Science Pedagogy: A Critical, Radical and Utopian Perspective*, New York: Palgrave Macmillan.

Strauss, L. (1957), "What is Political Philosophy?," *The Journal of Politics*, **19** (3), 343–68.

Strauss, L. (1999), *Natural Right and History*, Chicago, IL: University of Chicago Press.

Strauss, L. (2000), *On Tyranny*, Chicago, IL: University of Chicago Press.

Tampio, N. (2017), "Why Rule by the People Is Better Than Rule by the Experts," *Aeon*, October 18, accessed July 17, 2019 at https://aeon.co/essays/why-rule-by-the -people-is-better-than-rule-by-the-experts.

Van Norden, B. W. (2017), *Taking Back Philosophy: A Multicultural Manifesto*, New York: Columbia University Press.

6. Teaching Chinese political thought, with a focus on Zhuangzi

INTRODUCTION

In the summer of 2019, I participated in the Wuhan University political philosophy summer school program. Although I was teaching the pre-Qin masters before then, I returned to the United States with a renewed commitment to teaching the pre-Qin masters and contemporary Chinese political thought. In this chapter, I explain why I teach texts such as the *Analects*, the *Mengzi*, the *Xunzi*, and the *Zhuangzi*—namely, to gain insight into the deepest currents of Chinese political thinking and to stage a conversation with contemporary Chinese political theorists who draw upon these authors. Initially, I teach Confucians (*Rujia*) and Legalists (*Fajia*) who justify the sovereign steaming straight the crooked timber of humanity. I then teach the *Zhuangzi*, a classical Daoist text that encourages carefree wandering and an awareness that our perspective always shapes our understanding. One of the challenges of teaching early Chinese political thought is that there is little overlap—in authors, historical references, concepts, argumentative strategies, and so forth—between the kinds of political thinking happening in Greece and the Warring States between the fifth and third century bce. One should not let the caveats, however, stop one from seeing parallels and similarities. Just as Sextus Empiricus influenced Montaigne and through him a wide range of Enlightenment philosophers who praised freedom of speech and toleration for other ways of life, the *Zhuangzi* can energize Chinese thinkers who would like to see versions of skepticism, liberalism, democracy, and pluralism in their own country. In the concluding section, I identify some of the pitfalls of comparative political theory—including that we are probably always underinformed—but argue that the political and philosophical payoffs justify teaching it to students.

WHY TEACH CHINESE POLITICAL THOUGHT?

As a graduate student, I spent countless hours reading Hume, Kant, Hegel, Nietzsche, Arendt, Foucault, Rawls, and Nussbaum, but I rarely read anything written by someone living outside the North Atlantic. In 1997, *The Review of*

Politics published an issue with essays by Fred Dallmayr, Roxanne L. Euben, and others inviting Euro-American political theorists to engage in a conversation with authors around the world and across time. More recently, Michael Freeden has identified two reasons why political theorists today should do comparative political theory. One is to draw attention to traditions, authors, ideas, and practices that have been unfairly neglected due to the legacy of imperialism. The second is that political theorists should find wisdom about politics wherever they can find it, and non-Western political thought can often offer a treasure trove of insights. Comparative political theory's "role is not simply that of decentering or 'provincializing' an era or an historical epoch, but of identifying the major political thought-practices in which all societies engage" (Freeden 2021: 3).[1] While I am wary of mandating things for scholars to read, teach, or research, I have discovered that learning about political traditions based outside Europe or the United States opens one's eyes to new aspects of the political universe.

In my classes on political theory, I often discuss current events, and students of global affairs need to pay attention to China. How is it possible to know what China—a country of over a billion people—is thinking? For many scholars discussed in this chapter, studying classic books written during the Warring States period (476–221 bce) provides one way to access the deepest currents of Chinese habits of mind. Leigh Jenco warns us against identifying a relatively stable tradition of Confucianism that somehow explains Chinese behavior for over two millennia. Confucianism has become "a protean term that glosses over … variations in geography, textuality, genre and scholarly affiliation in favor of a drastically reduced set of texts identified with the historical figure Confucius" (Jenco 2017: 467). Jenco is right that scholars need to be wary of imposing order on a complicated and evolving intellectual-practical tradition. At the same time, oral and literary traditions create the folklore that shapes how societies view things like gender roles, attitudes towards risk, and trust (Michalopoulos and Xue 2021). Political theorists can add their piece to the puzzle of making sense of China alongside other approaches inside and outside of political science.

I am still a relative newcomer to Chinese political thought and rely on specialists and translators to provide access to the texts. Here, though, I may share one observation about a parallel between classical Greek political philosophers—who saw political things "with a freshness and directness which has never been equaled" (Strauss 1957: 356)—and Chinese masters who wrote in the centuries before the unification of China by the Qin dynasty in 221 bce. My experience reading and teaching the pre-Qin masters is that they too make profound observations about politics with concrete imagery. In *Philosophy in the Flesh*, George Lakoff and Mark Johnson posit "the body-based properties of basic-level categories." What they mean by that is that "our categories arise from the fact that we are neural beings, from the nature of our bodily capacities, from our experience interacting in the world, and from our evolved capacity for basic-level categorization—a level at which we optimally interact with the world" (Lakoff and Johnson 1999: 30). In other words, human beings have a certain level of category that enables them to move through the world at the right speed. A green blob is too vague a category; a *Dryophytes cinereus* (American green tree frog) is too specific a category, but "frog" seems to serve human beings well as they walk by a pond or see an animal crossing the road on a rainy day. One of the things I notice from reading classical Chinese philosophy is that the writing often describes basic-level categories like stars, wind, grass, children, wells, eels, and monkeys. Bryan W. Van Norden says that we should not believe "the ideographic myth" that Chinese words are always images of the things they represent (Van Norden 2019: xxi). Point taken. Reading several translations of the same text confirms that translators must make choices about the right words to convey the meaning of the *Analects* or the *Zhuangzi*. Still, the Greek and Chinese classics make their points as simply and concretely as possible—in a way that facilitates comparisons between European and Asian ways of thinking, while still recognizing that there is great variation within both bodies of thought.[2]

In this chapter, I explain how I teach a unit on Chinese political thought. Many books on Chinese political thought dedicate chapters to authors and/or the schools that they ostensibly founded. Given that contemporary scholars have access to roughly the same set of texts—though there are occasional archaeological discoveries that unearth a new one—contemporary scholars may construct their own political theories by how they present the classical material. In this chapter, I explain how I teach Chinese political thought to culminate in the philosophy of Zhuangzi, a pre-Qin thinker who has affinities with the Greek skeptic Sextus Empiricus, and who, like him, may provide classical resources for contemporary liberals, democrats, and pluralists.

First, Box 6.1 explores the advantages of running simulations in class as an active-learning approach.

BOX 6.1   RUN SIMULATIONS

Political theorists teach the history of ideas. In this book, I have mostly discussed preparing lectures, but you can also run a seminar in which students lead the discussion and the professor asks questions, raises points, and keeps the class moving in a certain direction.

A third approach is to run simulations in which students learn the material in the process of playing games or solving puzzles. Here are a few ways that theorists use active-learning approaches in their classes:

- *Reacting to the Past.* William Gorton and Jonathan Havercroft have run *Reacting to the Past* simulations so that students may imagine that they are alive during the Golden Age of ancient Greece or the French Revolution. Students pretend to be certain characters from that era and write articles, give speeches, and try to convince their peers to join their cause. In these simulations, students learn about the historical context of classic works of political theory, hone their persuasive skills, and appreciate that many political theorists participate in the debates of their time. The professors report that playing *Reacting to the Past* simulation brings abstract ideas down to earth, raises student test achievement compared to classes that did not play the game, and leads to higher student evaluations of teacher effectiveness (Gorton and Havercroft 2012: 54).
- *Enacting the Social Contract.* Given the importance of the social contract tradition, many political theorists teach canonical texts by Thomas Hobbes, John Locke, Jean-Jacques Rousseau, David Hume, and others. One way to liven up the discussion, according to Derek Glasgow, is to run a simulation in which students are placed in groups and a situation like the original parties in Locke's state of nature. At each turn, students in their groups decide whether to invade another square on the board, do nothing and pass, or call an arbitration. Glasgow reports that most students surveyed in the post-class poll enjoyed participating in the game and thought it helped them learn about Locke's argument in the *Second Treatise of Government* (Glasgow 2015). Glasgow suggests that teachers could modify the simulation for different social contract theorists—an idea that could pose intriguing possibilities for teaching Bruno Latour's idea of a "Parliament of Things" (Latour 2018) or Ursula K. Le Guin's dystopian story, "The Ones Who Walk Away from Omelas" (Kirkpatrick 2021).
- *Freeze!* The simulations we have considered involve a fair amount of planning, but spontaneous activities may also energize a classroom. Halit Mustafa E. Tagma has students talk in front of the classroom for a few minutes and then calls on them to freeze. He then shows a slide, or draws on the board, a map of the personal space surrounding individuals as an illustration of the phenomenon of territoriality. "Using simple gimmicks can be effective in teaching political science methodology" (Tagma 2021: 770).

Teachers should feel the pulse of their class, and if students are looking out the window or at their cell phones, then it may be time to try a new classroom activity.

AN OVERVIEW OF THE PRE-QIN MASTERS

I research and teach the history of ideas with an eye towards contributing to contemporary debates about politics. Today, I am particularly interested in the debate between Confucian meritocrats who maintain that modern-day *junzi* (noble sons, or gentlemen) should rule and liberals who appreciate individual freedom and draw inspiration from Zhuangzi. In this section, I say a few words about how I teach the pre-Qin masters to set up the discussion of Zhuangzi.[3]

Pre-Confucian Warrior Ethics

Confucius performed a transvaluation of values, lowering the status of the soldier and elevating the status of the scholar. A Korean student of philosophy once wrote me that Confucius had "in fact annihilated the party of Agamemnon more thoroughly—and permanently—than any ancient philosopher, anywhere."[4] Confucius elevated the life of the mind over the life of combat, and though Confucius still wanted *junzi* to know how to ride horses and shoot arrows, these physical activities were subordinate to knowing the rites and music. Alas, one of the features of warriors like Agamemnon is that they tend not to write a lot, so modern scholars cannot easily teach a text that represents their point of view. Whalen Lai wrote an article that assembles what evidence we do have about aristocratic knights and feudal ethics in ancient China: "The reason why every noble son [*junzi*] could fight was that war was still relatively simple; strength more or less laid then in numbers and weaponry such that some basic training was all that was required for preparing the young for war. The picture corresponds to what we expect of Homeric or heroic society" (Lai 1985: 187). To be clear: this account of pre-Confucian warrior ethics is stylized to fit an account of the trajectory of human history propagated by the *ru* (literati, scholars) tradition to which Confucius belonged. An archaeological account of the Neolithic period (c. 8000–1900 bce) would document the domestication of plants and animals, the transition from nomadism to more sedentary communities, the use of ceramics and grinding technologies, demographic growth, regional diversity, and so forth (Feinman, Fang and Nicholas 2018). Even if history is more complex than a clash between nerds and jocks, the Plato–Homer and Confucius–Agamemnon binaries help us understand historical and contemporary debates about who ought to lead society.

Confucius

When teaching Confucius (551–479 bce), I emphasize two things. First, the ministers who ought to advise the monarchs possess valuable knowledge acquired from a study of antiquity, particularly how things were done in the Zhou dynasty: "The Master said, 'I am not someone who was born with knowledge. I simply love antiquity, and diligently look there for knowledge'" (Ivanhoe and Van Norden 2005: 22). Second, those who know the standards of righteousness and rituals should rule over those who are ignorant of them. Confucius told Fan Chi that a wise ruler would "'Raise up the straight and apply them to the crooked, and the crooked will be made straight.'" Zixia then told Fan Chi: "What a wealth of instruction you have received! When Shu ruled the world, he selected from amongst the multitude, raising up Gao Yao, and those who were not Good then kept their distance. When Tang ruled the world, he selected from amongst the multitude, raising up Yi Yin, and those who were not Good then kept their distance" (Ivanhoe and Van Norden 2005: 37). In my courses, I teach both Mengzi, who encourages rulers to nurture the sprouts of benevolence in subjects, and Xunzi, who tells the ruler to flatten the crooked wood in his subjects. Confucius, Mengzi, and Xunzi all subscribe, like Aristotle, to a notion of politics as soulcraft.

Mozi

According to the historian Sima Qian, the Qin dynasty burned books and buried scholars (*Ru*) to consolidate power, and Emperor Wu of the Han dynasty (r. 141–87 bce) made Confucianism the state ideology, including by testing administrators on their mastery of the Confucian classics. Mohism never found a champion in later Chinese history, so its primary fascination for contemporary scholars is that it served as a foil for both Mengzi and Zhuangzi. Mohism was a kind of utilitarian ideology that told rulers to consider adopting a policy only if it would "enrich the poor, increase the population, [and] bring stability to precious situations and order to chaos" (Ivanhoe and Van Norden 2005: 81). And the ruler could tattoo faces, cut off noses, or use other gruesome techniques to make subjects obey: "This is why our teacher Mozi says, 'In ancient times, sage-kings created the Five Punishments to facilitate good order among the people. These are like the main thread of a skein or the drawing of a net. They are how the sage-kings gathered in those in the world who refused to obey their superiors'" (Ivanhoe and Van Norden 2005: 67–8). Mohists and Confucians disagreed about things like music and burial rites, but they all wanted to end war between the regions, reap the advantages of a unified state for safety and commerce, and identify rites and maxims that would create social bonds within and beyond families. With less concern for the ethical disposition of the people, Legalists like Lord Shang and Han Feizi shared a similar vision of a strong ruler presiding over an obedient and hard-working population (see Chapter 3).

REASONS TO READ THE *ZHUANGZI*

Zhuangzi lived around the fourth century bce, roughly the same time as Aristotle in ancient Greece and Mencius in ancient China. The Han historian Sima Qian reports that Zhuangzi was born in the state of Meng; his personal name was Zhou; he served as a minor official in his home state of Qiyuan; he lived during the reign of Prince Wei of Chu; and he drew his teachings from Laozi. Scholars tend to agree that the first seven chapters of the *Zhuangzi* are the "inner books" composed by Zhuangzi himself, and his disciples wrote the outer books (Chapters 8–22) and miscellaneous books (Chapters 23–33) (Ware 2019).[5] In *Zhuangzi and Modern Chinese Literature*, Jianmei Liu explains Zhuangzi's unique role within the history of Chinese philosophy: "The cultural spirit [Zhuangzi] represents emphasizes individuality, freedom, and nature, whereas the cultural spirit espoused by Confucius highlights moral teaching, order, and ethics… Zhuangzi's philosophy has been the source of the idea of 'freedom' under the strictly regulated moral and ethical orders, offering a spiritual home for personal emancipation" (Liu 2016: 1–2). If one is going to counterpose a classical Chinese thinker to the rigid social orders of Confucianism, Mohism, or Legalism, then Zhuangzi is the best candidate.

In the summer of 2021, I taught Introduction to Political Philosophy by juxtaposing a Greek and a Chinese political thinker and a big question in political theory. Here were the four units:

- Who should rule? Plato and Confucius on rule by the wise.
- How should the state train citizens? Aristotle and Mencius on moral cultivation.
- How should the ruler govern? Machiavelli and Han Feizi on fear, love, and rules (*fa*).
- Can skepticism point the way to a more humane future? Sextus Empiricus and Zhuangzi on skepticism and politics.

I have found these units useful for comparing the deepest levels of Euro-American and Chinese political philosophy. Reading Sextus Empiricus and Zhuangzi alongside one another, we appreciate how both Greek and Chinese skeptics recognized that loosening our claims to knowledge permits humans to be more generous to other ways of thinking and living (Kjellberg 1996).

Zhuangzi is fun to teach. C. C. Tsai has made wonderful cartoons of passages from the *Zhuangzi* that I fold into my lectures and discussions. Stories like the one about Butcher Ding carving an ox or Zhuangzi dreaming that he was a butterfly—more about both passages below—are simple enough for my eight-year-old son to appreciate, but scholars continue to offer new interpretations. Peng Yu, a political theorist who specializes in Daoism, tells me that he asks students to draw pictures from the *Zhuangzi* in a spontaneous and intuitive manner and that this exercise allows to them to "'feel' politics in its plural form like Zhuangzi."[6] If you are an English-speaking political theorist new to Chinese political thought, I recommend teaching the first two chapters of the *Zhuangzi*: the first, "Free and Easy Wandering," presents a vision of "absolute spiritual emancipation of the individual," and the second, "On the Equality of Things," questions and rejects "absolute and fixed views on 'right and wrong'" (Liu 2016: 5). Though the *Zhuangzi* is full of entertaining and thought-provoking passages, sometimes it is good to focus on just a few pages with students in class.

The next few sections discuss a few of Zhuangzi's arguments for perspectivalism, his use of language, and the political teaching of the *Zhuangzi*.

EELS, MONKEYS, AND HUMANS

When I teach the history of political philosophy, I often draw circles and a line through the center. In the top part of the circle, I identify what distinguishes human beings from other animals, and in the bottom half, I write the words that the philosopher uses to describe what we share with other animals. Kant, for example, all but invites the teacher to draw this image when he separates human beings into *personality* that signifies their rationality and responsibility, their *animality* that signifies that they are a living being, and their *humanity* that signifies that a human being is "living and at the same time *rational* being" (Kant 2001: 74; original emphasis). Chinese political thought does not make such a neat division between our higher and lower self, in part because the locus of decision-making, the *xin*, resides in the heart rather than the head. Still, Confucius and his disciples make it clear that the superior person has elevated capacities to learn (*xue*) and think (*si*) and possesses wisdom (*zhi*) (Hall and Ames 1987). As many commentators have noted, Plato and Confucius both contend that the wise should rule because they know the pattern that governs the universe.[7] Zhuangzi, like Sextus Empiricus, maintains that the wise may not be as smart as they think they are and ought to relax their insistence that they should be in charge of building a society according to their blueprints.

Chapter 2 of the *Zhuangzi* is filled with invitations to recognize that our knowledge is confined to our perspective or that reality itself eludes our grasp. Brook Ziporyn offers a useful explanation of the challenge that translators face in rendering the title, "Qiwulun." *Lun* means assessment; *wu* means things; and the title can indicate either the equalizing of words or things. "Qiwulun" can mean "Assessments that Equalize Things" and/or "Equalizing the Assessments Made by All Things" (Zhuangzi 2009: 9). In other words, despite the efforts made by Confucius, Mozi, and Xunzi to "rectify names" and forbid the use of language that confuses subjects about their duties, Zhuangzi's title suggests that human beings will never be able to say that a human knows what beauty is and a frog does not: both animals, so to speak, have the equal right to say what they think is beautiful.

The chapter contains a passage filled with hilarious images of animals looking at each other quizzically for what the other thinks is right or wrong. The passage begins with Nie Que and Wang Ni discussing whether it is possible for all things to agree in their assessment of what is right. Wang Ni says, "How could I know that what I call 'knowing' is not really 'not-knowing'? How could I know that what I call 'not-knowing' is not really 'knowing'?" (Zhuangzi 2009: 17). Like a Pyrrhonian skeptic, Zhuangzi is not suggesting with pure confidence that he or anything else can know or not know how things are in reality; he is merely sharing his own doubts about whether anything can possess the truth beyond that which is available to it from its own perspective. Here is the passage filled with animals disagreeing with each other about the right place to live, eat, or judge the beautiful:

> When people sleep in a damp place, they wake up deathly ill and sore about the waist—but what about eels? If people live in trees, they tremble with fear and worry—but how about monkeys? Of these three, which "knows" what is the right place to live? People eat the flesh of the livestock, deer eat grass, snakes eat centipedes, hawks and eagles eat mice. Of these four, which "knows" the right thing to eat? Monkeys take she-monkeys for mates, bucks mount does, male fish frolic with female fish, while humans regard Mao Qiang and Lady Li as great beauties—but when fish see them they dart into the depths, when birds see them they soar into the skies, when deer see them they bolt away without looking back. Which of these four "knows" what is rightly alluring? (Zhuangzi, 2009: 18)

After reading this passage together, it is a great exercise to put students into groups to discuss the political import of these thought experiments. Why should anyone care where an eel sleeps or what a deer eats?! Near the end of the passage, Wang Ni admits that he is not really talking about eels or deer at all: these are a metaphor for human beings who think, feel, and act in different ways. "From where I see it, the transitions of Humanity and Responsibility and the trails of right and wrong are hopelessly tangled and confused. How could I know how to distinguish which is right among them?" (Zhuangzi 2009: 18).

Zhuangzi has a normative vision: eels should sleep in a damp place, monkeys should live in trees, and all things should follow their own way (*dao*) (Allinson 1989; Ivanhoe 1996). But if we assume that these animals are also stand-ins for other human beings and their values, then Zhuangzi's philosophy is more tolerant and flexible than the ethico-political visions of the Confucians and Mohists, dogmatists whom Zhuangzi groups together as *RuMo* (Jiang 2021: 290).

DEAD OR ALIVE, AWAKE OR ASLEEP

One of Zhuangzi's strategies to deflate human claims to possess knowledge is to compare human beings with animals. Another is to show how the human being's perspective changes depending on what is going on with their own bodies. One example is the fact that human beings assume that life is better than death. But Zhuangzi invites us to consider the example of Lady Li to show that we have no grounds for assuming that that is so:

> Lady Li was the daughter of the border guard of Ai. When she was first taken captive and brought to the state of Jin, she wept until her tears drenched the collar of her robe. But later, when she went to live in the palace of the ruler, shared his couch with him, and ate the delicious meats of his table, she wondered why she had ever wept. How do I know that the dead do not wonder why they ever longed for life? (Zhuangzi 2003: 42–3)

There are other examples in the *Zhuangzi* of people dancing, singing, and carrying on after the death of a spouse or a teacher. Zhuangzi's point, I take it, is that human beings do not know as much as we assume we do, even something as apparently obvious as that it is better to be alive than dead. Zhuangzi is also conveying the message that the universe does not owe us anything and we need to let go of our demands for knowledge and control. Zhuangzi, to borrow a term from Nietzsche, criticizes *ressentiment* that can often manifest in violence against groups blamed for the universe not conforming to our expectations.

The *Zhuangzi* is also filled with examples of people sleeping and dreaming.[8] Here is the final passage in Chapter 2 in which Zhuangzi dreamt he was a butterfly:

> Once Zhuang Zhou dreamt he was a butterfly, a butterfly flitting and fluttering around, happy with himself and doing as he pleased. He didn't know he was Zhuang Zhou. Suddenly he woke up and there he was, solid and unmistakable Zhuang Zhou. But he didn't know if he was Zhuang Zhou who had dreamt he was a butterfly, or a butterfly dreaming he was Zhuang Zhou. Between Zhuang Zhou and a butterfly there must be *some* distinction! This is called the Transformation of Things! (Zhuangzi 2003: 44; original emphasis)

This passage has many possible lessons, all of which undermine human claims to understand reality. Human beings have no way of knowing for sure whether they have a more privileged access to the truth when they are awake than when they are asleep. Human beings do not know whether reality corresponds to the way that humans see it versus how butterflies see it. And in the last sentence, Zhuangzi opens the possibility that what human beings perceive is just a snapshot of a process that is in constant motion: the unending transformation of one thing into another. In *Creative Evolution*, Henri Bergson said that human beings believe that life is organized into distinct units like beads on a necklace; in fact, reality is "a flux of fleeting shades merging into each other" (Bergson 1998: 3). Likewise, Zhuangzi suggests that human cognition has only a dim view of the way that things interconnect and merge into one another. It is folly to say that we have any access to reality other than how we perceive it here and now, with processes eluding the human cognitive apparatus.[9]

RIGHT AND WRONG

Often, Zhuangzi buries the ethical or political point in a story about a fish turning into a giant bird, a monkey trainer giving a different ratio of nuts to monkeys to make them calm, or a man having a conversation with a skull. Occasionally, Zhuangzi foregrounds the ethical and political dimensions of his perspectivism. Here is one passage in which Zhuangzi makes it clear how difficult, if not impossible, it is for somebody to adjudicate a dispute about facts or values:

> Once you and I have started arguing, if you win and I lose, then are you really right and am I really wrong? If I win and you lose, then am I really right and are you really wrong? Is one of us right and the other one wrong? Or are both of us right and both of us wrong? If you and I can't understand one another, then other people will certainly be even more in the dark. Whom shall we get to set us right? Shall we get someone who agrees with you to set us right? But if they already agree with you how can they set us right? Shall we get someone who agrees with me to set us right? But if they already agree with me, how can they set us right? (Ivanhoe and Van Norden 2005: 223)

For Zhuangzi, the point is that there is nobody who transcends the human condition and is qualified to be an impartial judge. Zhuangzi does discuss an authentic person or sage who has achieved a kind of higher vantage point on the human condition (Allinson 1989). In my reading of the *Zhuangzi*, the authentic person still does not take sides in disputes as currently formulated. It is more that the authentic person sighs at the predicament in which human beings find themselves rather than renders a fair judgment in a dispute about values. They are like the giant bird named Peng—mentioned in the opening pages of the book—that flies from the Northern Oblivion to the Southern Oblivion, above mundane debates about right and wrong.

Elsewhere, Zhuangzi makes it clear that his target is the Confucians and Mohists who believe that they are right and that others are wrong. "Words are obscured by the ostentatious blossoms of reputation that come with them. Hence we have the rights and wrongs of the Confucians and Mohists, each affirming what the other negates and negating what the other affirms"

(Zhuangzi 2009: 11–12). In a way, the Confucians and Mohists need each other. If the Confucians say that *this* (*shi*) is right and *that* (*fei*) is wrong, then they need a party that stands in the position of the wrong. And the same goes for the Mohists. The political theorist William E. Connolly calls this relationship the *paradox of difference*: "My personal identity is defined through the collective constituencies with which I identify or am identified by others...it is further specified by comparison to a variety of things I am not. Identity, then, is always connected to a series of differences that help it be what it is" (Connolly 2002: xiv). For Zhuangzi, recognizing the interdependence of opposed positions gives one a certain clarity that neither side has a monopoly on the truth; and that both positions together simply cover one corner of nature (*tian*). "[T]he Sage does not proceed from any one of them alone but instead lets them all bask in the broad daylight of Heaven. And that too is only a case of going by the rightness of the present 'this'" (Zhuangzi 2009: 12). For Zhuangzi, there are no mechanical rules to separate the right and the wrong; the only normative criterion is the way, the *dao*, of each thing. At a minimum, so far, we can see that this entails denying the Confucians or Mohists or subsequent Legalists the right to impose their pattern on other individuals or society.

ZHUANGZI'S STYLE

We are getting closer to discerning the political teaching of the *Zhuangzi*. Zhuangzi does not discuss many topics that are at the heart of political theory, including the proper institutional arrangements. Nor does Zhuangzi even consistently speak in his own voice about what principles a ruler should follow. What Zhuangzi does is change how one speaks and thinks, which in turn influences how one speaks and thinks about politics. In this section, I discuss how Zhuangzi's perspectivism leads to a certain style of writing and communicating that thwarts any effort to rectify names once and for all.[10]

One thing that Zhuangzi does is draw attention to the fact that human concepts do not cut nature at the joints. In other words, human beings may point to *this* or *that*, the *right* or the *wrong*, but these gestures are not all that precise. Debates always need additional words to define terms, and infinite regress means that human words float on air. "Now, courses have never had any sealed borders between them, and words have never had any constant sustainability" (Zhuangzi 2009: 16). Here is one point on which Laozi and Zhuangzi agree: words are at best a crude tool to help people reach a more holistic intuition of how things fit together. Furthermore, nature itself seems to resist being boxed into human concepts. "Wherever debate shows one of two alternatives to be right, something remains undistinguished and unshown. What is it? The sage hides it in his embrace, while the masses of people debate it, trying to demonstrate it to one another. Thus I say that demonstration by debate always leaves something unseen" (Zhuangzi 2009: 16). In *Political Theory and the Displacement of Politics*, Bonnie Honig calls these the *remainders of politics*, the resistances "engendered by every settlement" and calls attention to them "to secure the perpetuity of political contest" (Honig 1993: 3). The *Zhuangzi* does not seem to encourage readers to participate in political contestation; there are many passages in the *Zhuangzi* that counsel withdrawal from political affairs. But Zhuangzi and Honig share an awareness that political actors should recognize the contestability of their claims and judgments.

A second literary device that Zhuangzi uses to undermine certainty is paradox, a statement that appears on its face to be absurd. One of these is the story of Butcher Ding skillfully carving an ox before King Hui of Liang who exclaims that the butcher has taught him "how to nourish life" (Zhuangzi 2009: 23)! The point of the story seems to be that good rulers should rule with grace and that resistance is a sign that they are doing it wrong. But it is still funny to imagine a king in front of a butchered ox, with blood pooling on the floor, drawing a lesson about how to nourish life (Kwek 2019: 423–8). Zhuangzi also uses paradox to disrupt habitual ways of thinking that we know something as simple as something's size. "Nothing in the world is bigger than the tip of an autumn hair but Mount Tai is small. No one lives longer than a dead child and Peng Yu died young. Heaven and earth were born alongside me, and the ten thousand things and I are one" (Ivanhoe and Van Norden 2005: 219–20). I take it that the point is that if we put our finger up it looks larger than the mountain in the distance, and that if we bring a tip of hair to our eyeball that it will fill our field of vision. Regardless, Zhuangzi's paradoxes "shake complacent readers and make them question their unnatural assumptions about the world" (Goldin 2020: 17).

A third literary device is what the Chan/Zen Buddhists took from Zhuangzi and called *koan*s: "riddles, nonsense statements, or interpersonal encounters that…have no logical meaning" (Slingerland 2014: 153). Chapter 2 opens with a conversation between two men with apparently fictitious names discussing the sound of the wind blowing through huge trees: "In the mountain forests that lash and sway, there are huge trees a hundred spans around with hollows and openings like noses, like mouths, like ears, like jugs, like cups, like mortars, like rifts, like ruts. They roar like waves, whistle like arrows, screech, gasp, cry, wail, moan, and howl, those in the lead calling out *yeee!*, those behind calling out *yuuu!*" Later in the chapter, Zhuangzi explains, "I'm going to try speaking some reckless words and I want you to listen to them recklessly" (Zhuangzi 2003: 31–2, 42). For Zhuangzi, words glide on the surface of things and the best chance for words to help us get to a deeper understanding is to jolt us out of habitual ways of thinking and speaking. In *Thus Spoke Zarathustra*, Nietzsche has Zarathustra say that "the world is deeper—and deeper than day had ever been aware" (Nietzsche 1977: 166). Nietzsche's idea that philosophy should be poetic and incorporate Dionysian elements has influenced a tradition called, for better or worse, Continental philosophy. Like Nietzsche, "Zhuangzi models a new way of speaking that opens one's spirit to appreciate strangeness and wonder" (Froese 2018: 15).

One could argue that Zhuangzi is a mystic whose writing aims to make one tranquil after seeing the interconnectedness of things. In this case, Zhuangzi's stories about relativism aim to loosen one's mind for the mystical intuition. "[T]he Radiance of Drift and Doubt is the sage's only map. He makes no definition of what is right but instead entrusts it to the everyday function of each thing. This is what I call the Illumination of the Obvious" (Zhuangzi 2009: 15). The *Zhuangzi* may make one suspend judgment about what is right or wrong and go along with the norms of one's community. In the next section, we consider several readers of the *Zhuangzi* who maintain that Zhuangzi counsels conservativism and lethargy. In the subsequent section, I argue that contemporary political theorists may reconstruct Zhuangzi's ideas for a more energetic political stance.[11]

CRITIQUES OF ZHUANGZI'S POLITICS

In my Introduction to Political Philosophy course, I pair Zhuangzi with Sextus Empiricus, and one critique of the Greek skeptics is that they "have removed the intensity of commitment to virtue that makes people risk their lives for justice" (Nussbaum 1996: 314; Ribeiro 2021: 20). Do people make the same *apraxia* objection to Zhuangzi? In fact, they do. This section will consider three critiques that Zhuangzi is not a political thinker or, if he is one, he affirms the status quo whatever it happens to be. Bryan W. Van Norden argues that the *Zhuangzi* is a "recipe for political passivity" and "apathy toward politics." Van Norden acknowledges that the *Zhuangzi* contains passages that suggest that it is wrong to coerce people to conform to social norms about gender roles, sexual preferences, religions, artistic tastes, and so forth. Here is one passage that provides support for the reading of Zhuangzi as a teacher of tolerance:

> The emperor of the South Sea was called Shu [Brief], the emperor of the North Sea was called Hu [Sudden], and the emperor of the central region was called Hundun [Chaos]. Shu and Hu from time to time came together for a meeting in the territory of Hundun, and Hundun treated them very generously. Shu and Hu discussed how they could repay his kindness. "All men," they said, "have seven openings so they can see, hear, eat, and breathe. But Hundun alone doesn't have any. Let's trying boring him some!" Every day they bored another hole, and on the seventh day he died. (Zhuangzi 2003: 95)

The Confucian and Mohist traditions worked within a moral–political paradigm committed to cultivating personal virtues, regulating the family, governing the state, and bringing peace to all under Heaven (Jiang 2021: 37). In other words, the *RuMo* taught what Aristotle called soulcraft, shaping people to speak, work, raise families, bury the dead, and obey the ruler in a certain way. Zhuangzi suggests that trying to help people in this way is analogous to Shu and Hu boring an extra hole into Hundun. Van Norden sees why liberals may like Zhuangzi, but he thinks that in the last analysis Zhuangzi is an ironist whose philosophy cannot give one the principles or the confidence to act for justice. Borrowing a line from Hegel, Van Norden contends that Zhuangzi's philosophy is "the night in which all cows are black," that is, it is incapable of making distinctions necessary for ethics and politics (Van Norden 2016).

In *Trying Not to Try*, Edward Slingerland suggests that the *Zhuangzi* is a kind of self-help book that helps people go along smoothly in the world and not change it. Slingerland discusses the passage about Butcher Ding as an example of how practicing certain techniques helps one achieve spontaneous action (*wuwei*), or, in modern psychological terms, a state of flow. The story is about Butcher Ding carving up an ox for Lord Wenhui. Initially, Butcher Ding looked at the ox as a huge animal, and then he looked at it as a collection of parts. "And now—now I go at it by spirit and don't look with my eyes. Perception and understanding have come to a stop and spirit moves where it wants. I go along with the natural makeup, strike in the big hollows, guide the knife through the big openings, and follow things as they are. So I never touch the smallest ligament or tendon, much less a main joint" (Zhuangzi 2003: 46). On Slingerland's reading, the *Zhuangzi* recommends certain techniques, perhaps even drug use, to downshift the conscious mind and let "the adaptive unconscious take over." Like the early Christians or latter-day hippies, Zhuangzi is more concerned with individual salvation or enlightenment rather than societal change. "Zhuangzi seems to accept the political social status quo, merely giving us a method for moving within it successfully" (Slingerland 2014: 145, 159).

Tao Jiang argues that the *Zhuangzi* presents an inspiring vision of carefree wandering at the margin of the lifeworld (*fangwai*) and within the lifeworld (*fangnei*) (Jiang 2021: 320–34). If there is a seed for a Chinese version of liberalism, it is the *Zhuangzi*, but unfortunately the text is primarily written for extraordinary individuals who can attune to the way (*dao*) while still performing their social roles well. There is no sufficient account of a politics or state that can create room for ordinary misfits in the *Zhuangzi*. To make this point, Jiang compares Zhuangzi and Isaiah Berlin on the topic of freedom. On the one side, Jiang argues that the *Zhuangzi* contributes to the liberal project by its richer spiritual account of what it is like to transform the self (*hua*), gracefully roam indifferent to worldly entanglements, and let each other be (*wang*). One way that Zhuangzi does that is by presenting a social order in which humans following their individual way (*dao*) are like fish swimming by each other in a lake. Ironically, Zhuangzi puts this teaching in the words of a historical figure, Confucius, who thought that social order depended on fixed rituals and hierarchies:

> Confucius said, "Fish come together in water, and human beings come together in the Course. Those who meet each other in the water do so by darting through the ponds, thus finding their nourishment and support. Those who meet each other in the Course do so by not being bothered to serve any one particular goal, thereby allowing the flow of their lives to settle into stability. Thus it is said, fish forget one another in the rivers and lakes, and human beings forget one another in the arts of the Course." (Zhuangzi 2009: 47)

What Zhuangzi does not realize, according to Jiang, is that politics sometimes involves digging the lakes and directing the rivers so that fish may swim without bumping into one another. Stated less poetically, Isaiah Berlin recognized in a way that Zhuangzi did not that liberals need to create institutions that create space and protection for freedom-seeking individuals. "Given the richness of the Zhuangzian *imaginaire*, it is puzzling, and, indeed, unfortunate that it has a rather limited imagination about the state and politics" (Jiang 2012: 84; original emphasis).

It is true that the *Zhuangzi* lacks many of the elements that contemporary political theorists look for when reading the history of political philosophy. That said, for those who are interested in encouraging the cultivation of something like a liberal, democratic sensibility in China, the *Zhuangzi* provides the prime candidate among the pre-Qin masters to reconstruct.

ZHUANGZIAN POLITICAL THEORY

As a comparative political theorist rather than an area specialist, I hesitate to make an original interpretation of the *Zhuangzi*. Instead, I assign work by Chinese political theorists Dorothy Kwek and Peng Yu who explore ways to reconstruct Zhuangzi's political theory for our era. Here are the ways that they do it and my own modest contribution to bring Zhuangzi into pluralist political theory:

Be Useless

There are many passages in the *Zhuangzi* that seem to counsel withdrawing from politics entirely:

> Once, when Zhuangzi was fishing in the Pu River, the king of Chu sent two officials to see him and announce to him: "I would like to trouble you with the administration of my realm." Zhuangzi held on to the fishing pole and, without turning his head,

said, "I have heard that there is a sacred tortoise in Chu that has been dead for 3,000 years. The king keeps it wrapped in cloth and boxed, and stores it in the ancestral temple. Now would this tortoise rather be dead and have its bones left behind and honored? Or would it rather be alive dragging its tail in the mud?" The two officials said, "It would rather be alive and drag its tail in the mud." Zhuangzi said, "Then go away, I'll drag my tail in the mud!" (Chang 2016: 146)

Laozi supposedly wrote the *Daodejing* on his way into the hinterlands because of a request from a border guard, and Zhuangzi seems to be doing and counseling willful abandonment of a political life. What Kwek argues, however, is that Zhuangzi's message gains focus once we realize his audience and context. In this era, the audience of people who could read, and who could read complex texts, was small, and was largely composed of the *shi*, scholar-officials, responsible for helping their state gain economic and military power and impose order on their subjects. "The service that the *shi* performed for the ruler often consisted of surveillance, discipline, and punishment exercised *over* the commoners" (Kwek 2019: 415; original emphasis). According to Kwek, Zhuangzi is not arguing against politics as such but against the kind of politics that administrators performed in the Warring States period.

What does it mean to participate in politics? Ideally, Zhuangzi envisions people living together like fish in a lake, barely noticing one another as they swim peacefully past one another. But to get to that point requires challenging rulers and ministers who wish to micro-manage the social order. In a passage that calls to mind James C. Scott's (1998) critique of large-scale government projects in *Seeing Like a State*, Zhuangzi tells the story of a man named Tian Chengzi who killed the ruler of Qi and took advantage of the existing "laws and regulations devised by the sagely wisdom" (Zhuangzi 2009: 63). Even though the architects of the laws and regulations may have assumed that the rulers would possess virtue (*de*), Zhuangzi observes that people with poor moral character can also rule. In fact, Zhuangzi seems to suggest that the Confucians and the Mohists both contribute to the problem. Zhuangzi's radical suggestion is to destroy the tools of governance that include the words of the so-called sages:

> Hence, only when sagacity is destroyed and wisdom abandoned will the great robbers disappear. Smash the jades and crush the pearls, and the small robbers will not arise. Burn the tallies and shred the seals, and the people will become plain and straight. Break the measures and split the scales, and the people will no longer bicker and fight. Only when we decimate the sagely laws throughout the world will the people be able to listen to reason. (Zhuangzi 2009: 64)

According to Kwek, "the sageliness that orders and organizes the state in fact makes it easier for the usurper and tyrant to assert their control. *Zhuangzi makes problematic the efficacy of governance itself*" (Kwek 2019: 417; original emphasis). Depending on the level and mood of the class, this could be a moment to discuss the relationship between epistemology, ontology, and politics. In playful stories and aphorisms, the *Zhuangzi* induces readers to see that human categories and perceptions do not "fit" the world.[12] In his demand to "[b]reak the measures and split the scales," Zhuangzi is like many of the great skeptics and nominalists in Western philosophy who dispute Plato's account of transcendent Ideas or the authority of anybody who claims to know them. For my class right now, I put Zhuangzi into conversation with Sextus Empiricus, but one could also juxtapose him with David Hume, Friedrich Nietzsche, Jacques Derrida, or Jane Bennett (Kwek 2018).

In an article on "The Importance of Being Useless," Kwek notes that the *Zhuangzi* has many versions of stories of trees that are not chopped down because their wood would make boats sink, coffins rot, vessels break, doors sweat sap, and be eaten by worms. One dream-like episode includes a conversation between Carpenter Shi and a serrate oak that explains that, "if I had been of some use, would I ever have grown this large?" (Kwek 2018: 29). On the one hand, these passages seem to recommend that people become useless to survive in an era of ruthless struggles for power—do not draw attention to yourself in a dangerous time. But Kwek also reads these passages as offering a profound teaching of "letting-be." "In *Zhuangzi*, the tree's uselessness is what is 'natural' to itself, or *zìrán*. This is opposed to the forms of utility at first envisaged by the carpenter, which are not only externally imposed, but also utterly opposed to the tree's way of being." Zhuangzi's teaching of letting-be "involves a sensitization to things and expressions we may not even have begun to dream of" (Kwek 2018: 38). After reading aloud one of the passages about useless trees in the *Zhuangzi*, I ask my students: What is the purpose of this story? What are examples, good and bad, of useless trees? How could we as political actors create more room and appreciation for useless trees?

Lose the Body

In Chapter 3, I argued that teaching the history of political philosophy benefits from focusing on the topic of human nature. How do human beings differ from animals? How do human beings differ from one another? Virtually every Western political philosopher addresses these questions, and though Confucius was reticent about the question of human nature (*xing*), one can find or reconstruct a view of human nature from most of the pre-Qin masters (Sung 2016). In an article on "Indeterminate Self: Subjectivity, Body and Politics in *Zhuangzi*," Peng Yu shows how Zhuangzi recommends losing the body (*sangwo*) to attain a state of free and easy wandering (*xiaoyao*). Though Zhuangzi did not pursue the political ramifications of this view of human nature and ethics, Peng Yu suggests that Zhuangzi can join contemporary political theorists seeking to move beyond the strictures of the mind, reason, clear language, and fixed rituals.

Here is one passage in the *Zhuangzi* in which Confucius, of all people, praises human beings who "roam outside of the lines," including by not participating in funeral rituals:

> Men such as these look upon life as a dangling wart or swollen pimple, and on death as its dropping off, its bursting and draining. Being such, what would they understand about which is life and which is death, what comes before and what comes after? Depending on all their diverse borrowings, they yet lodge securely in the one and only selfsame body. They forget all about their livers and gallbladders, cast away their eyes and ears, reversing and returning, ending and beginning, knowing no start or finish. Oblivious, they drift uncommitted beyond the dust and grime, far-flung and unfettered in the great work of doing nothing in particular. Why would they do something as stupid as practicing conventional rituals to impress the eyes and ears of the common crowd? (Zhuangzi 2009: 46–7)

Human beings, according to Zhuangzi, are made of pus, blood, spit, semen, and feces, and we have organs, livers, gallbladders, eyes, and ears possessed by other animals. For philosophers in the East or West who subscribe to a constitutional model of the soul in which one part—the mind or *xin*—governs the rest, Zhuangzi's philosophy is relativistic and dangerous. Zhuangzi takes the insult and turns it into a compliment: such human beings drift "uncommitted beyond the dust and grime." It's hard to find a complete ethics or politics in passages like these, but at least they contest the rituals of Confucianism. Here is how Peng Yu draws the lesson: "*Sangwo*, or losing the self, pertains to the state in which one detaches from perpetuated self and instead embraces nomadic self. This dynamic results in what is called *xiaoyao* in *Zhuangzi* – a stage in which political relations are radically rearranged in opposition to predetermined structure" (Yu 2020: 344; original emphasis).

Here is another passage in which Zhuangzi challenges what Alan Jasanoff calls *the cerebral mystique*, the notion that the brain can perform the leadership functions often attributed to the nonphysical mind (Jasanoff 2018):

> There's Crippled Shu—chin stuck down in his navel, shoulders up above his head, pigtail pointing at the sky, his five organs on the top, his two thighs pressing his ribs. By sewing and washing, he gets enough to fill his mouth; by handling a winnow and sifting out the good grain, he makes enough to feed ten people. When the authorities call out the troops, he stands in the crowd waving good-bye; when they get up a big work party, they pass him over because he's a chronic invalid. And when they are doling out grain to the ailing, he gets three big measures and ten bundles of firewood. With a crippled body, he's still able to look after himself, and finish out the years Heaven gave him. How much better, then, if he had crippled virtue! (Zhuangzi 2003: 61–2)

Again, we see the pattern: view of human nature → political implications. Zhuangzi's view is that an authentic person (*zhenren*) does not reside in a body with discrete organs performing defined roles. Rather, "the body no longer identifies itself with specific organs but instead immerses in the ceaseless variations of the Way." Rather than try to govern himself through reason alone, or by following established rituals and standards of righteousness, the enlightened hero of Zhuangzi's story finds a way to survive, and flourish, by living in a somewhat chaotic body: "the unsettled body matters" (Yu 2020: 346, 344).

Philosophy can be political without explicitly mentioning politics. Sometimes, philosophy can focus on *how* we think about politics than *what* we think about politics. Peng Yu describes beautifully how rearranging the bodily organs—becoming what Gilles Deleuze and Félix Guattari call the Body without Organs (BwO)—individual and collective experimentation in ways of thinking, living, legislating, and governing:

> While many stressed systematic reconstructions that placed state and authority at the center of social reforms, *Zhuangzi* looked to the volatility of life per se as a crucial site to change politics. Seeing how moral rule further consolidated rather than mitigated inequality and injustice and hence only worked nominally, *Zhuangzi* found alternatives in the quotidian lived by those who were condemned as unworthy and useless. What entices is not only the resilience of the volatile body but also what arises from the unsettled process of subjectivation that is caught in the chaos of social degradation. (Yu 2020: 357; original emphasis)

On the board, I draw the critiques made of Zhuangzi and Peng Yu's replies. Edward Slingerland suggests that the *Zhuangzi* is a kind of self-help book with advice about how to enter a state of flow; Peng Yu replies that becoming a spontaneous (*ziran*) body can also empower one to challenge the political status quo. Peng Yu would agree with Bryan W. Van Norden that the *Zhuangzi* lacks the specific advice about ruling and rituals that you would find in the *Analects*, *Mengzi*, or *Xunzi*; but he would also say that people can confidently commit acts of injustice while spouting moralistic rhetoric. In the actual practice of governing, Zhuangzian Daoists may be more attuned to the specifics of the situation before them. And to Tao Jiang's argument that the *Zhuangzi* lacks a fully developed political theory, Peng Yu would say that it is our task, here and now, to fill it out: "While I agree with Jiang about *Zhuangzi*'s espousal of political reality *as is*, I would like to contend that it is precisely because of the acute awareness of the capricious reality does *Zhuangzi* venture to an imagination of politics outside conventional forms" (Yu 2020: 358; original emphasis). If political theory at the highest level entails imagining a world that the theorist "can never 'know' in an intimate way" (Wolin 2016: 19), then the *Zhuangzi* fits the category of a canonical work of political theory.

I think that pluralist political theorists may profitably use images from the *Zhuangzi*. Here is a passage from the "Qiwulun":

> In ancient times, Yao asked Shun, "I want to attack Zong, Kuai, and Xu'ao, for though I sit facing south on the throne, still I am not at ease. Why is this?" Shun said, "Though these three may continue to dwell out among the grasses and brambles, why should this make you ill at ease? Once upon a time, ten suns rose in the sky at once, and the ten thousand things were all simultaneously illuminated. And how much better are many Virtuosities than many suns?" (Zhuangzi 2009: 17)

In the original story, the mythic sage-king Yao shot down ten suns out of the sky so that the plants and grains would not burn, suggesting that a ruler needed to consolidate power for the people to flourish (Zhuangzi 2009: 17, n.24). Zhuangzi invites us to consider "many Virtuosities" that complement one another and compete against one another in a relation of "agonistic respect" (Connolly 1995). To my students, I would pose the following question: What are examples of many Virtuosities coexisting peacefully?

FINAL THOUGHT ON TEACHING COMPARATIVE POLITICAL THEORY

What are the benefits and risks of non-specialists teaching Chinese political theory to undergraduates? Leigh Jenco has identified at least three risks. The "unpunctuated, uninflected, and severely sparse language of classical Chinese" (Jenco 2007: 751) means that any reader must use their own judgment about what the passage means. Someone who doesn't speak Chinese is at the mercy of translators. The ancient *ru* (scholars), including Confucius, did not communicate primarily or exclusively through treatises but also in funeral orations, tombstone inscriptions, paintings, monuments, temples, performances, burial rituals, oral histories, and teacher–student transmissions. Modern Western scholars who focus on canonical texts are bringing in their own biases to the study of another tradition. Finally, Confucianism is a complex tradition that participants in the *ru* tradition modified in different ways. An American cannot simply pick up a text and infer how the Chinese have read and used the *Analects* for over two millennia. Leigh Jenco recommends that Westerners do language study, historical research, and fieldwork before claiming to be an expert in the subject. The "process of attaining this wisdom takes a lifetime of practice and study" (Jenco 2007: 752–3). Given that most political theorists will not make this kind of commitment to the study of classical Chinese political thought, should they even try to teach or write about it?

In this chapter, I have suggested why Westerners should risk engaging and teaching Chinese political theory even if they make mistakes along the way. You cannot understand global politics unless you study China, including its political and intellectual traditions. Reading Chinese political thought opens your mind up to new ways of thinking about things like language and its paradoxes and snares. Chinese political thinkers often want Western theorists to talk with them even if people stumble with pronunciation and prepositions. Political theorists always work with incomplete awareness of all that an author has written, their historical context, the authors that preceded and followed them, and so forth. Political theorists may still learn from others even if we cannot speak their languages.

Political theorists should strive to understand non-Western political thought; they may also criticize and challenge it. As a democrat who believes that ordinary people ought to raise their voices and participate in politics (Tampio 2017), I know that some of the sharpest objections to democracy emanate from Chinese political theorists. Take Tongdong Bai, author of *Against Political Equality: The Confucian Case*. In this book, Bai draws upon Confucius and Mencius to make a case for political meritocracy or epistocracy, the idea that "the right of political participation in decision-making processes should be based on intellectual, moral, and political competence" (Bai 2019: 70). The uneducated are not welcome in public conversations about political affairs: "we should have more institutional arrangements in place that help prevent incompetent citizens from having too much of a voice in political matters" (Bai 2019: 70). Bai wants the Chinese to adopt certain liberal tenets without embracing democracy. Confucian societies should protect free speech so that the elites know the will of the people, the presence of corruption, and can make good policy. But "Confucians have no trust in the masses' ability to handle the truth" (Bai 2019: 259–60). Bai wrote this book in English and published it with Princeton University Press. He has visited my global justice seminar at Fordham University to discuss the book, we went to dinner on Arthur Avenue afterwards, and we remain in touch. He wants to have a conversation with English-speaking theorists.

What is the best way to discuss politics with Chinese thinkers like Tongdong Bai? One strategy is to study Western political thought and expect Chinese thinkers to speak our language. A better strategy, it strikes me, is to meet Chinese thinkers if not half way, at least at a point where we have made a good faith effort to learn the names, ideas, and arguments of key figures in Chinese intellectual history. Does it work? Perhaps I may end this chapter with a quote from a course evaluation in the summer of 2021: "Professor Tampio spent a great deal of our class time bringing in texts and thinkers who fall outside of the Western canon. This provided a much more diverse and productive discussion as well as introduced new material to those who were already familiar with the subject through other classes that only focus on Western thinkers."[13]

NOTES

1.   Roxanne L. Euben and Andrew F. March argue that political theory has been comparative at least since Athens sent envoys to watch religious practices in other city-states and that political theory has always had a comparative dimension (Euben 2006; March 2009).

2.   Ihnji Jon has encouraged me to read *The Analects of Dasan* to understand how Confucius was received and revised in Korea. She is right that the Confucian tradition has mutated over time and place, even fusing with Christianity in Korea.

3.   In class, I assign readings from Philip J. Ivanhoe and Bryan W. Van Norden's *Readings in Classical Chinese Philosophy*, but in this chapter, I will explain my thinking as I teach the course and will draw, as is customary in the scholarship on Chinese political thought, from multiple translations.

4.   Joon Choe, personal correspondence with the author, September 19, 2016.

5.   On the issue of how to read texts with multiple authors such as the *Zhuangzi*, see Jiang (2021: 7–26).

6.   Peng Yu, personal correspondence with the author, January 3, 2022.

7.   Around 1000 ce, the neo-Confucians, partly in response to Buddhism, emphasized the concept of pattern (*li*) that introduced a more metaphysical aspect into Confucianism. See Angle and Tiwald (2017).

8.   Dorothy H. B. Kwek translates this passage to remove the "dreaming subject," an interposition, she says, of Western interpreters. She also argues that the passage is more about the deep nature of reality (ontology) than how humans perceive it (epistemology). "The absolute cut between the two dreams, between butterfly and man, points toward the transformations (of state, of degree *and* kind) that all things undergo" (Kwek 2018: 33; original emphasis). Kwek and I do not disagree so much as have different reasons to read Zhuangzi. I want to stage a conversation between Zhuangzi and Western skeptics and liberals, and she wants Zhuangzi to engage new materialists like Bruno Latour and Jane Bennett.

9.   One benefit of teaching Zhuangzi's story of the butterfly is that one can compare it to other famous accounts of dreaming in Western philosophy, including in Descartes' *Meditations*, Charles S. Peirce's article "How to Make our Ideas Clear," and Sigmund Freud's *The Interpretation of Dreams.*

10. For Confucius, the ruler should use names as they were used in the Zhou dynasty; for Xunzi, the ruler had more discretion about what kind of language would best order the population. For both philosophers, verbal ambiguity leads to social chaos. See Chapter 22, "Correct Naming," in Xunzi (2016: 236–47).

11. On how Chinese liberals such as Hu Ping, editor of the journal *Beijing Spring*, think that history may inspire movements for democracy and free speech in China, see Luo (2021). Reading the *Zhuangzi* may not be sufficient to spark a Chinese democracy movement, but it can inspire Chinese to fight for values that are not seen as merely Western.

12. In a chapter, "Nothing is Fundamental," in *The Ethos of Pluralization*, William E. Connolly encourages political theorists to relax their demand for epistemological certainty and recognize that our ontological assumptions may be subject to contestation. At one point, Connolly refers favorably to the Chinese concept of *hsu* (in Pinyin: *xu*), nothingness/fullness, and it would be fruitful to explore the resonances between his political theory and Zhuangzi's (Connolly 1995: 39; Yu 2016).

13.   Fordham University, *Summer 2021 Report for [POSC2401 R11-Intro to Political Philosophy (Nicholas Tampio)]*.

REFERENCES

Allinson, R. E. (1989), *Chuang-Tzu for Spiritual Transformation: An Analysis of the Inner Chapters*, Albany, NY: State University of New York Press.

Angle, S. C. and J. Tiwald (2017), *Neo-Confucianism: A Philosophical Introduction*, Malden, MA: Polity.

Bai, T. (2019), *Against Political Equality: The Confucian Case*, Princeton, NJ: Princeton University Press.

Bergson, H. (1998), *Creative Evolution*, Mineola, NY: Dover Publications.

Chang, W. (2016), *In Search of the Way: Legal Philosophy of the Classic Chinese Thinkers*, Edinburgh: Edinburgh University Press.

Connolly, W. E. (1995), *The Ethos of Pluralization*, Minneapolis, MN: University of Minnesota Press.

Connolly, W. (2002), *Identity/Difference: Democratic Negotiations of Political Paradox*, Minneapolis, MN: University of Minnesota Press.

Euben, R. L. (2006), *Journeys to the Other Shore: Muslim and Western Travelers in Search of Knowledge*, Princeton, NJ: Princeton University Press.

Feinman, G. M., H. Fang and L. M. Nicholas (2018), "China during the Neolithic Period", in D. A. Bekken, L. C. Niziolek and G. M. Feinman (eds), *China: Visions through the Ages*, Chicago, IL: University of Chicago Press, pp. 69–88.

Freeden, M. (2021), "Comparative Political Thought: What Are We Looking At?," *Comparative Political Theory*, **1** (1), 3–7.

Froese, K. (2018), "Machine Hearts and Wandering Spirits in Nietzsche and Zhuangzi," *Religions*, **9** (12), Article 411, 1–20.

Glasgow, D. (2015), "Political Theory Simulations in the Classroom: Simulating John Locke's *Second Treatise of Government*," *PS: Political Science & Politics*, **48** (2), 368–72.

Goldin, P. (2020), *The Art of Chinese Philosophy: Eight Classical Texts and How to Read Them*, Princeton, NJ: Princeton University Press.

Gorton, W. and J. Havercroft (2012), "Using Historical Simulations to Teach Political Theory," *Journal of Political Science Education*, **8** (1), 50–68.

Hall, D. L. and R. T. Ames (1987), *Thinking Through Confucius*, Albany, NY: State University of New York Press.

Honig, B. (1993), *Political Theory and the Displacement of Politics*, Ithaca, NY: Cornell University Press.

Ivanhoe, P. J. (1996), "Was Zhuangzi a Relativist?," in P. Kjellberg and P. J. Ivanhoe (eds), *Essays on Skepticism, Relativism, and Ethics in the Zhuangzi*, Albany, NY: State University of New York Press, pp. 196–214.

Ivanhoe, P. J. and B. W. Van Norden (eds) (2005), *Readings in Classical Chinese Philosophy* (2nd edition), Indianapolis, IN: Hackett Publishing Company.

Jasanoff, A. (2018), *The Biological Mind: How Brain, Body, and Environment Collaborate to Make Us Who We Are*, New York: Basic Books.

Jenco, L. K. (2007), "'What Does Heaven Ever Say?' A Methods-Centered Approach to Cross-Cultural Engagement," *The American Political Science Review*, **101** (4), 741–55.

Jenco, L. K. (2017), "How Should We Use the Chinese Past? Contemporary Confucianism, the 'Reorganization of The National Heritage' and Non-Western Histories of Thought in a Global Age," *European Journal of Political Theory*, **16** (4), 450–69.

Jiang, T. (2012), "Isaiah Berlin's Challenge to the Zhuangzian Freedom," *Journal of Chinese Philosophy*, **39** (S1), 69–92.

Jiang, T. (2021), *Origins of Moral-Political Philosophy in Early China: Contestation of Humaneness, Justice, and Personal Freedom*, New York: Oxford University Press.

Kant, I. (2001), *Religion and Rational Theology*, New York: Cambridge University Press.

Kirkpatrick, J. (2021), "Literary Devices: Teaching Social Contract Theory with a Short Story," *Journal of Political Science Education*, **17** (sup1), 554–66.

Kjellberg, P. (1996), "Sextus Empiricus, Zhuangzi, and Xunzi on 'Why Be Skeptical?'" in P. Kjellberg and P.J. Ivanhoe (eds), *Essays on Skepticism, Relativism, and Ethics in the Zhuangzi*, Albany, NY: State University of New York Press, pp. 1–25.

Kwek, D. H. (2018), "The Importance of Being Useless: A Cross-Cultural Contribution to the New Materialisms from Zhuangzi," *Theory, Culture & Society*, **35** (7–8), 21–48.

Kwek, D. H. B. (2019), "Critique of Imperial Reason: Lessons from the Zhuangzi," *Dao*, **18** (3), 411–33.

Lai, W. (1985), "Yung and the Tradition of the Shih: The Confucian Restructuring of Heroic Courage," *Religious Studies*, **21** (2), 181–203.

Lakoff, G. and M. Johnson (1999), *Philosophy in the Flesh: The Embodied Mind & Its Challenge to Western Thought*, New York: Basic Books.

Latour, B. (2018), "Outline of a Parliament of Things," *Ecologie Politique*, **56** (1), 47–64.

Liu, J. (2016), *Zhuangzi and Modern Chinese Literature*, New York: Oxford University Press.

Luo, S. S. (2021), "The Liberalism of Fear in China: Hu Ping and the Uses of Fear and Memory in Contemporary Chinese Liberalism," *Global Intellectual History*, accessed June 8, 2022 at http://doi.org/10.1080/23801883.2021.1977674.

March, A. F. (2009), "What Is Comparative Political Theory?," *The Review of Politics*, **71** (4), 531–65.

Michalopoulos, S. and M. M. Xue (2021), "Folklore," *The Quarterly Journal of Economics*, **136** (4), 1993–2046.

Nietzsche, F. (1977), *The Portable Nietzsche*, ed. and trans. W. Kaufmann, New York: Penguin Books.

Nussbaum, M. C. (1996), *The Therapy of Desire*, Princeton, NJ: Princeton University Press.

Ribeiro, B. C. (2021), *Sextus, Montaigne, Hume: Pyrrhonizers*, Leiden: Brill.

Scott, J. C. (1998), *Seeing Like a State: How Certain Schemes to Improve the Human Condition Have Failed*, New Haven, CT: Yale University Press.

Slingerland, E. (2014), *Trying Not to Try: The Art and Science of Spontaneity*, New York: Crown.

Strauss, L. (1957), "What Is Political Philosophy?," *The Journal of Politics*, **19** (3), 343–68.

Sung, W. (2016), "Mencius and Xunzi on Xing (Human Nature)," *Philosophy Compass*, **11** (11), 632–41.

Tagma, H. M. E. (2021), "Teaching Theory and Space: Human Territoriality in Political Science," *PS: Political Science & Politics*, **54** (4), 767–71.

Tampio, N. (2017), "Why Rule By the People Is Better Than Rule By the Experts," *Aeon*, October 18, accessed July 17, 2019 at https://aeon.co/essays/why-rule-by-the -people-is-better-than-rule-by-the-experts.

Van Norden, B. W. (2016), "Zhuangzi's Ironic Detachment and Political Commitment," *Dao*, **15** (1), 1–17.

Van Norden, B. W. (2019), *Classical Chinese for Everyone: A Guide for Absolute Beginners*, Indianapolis, IN: Hackett Publishing.

Ware, J. H. (2019), "Zhuangzi: Chinese Daoist Philosopher," *Britannica*, accessed September 7, 2021 at https://www.britannica.com/biography/Zhuangzi.

Wolin, S. S. (2016), *Politics and Vision: Continuity and Innovation in Western Political Thought*, Princeton, NJ: Princeton University Press.

Xunzi (2016), *Xunzi: The Complete Text*, ed. E. L. Hutton, Princeton, NJ: Princeton University Press.

Yu, P. (2016), "Zones of Indeterminacy: Art, Body and Politics in Daoist Thought," *Theory, Culture & Society*, **33** (1), 93–114.

Yu, P. (2020), "Indeterminate Self: Subjectivity, Body and Politics in *Zhuangzi*," *Philosophy & Social Criticism*, **46** (3), 342–66.

Zhuangzi (2003), *Zhuangzi: Basic Writings*, trans. B. Watson, New York: Columbia University Press.

Zhuangzi (2009), *Zhuangzi: The Essential Writings, With Selections from Traditional Commentaries*, trans. B. Ziporyn, Indianapolis, IN: Hackett Publishing Company.

7. Teaching neuroscience in a political theory course

INTRODUCTION

Political theorists are responsible for teaching students about the ocean flows of politics, and the best way to begin one's education in political theory is to read books by thinkers who have plumbed the depths of political life. The primary responsibility of academic political theory is reading and commenting on the canon. In our research and in our upper-level courses, however, we want to advance the tradition of political theory, and one way to do that is to teach, or co-teach, a course that covers recent developments in the natural sciences. In this chapter, I share thoughts about how and why political theorists may teach neuroscience. The chapter explains how recent research on the brain and hiking, dance, nutrition, smell, and sleep may offer possible remedies for in-your-face politics.

REASONS TO TEACH NEUROSCIENCE IN A POLITICAL THEORY COURSE

Political theory is the subfield of political science closest to the humanities, but profound political thinkers have often studied or contributed to the natural sciences. Plato expected members of the academy to learn geometry; Aristotle launched the natural sciences with his analysis and classification of living things; Thomas Hobbes challenged the claim that an air pump could produce immaterial bodies (Latour 1993); Hannah Arendt assigned a book on animal camouflage in her course on Thinking at the New School for Social Research in 1974 (Hill 2019); William E. Connolly and Jane Bennett have extracted political lessons from research about the amygdala and omega-3 fatty acids (Bennett 2010; Connolly 2002). One could multiply examples. Political theorists investigate human nature, the nature of reality, and how human beings acquire knowledge, and one way to sharpen our thinking is to learn what scholars in other parts of the academy are researching on these topics.

Political scientists have examined the relationship between sleep patterns and political ideology (Ksiazkiewicz 2020), free lunch programs and fights at school (Altindag et al. 2020), and insufficient sleep and voting behavior (Holbein, Schafer and Dickinson 2019). Political theorists can draw upon the history of political thought and normative political theory to suggest future research projects at the intersection of the natural sciences and politics. I recommend that theorists teach, or co-teach, courses that review developments in the natural sciences.

In this chapter, I walk through how a political theorist may construct a course that engages recent work in neuroscience. In *Smellosophy*, empirical philosopher and cognitive scientist A. S. Barwich says that neuroscience yields "new philosophical questions and angles from which to revisit historically grown, deeply engrained intuitions about the mind and its creation, structure, and environment" (Barwich 2020: 311). In *The Political Life of Sensation*, political theorist Davide Panagia says that philosophers still have trouble understanding how the mouth plays a vital role in both "the divinity of the mind and the baseness of the digestive tract" (Panagia 2009: 125). If we bring these insights together, I think that we see an opening for political theorists to do, and teach, groundbreaking work that yields a political payoff. Neuroscientists are generating new insights into how the body affects the brain/mind, and political theorists should update their account of human nature to reflect this research. Many political theorists still emulate philosophers like Plato and Kant in drawing a sharp line between the rational and animal parts of human nature.[1] If political theorists read cognitive neuroscientists, they may gain insights about how to rethink, or reconfigure, their political theories in ways that are both scientifically grounded and theoretically adventurous.

In this chapter, I explain what I am thinking when I teach cognitive neuroscience in a political theory course. I will identify a problem that interests many people today—in-your-face politics—and how political theory and cognitive neuroscience can team up to identify ways to create warmer feelings between political adversaries.

First, Box 7.1 describes the benefits of taking students off-campus.

7.1   GO ON FIELD TRIPS

Academic political theorists' main responsibility is to hand over accumulated wisdom about politics to our students.

Sometimes, teachers may bring their students off-campus to continue their political education. Over the years, I have brought students to the United Nations compound in Manhattan to learn about the UN and to visit the site where Malala Yousafzai spoke to the General Assembly. I have also taken students to dinner at Le Monde on the Upper West Side of Manhattan before bringing them to a book launch. Soon, I hope to take students to the

Schomburg Center for Research in Black Culture in Harlem.

Political theorist William Sokoloff has written about bringing his students at the University of Texas, Pan American (UTPA) to Reynoldo V. Lopez State Jail in Edinburg, Texas. His students met inmates, guards, and the warden, and discussed how the readings in the course—including by Nietzsche and Michel Foucault—shed light on the nature of modern punishment. Sokoloff also identified other benefits from the trip: students could discuss the role of prisons in the United States, the similarities between prisons and educational institutions, and could relate to each other and the instructor in a more egalitarian way (Sokoloff 2014).

If there is a way for you to take your students off-campus, or host an event on-campus that appeals to a wide range of students (Abernathy and Forestal 2020), then do it. Political theorists should teach students about the world inside and outside the classroom.

THE PROBLEM OF IN-YOUR-FACE POLITICS

Whenever you start a course, unit, or lecture, you want to explain at the beginning why the audience should care about the topic. One approach is to discuss breaking news stories and ask what deeper questions they raise. Another is to assign a recent work of political science and explore how political theory may help address the identified problem. In this section, I describe a problem raised by political scientist Diana C. Mutz in her book, *In-Your-Face Politics: The Consequences of Uncivil Media*.

Democracy requires a certain civility between political adversaries. Many democrats after James Madison acknowledge that people tend to separate themselves into factions, and these factions compete with other factions for resources and to get its candidates elected to office. Scandals, accusations, feuds, duels, and slander are part of U.S. history and arguably democratic life in general. What is new, according to Mutz, is that incivility— a "violation of norms for interpersonal interaction" (Mutz 2015: 6)—is permeating democratic societies. Even when partisan passions are high, ordinary people can be polite to one another. Today, we see more occasions when people are impolite to people with different partisan positions. Incivility leads to disrespecting other people and losing trust in politicians and the political process in general.

According to Mutz, one of the things driving a rise in incivility is television. Television producers want to increase ratings and revenue. People crave drama. Therefore, television producers create television programming in which people argue with one another. One way producers intensify the action is to fill the screen with people's faces. "Cognitive neuroscience demonstrates that the human brain is designed to be sensitive to information about physical distance… The close-up creates a sense of spatial intimacy that violates individuals' boundaries for personal space" (Mutz 2015: 10). Uncivil media is like corn syrup; people can know that it has negative side-effects, but they keep consuming it. Television shows, or video clips, zoom in on faces even though it feels like politicians are violating our personal space. Though Mutz was writing before Twitter, TikTok, and other social media companies displaced television as the place where young people get their news, her analysis explains why social media feeds are filled with enraging political content.

Mutz acknowledges the benefits of uncivil discourse. Television shows with in-your-face moments attract bigger audiences, are more likely to be remembered by viewers, and are more likely to be shared on social media. At the same time, television can contribute to a coarsening of culture where people make insults rather than engage in a productive dialogue. What can be done to address the role that social media plays in accelerating political polarization? How can our society find healthier ways to generate community than by isolated individuals sharing anger on social media?

Mutz's remedy is to create television programming that is educational and interesting like *Sesame Street*, funny like *The Daily Show*, engrossing like *American Idol*, and a place where politicians want to appear, like presidential candidate Bill Clinton on *The Arsenio Hall Show*. She envisions scholars and television executives collaborating "to produce political television that holds citizens' attention and attracts viewer interest, without suggesting to the public that political advocates are antisocial ne'er-do-wells" (Mutz 2015: 211). If scholars and producers make television programming that is thoughtful and entertaining, that's great, but her book provides compelling reasons why producers who care about ratings and money will produce shows that are more like fast food than fresh vegetables. I also think that Mutz's solutions focus on images that enter through the eyes rather than influences that enter through the rest of the body. This eye-centric view of human nature is pervasive in political science, I venture, including a recent *American Political Science Review* article describing an experiment in which researchers brought people together to deliberate about political issues and observed less political polarization at the end of the long weekend. Rather than call for people to be physically co-present with people in different political parties, the authors recommended "online deliberation with video-based discussions" (Fishkin et al. 2021: 1479). Mainstream political science cannot easily imagine how things like breaking bread together creates companionship.

If we are going to do something about incivility in our society, changing television or Internet content is only one part of what should be a comprehensive strategy. As to how we should think about that strategy, I suggest that we recover insights from the Swiss philosopher, Jean-Jacques Rousseau (1712-78).

ROUSSEAU'S INSIGHT ON POLITICAL ATTACHMENTS

Rousseau wrote *The Government of Poland* in 1772 to help Poland draft its Constitution, but the text remains captivating because it brings ancient ideas of soulcraft into a modern, egalitarian context. In this book, Rousseau acknowledges that words on paper will not generate a Polish identity that will compel Poles to care for, protect, and sacrifice themselves for one another. Rousseau's great insight is that the social order must generate warm feelings among citizens *before* they articulate their identities in words. Here is a quote in which he explains how legislators may generate these feelings of sympathy:

> By what means, then, are we to move men's hearts and bring them to love their fatherland and its laws? Dare I say? Through the games they play as children, through institutions that, though a superficial man would deem them pointless, develop habits that abide and attachments that nothing can dissolve. (Rousseau 1985: 4)

Think about the habits that children develop when they play cooperative games such as holding a parachute and lifting it up and running underneath that. Now, compare that game to one such as dodgeball that involves hurling objects at other children to knock them out of the game. Alternately, consider the ethical sensibilities nurtured when children work together on projects versus when they take standardized tests behind privacy shields so that classmates cannot see their answers. It is hard to run experiments to test Rousseau's theory because growing up takes decades and it is nearly impossible for researchers to isolate one variable as the determinative one.[2] But if Rousseau has a good intuition, then the question of how to generate sympathy among people requires attention to things that may not at first glance seem political, like childhood games.[3]

William E. Connolly brought Rousseau's insight into the present in his book *Neuropolitics: Thinking, Culture, Speed*. In this book, Connolly drew upon philosophers such as Friedrich Nietzsche and Maurice Merleau-Ponty, neuroscientists such as Francisco Varela and Joseph Ledoux, and cinema scholars to argue that political theorists need to attend to the soil from which our political thoughts and habits arise. In this book, Connolly offers suggestions to cultivate a democratic sensibility such as listening to Mozart while reading, enjoying music by the Talking Heads while taking a bath, and going for a run to process something you have read (Connolly 2002: 101). Inspired by Connolly's work on the body–brain–culture network, the rest of the chapter explores how political theorists may draw upon recent work on neuroscience to address the problem of in-your-face politics.

WALK OUTDOORS

During the pandemic, I have taken my sons on an outdoor adventure at least once a week. We have climbed Anthony's Nose, Bear Mountain, and Bonticou Crag and walked through the woods at Mianus River Gorge, the old-growth forest at the Bronx Botanical Garden, and properties of Gilded Age mansions that have become New York state preserves. We have not been alone in trying to reconnect with nature during the pandemic (Ronto 2021). On an intuitive level, people realize they will be healthier and happier if they breathe fresh air and challenge themselves physically. In *Physical Intelligence: The Science of How the Body and the Mind Guide Each Other Through Life*, Scott Grafton, a professor and director of a brain imaging center at the University of California, Santa Barbara explains how the body and brain coordinate to move human beings through the world. His work also raises the question of how political orders may cultivate the kind of physical intelligence that makes people more peaceful with one another.

Physical Intelligence is organized by chapters describing how different parts of the brain are primarily responsible for specific functions like feeling the space around our body, maintaining our balance, or knowing how far our arms may reach. But the book is not just a review of the scientific literature on the brain–body connection; it also challenges the deep-seated prejudice in Western philosophy that the mind somehow transcends the viscera. Intelligence is not just a possession of the stationary person reading and thinking about words; the person who moves their bodies in treacherous outdoor conditions also possesses a kind of intelligence:

> For many of my colleagues who study the mind, the very notion that physical action also requires some intelligence draws a blank stare. They focus on thinking and perceiving. Other than ears and eyeballs, the body is largely irrelevant for their kind of science. However, to study a mind without a body ignores some of the greatest pleasures of being alive: experiencing the world directly, as we perform and create. (Grafton 2020: x–xi)

In *Physical Intelligence*, Grafton summarizes the findings of peer-reviewed articles on what part of the brain lights up in an MRI machine when subjects think about or do certain things. He grafts this research onto a narrative of hiking by himself in the High Sierra. Though the book does not directly address questions of ethics or politics, the book provides political theorists with a rich account of how the body acts and thinks—that is, human nature.

Most people know that the brain is the part of the human body responsible for higher-order thinking. Grafton is interested in lesion studies, or studies that examine what goes wrong when a part of the brain is injured. During World

War I, scientists investigated how certain injuries to the brain led to losses in hearing, speaking, and spatial awareness. In this way, scientists could make a certain map of the brain and each module's main functions. Grafton also describes research in the 1930s on the homunculus, the "little man," in the motor cortex. As it turns out, scientists can identify which neurons fire in the brain to move certain parts of the body. What, then, is new in neuroscience? According to Grafton, it is research showing how different parts of the brain work together to perform complicated movements. "This intermingled spatial arrangement of neurons is fundamentally different from the modular view. It is far more disorganized as a spatial map. Nevertheless, the mixing of different body parts could be a great way for the brain to control all sorts of movements across different joints at once." One thing that this research explains is how the body can create new movements. "The motor cortex neurons are like a bunch of intramural athletes who can be chosen to play different sports and on different teams every afternoon" (Grafton 2020: 121). Grafton's book raises the question of how people are going to train their motor cortex neurons to perform what functions.

How do you become more intelligent? If you are trained in the Western intellectual tradition, the emphasis is on reading, writing, taking tests, or sitting in the lecture hall or the library. By tracing how the different parts of the brain work together, and are constantly growing, making connections, or atrophying, Grafton shows that physical intelligence requires regular use of the body: "One never stops learning to cook, to drive, or even to talk, for that matter. It is also a knowledge that is lost from disuse; without practice you will fall on ice or off ladders" (Grafton 2020: xv). The Greek conceptual tradition—perhaps reflecting its origin in a society divided by ruling elites and slave laborers—makes a sharp distinction between thinking and doing, looking with one's eyes and working with one's hands. Grafton's argument is that these dualisms misrepresent the way in which living, acting, feeling, and thinking are all sloshed together in a living organism filled with nerves, blood, pus, hormones, and so forth. "The interconnectedness of cortical systems for thinking, sustaining physical life, and setting tangible goals is hardwired into all of us. Insofar as physical intelligence is concerned, the distinctions between mind and body are illusory" (Grafton 2020: 221). If we are going to take our own education seriously, we need to appreciate that mind and body, book smarts and life smarts, are mutually imbricated.

Problems arise when people neglect physical intelligence. One is that some elderly people injure themselves because they forget how to use their bodies, say, when walking outside or shoveling snow. "The epidemic of ground-level falls reveals how detached people can become from some of the most elemental affordances of the natural world" (Grafton 2020: 49). Looking at physical intelligence through a Spinozist lens, we can see that ignoring physical intelligence brings about a kind of sadness, in the person affected but also those with whom they interact. Grafton discusses research about the relationship between fatigue and depression. Researchers could change the risk–reward calculations in monkeys by stimulating their anterior cingulate cortex and, in effect, turning them into pessimists. "In related research in patients with severe depression, it is clear that this region of the cortex is also intertwined with circuits that powerfully manipulate a person's mood, and it is thought to play a critical role in generating depressive symptoms" (Grafton 2020: 216). Grafton draws analogies between monkeys and humans, and stimulations and fatigue, to show that researchers are tracing how interactions between the environment and the brain generate emotions. It does not have to be a mystery why people are sad or angry.

Grafton observes that people feel stronger and happier when they are hiking on trails. He also remarks that intense physical challenges in nature generate a purer form of the emotion that people seek when they meditate. If you want to "reboot intrinsic cognitive abilities" but do not want to sit and quiet your mind, "go to the mountains and these abilities arise on their own" (Grafton 2020: 24). Perhaps anticipating the charge that this argument is ableist, Grafton notes that even Stephen Hawking, the famed physicist who had amyotrophic lateral sclerosis (ALS), traveled the world and tried to "lead as full a life as possible" (Grafton 2020: xi).

Grafton avoids making explicit ethical or political recommendations in *Physical Intelligence*, but one of his main points is that "physical engagement, particularly walking outdoors, is one of the top performers in sustaining cognitive health" (Grafton 2020: 223). Other researchers have shown that spending time outdoors contributes to healthy childhood growth and development (Lee et al. 2021) and, for older people, leads to "improved mood, increased wellbeing and quality of life, better sleep, decreased agitation and disruptive behaviors, and reduced use of medications used to treat changed behaviors" (van den Berg et al. 2020: e254–55). Here, then, we have a clue about how to address in-your-face politics. People tend to become angry and uncivil when they watch television programming about politics, and this anger becomes addictive. Bringing people outside replicates the experience of meditating and loosens the hold that provocative media has on our attention. Sending kids to summer camp, placing parks in city centers, hiring landscape architects so that nursing homes have beautiful outdoor space, ensuring that students can play outside during recess, and so forth, tend to make people happier and healthier. But they also provide people with opportunities to increase their joy with other people, thereby counteracting the effects of uncivil media on social life.

JUST DANCE

People dance at parties, weddings, and celebrations. It does not seem necessary to argue that dancing can make you feel good. At the same time, many public schools lack dance programs, and people can go for years without dancing. Is there a serious case to be made for dance? Dance educators Sandra Minton and Rima Faber make such a case in their book, *Thinking with the Dancing Brain: Embodying Neuroscience*. If Minton and Faber succeed in their argument, then the task for theorists is to consider how to use this insight for political ends.

Our body expresses its feelings in dance. If we feel unhealthy, we dance in one way, and if we feel sick, we dance in another way. "Movement is the embodiment of thought; thinking directs action" (Minton and Faber 2016: 1). Minton and Faber use neuroscience to peer inside the black box of the brain of the dancer—in particular, the insula that acts as a conduit between the emotional centers of the brain such as the amygdala, the hypothalamus, and the orbitofrontal cortex. "Internal sensations come from the major organs of the body, bones, and kinesthetic receptors in joints, ligaments, fascia, muscles, and skin. The insula uses these sensations to assess feelings about the outside world" (Minton and Faber 2016: 65). The famed dancer Martha Graham "probed the depth of human passion and embodied expressions of grief, struggle, or anger and the open release of joy" (Minton and Faber 2016: 67). Neuroscience can help trace stimuli from the world, through the sense organs and brain, into the dancer's movements.

For me, the more interesting argument in the book reverses the causality arrows and looks at how dance affects the body, which then affects the brain/mind. Consider, for example, the effect of movement on blood oxygenation: "When students sit for long periods of time, blood pools in the buttocks and legs, and less circulates to the brain. Increasing the heart rate through exercise delivers more oxygen to the brain, creating conditions for more effective learning" (Minton and Faber 2016: 37). As a veteran of debates about education, I can attest that scholars and policymakers mostly ignore the role of the body in learning (Tampio 2018b). Minton and Faber's work challenges the reader to think about how movement, including but not only dance, affects our higher-order cognitive functioning: "exercise provides an increased supply of oxygen and glucose that are an unparalleled stimulus from which the brain functions to learn" (Minton and Faber 2016: 37). Rather than isolate the brain as the locus of thought, Minton and Faber propose a new concept: *body thinking* (Minton and Faber 2016: 14).[4]

Dancing, or the absence of it, has consequences for whether people cope with stress or become depressed.[5] Neuroscientists have traced how stress causes the adrenal glands "to release cortisol and other steroids that negatively affect the amygdala and hippocampus and interfere with neurotransmitters." When we are stressed, the release of cortisol causes our metabolism to slow down, the amygdala to become hyperactive, and the cortex to shrink (Minton and Faber 2016: 65, 68). In a word, when we do not find a way to burn off stress, our world shrinks, and it becomes harder to listen to other people or sympathize with them. We are just trying to hang on. Alternately, when we recognize the role that dance plays in making us happier, then we have a tool to change our brain, mood, and, on my extrapolation, political sensibility. When we dance, the brain releases hormones known as endorphins. Endorphins "cause relaxation, opening of the body frame, and facial expressions of confidence and well-being"; endorphins bind to specific regions in the brain "to produce a natural analgesic" (Minton and Faber 2016: 65). Minton and Faber cite a study showing that rats that run as a group create more new brain cells than isolated rats, and infer from this that humans should see an increase in neurogenesis when they dance together (Minton and Faber 2016: 70). Neuroscientists confirm what people who like to dance take for granted: dancing puts you in a good mood, and you don't care about the politics of the other people on the dance floor. People share energy and feel joy when they are moving their bodies together to music.

Minton and Faber are dance educators, and they see benefits in things like middle school choreography classes and the International Baccalaureate dance program (Minton and Faber 2016: 73–4). One natural policy extension of their work is to support more dance education programs in schools, communities, nursing homes, and so forth. As a political theorist, though, I am inclined to enlist dance educators in a battle against other conceptions of somatic education. Right now, educators and policymakers are interested in socio-emotional learning, and many people are interested in the idea of "grit" associated with the Positive Psychology movement. Elsewhere, I have written about why the concept of grit teaches young people to survive stressful situations rather than work together to make things better (Tampio 2016). Here, I identify a danger to students spending countless hours training for Spelling Bees, practicing the violin, or training in ballet. When students work by themselves on grueling tasks, then they can view other people as weak and deserving of contempt. If we care about creating a community where people enjoy each other's company, then we need to create opportunities for people who are not elite dancers or athletes to still be able to move their hips, laugh, sing, listen to music, and do things that release endorphins in a way that nurtures civic friendship. It may be too late to bring back square dancing in public schools, but I would like to see schools introduce more students to joyful, synchronized movements such as dance, tai chi, or yoga.[6]

Canonical figures in the history of political philosophy, including Sophocles, Xenophon, John Locke, and Rousseau, discuss the role of dance in training political sensibilities (Taylor 2021).[7] Recently, a political theorist and a scholar of dispute resolution have explored how neuroscience provides insight on how dance may ameliorate bitterness arising from wars or family conflicts. They suggest that "physical training and experience with dance [can] help expand mediators' mental models, enlarge their maneuverability in practice, and even serve parties in the midst of mediation" (Beausoleil and LeBaron 2013: 134). Stress floods the brain with adrenaline and makes it hard for people to hear, think about, or care for people perceived as a possible threat. Dancing can change interpersonal dynamics by helping people sweat, relieve stress, smile, generate new thoughts, attend to other people's body language, and leave the dance floor in a state of relaxed openness. Political theorists have a wide-open vista before them, drawing upon recent neuroscience to address questions that have consumed political philosophers for millennia, including the role of dance in generating an ethico-political sensibility.

EAT WELL

In graduate school, I took a seminar at Villa Spellman, the Johns Hopkins University campus in Florence, and lived in Arezzo, a Tuscan hill town. If you look at pictures of the medieval piazza on the Internet, you will see that the town square slopes down. There are few flat streets in Arezzo, and every walk to and from the train stop, library, and food market is a challenging physical exercise. One day, I walked into a macrobiotic restaurant and ate a meal that made me feel much lighter on my feet than the more cheese- and starch-heavy meals I had become accustomed to. For the remainder of my time in Arezzo, I ate most of my meals at the communal table of the restaurant and learned about macrobiotic cooking. When I was saying my goodbyes before returning to the United States, the manager told me with the utmost seriousness: "*Mangia bene*" [Eat well]. Does it really make a difference if one eats well? In *Eat to Beat Depression and Anxiety: Nourish Your Way to Better Mental Health in Six Weeks*, Drew Ramsey, M.D. presents a case that eating the right nutrients makes a difference for your health and mood. I think that the field of nutritional psychology has important implications for nurturing bodies that are kind to one another.

Ramsey's argument can be diagrammed simply: food → health → mood. Nineteenth-century writers like Henry David Thoreau and Friedrich Nietzsche maintained that eating huckleberries or "warrior's food," respectively, affects one's actions, thoughts, and feelings (Bennett 2010: Chapter 3). Ramsey takes up this line of argument with a bevy of research that traces the pathway between specific nutrients, bodily affects, and conscious thoughts and feelings. "Over the past few decades, the field of psychiatry has gained remarkable insights into the biological factors that may underlie changes in mood and anxiety levels" (Ramsey 2021: x). Ramsey writes a chapter, for example, called "Optimize Your Gut for Mental Health." The microbiome is composed of trillions of micro-organisms that live in one's gastrointestinal (GI) tract and digest food and send signals to one's brain. Ramsey describes research showing that mice without a microbiome cannot handle stress as well as normal mice. These microbe-free mice were then given a probiotic, *Bifidobacterium infantis*, that helped them handle stress. "Researchers showed that having the right bacteria in your GI tract could change the way your brain responded to stress" (Ramsey 2021: 84). Researchers should be careful about extrapolating findings from mice to humans and attend to specific interactions between probiotics and groups of people (Groopman 2021). Still, changing people's gut, through probiotics, may change their health and emotions in ways that could have macrolevel political effects.[8]

According to Ramsey, many people are setting themselves up for depression and anxiety with how they eat. People in the West often eat processed meats, refined carbohydrates, and trans fats that lead to high levels of inflammation, the immune system's response to injury and infection.[9] Inflammation, in turn, increases worry, irritability, and fatigue. Often, people "who've been diagnosed with depression or anxiety show elevated levels of inflammatory proteins—and those molecules may be behind symptoms like anhedonia, or the inability to feel pleasure, and sleep issues" (Ramsey 2021: 12). People in the West are also not getting enough serotonin, a neurotransmitter linked to mood. "Without eating foods that contain adequate levels of nutrients like iron, folate, and vitamin B12, your body cannot produce adequate levels of this mood-enhancing chemical" (Ramsey 2021: 22). Ramsey is not offering quick fixes, and he emphasizes that everyone is unique, and what is good for one person might not necessarily have the same effect on someone else. Still, Ramsey and Laura LaChance created an Antidepressant Food Scale (AFS) to identify 12 nutrients that can help people combat depression and sustain good physical and mental health: folate, iron, long-chain omega-3 fatty acids, magnesium, potassium, selenium, thiamine, vitamin A, vitamin B6, vitamin B12, vitamin C, and zinc.

Here are a few of the pathways that Ramsey identifies between nutrients, health, and food:

• *Folate.* Folate, also known as vitamin B9, makes myelin, a fatty substance that covers neurons to relay electrical impulses swiftly, and neurotransmitters to regulate your mood, sense of pleasure, and the clarity of your thinking. Folate regulates your DNA and processes an amino acid called homocysteine and thereby wards off depression and heart disease. Folate is from the Latin word for foliage, and people can get folate from chickpeas, lentils, chicken liver, brussels sprouts, asparagus, and cooked spinach (Ramsey 2021: 34–5).

- *Iron.* Iron, in the form of hemoglobin, transports oxygen from the lungs to the brain, and in the form of myoglobin, stores oxygen in the muscles for when you need a quick energy burst. The body also uses iron to produce two neurotransmitters, dopamine and serotonin, to regulate mood, focus, and pleasure. Vegetarians can get enough iron through pumpkin seeds, sesame seeds, spinach, and dark chocolate, but many people need to eat meat to get enough iron. Approximately 2 billion people around the world lack sufficient iron and suffer from low energy, focus problems, and irritability (Ramsey 2021: 35–6).
- *Magnesium.* Magnesium is a micromineral that plays a vital role in many body processes, including supporting the proper function of nerve cells and brain cells, stimulating brain growth, and controlling blood sugar levels. In 1923, researchers gave patients with "agitated depression" an IV infusion of magnesium and observed that they became calm and felt better. Without sufficient magnesium, people become vulnerable to GI diseases, type 2 diabetes, and alcohol dependence. Ramsey notes that magnesium is the mineral at the center of photosynthesis; it is "a way to conduct the flow of energy from the sun all the way to your brain." The way to get enough magnesium, then, is to eat fruits, vegetables, and leafy greens (Ramsey 2021: 38–40).

The nineteenth-century German philosopher Ludwig Feuerbach said "*Der Mensch ist, was er isst*" [Man is what he eats]: Ramsey agrees that you are what you eat, or that "your brain is made of food," and he draws upon research to show how specific nutrients can help you relax, think clearly, and beat depression and anxiety (Ramsey 2021: 22). Ramsey acknowledges that antidepressants and other pharmaceuticals can help people with mental health struggles, but he invites us to consider food as medicine, and one that people can use daily and not just in times of crisis.

According to Ramsay, "food is a mental health factor that is entirely within your control" (Ramsey 2021: 15). I respectfully disagree. When circumstances line up just right, adults can exercise some control of their diet, but often, people in schools, prisons, airplanes, cafeterias, office parties, and so forth are at the mercy of people providing the food. Ramsay's book is filled with good ideas, but to take his ideas to scale, we need to leave the field of nutritional psychology and enter the field of public policy.

I have learned from reading *Public Health Nutrition: Essentials for Practitioners* (Jones-Smith 2020) that public health officials run community health assessments that collect data about what people are eating from direct observation, informant interviews, surveys, laboratory tests of blood and urine, and focus groups. The National Health and Nutrition Examination Survey (NHANES) collects nutritional surveillance data to monitor trends, inform public policy, and support research agendas. For example, the NHANES discovered that a low intake of folate in women was associated with an elevated risk of neural tube defects in babies. In 1992, the United States Public Health Service recommended that food be fortified with folic acid, and in 1998, the Food and Drug Administration (FDA) mandated the fortification of enriched grain products with folic acid. "Using biomarker data of folate concentrations from NHANES (as measured by serum and RBC folate concentration), researchers have reported that folate concentration levels among the US population significantly increased after fortification was implemented" (Zwald and Ogden 2020: 19). This seems to be an example of a successful public health intervention to address a widespread nutritional deficiency. And yet I have also raised concerns, in another context, that public health mandates can infringe on the right to bodily integrity (Dotson and Tampio 2021; Tampio 2021). It is not always obvious what the right public health policy is in a liberal democracy.

We have reached a gap in the scholarly literature that advanced undergraduates and graduate students may fill in with research papers, theses, and the like. On one side of the gap, political theorists rarely discuss the interaction between politics and nutrition.[10] One exception is Jane Bennett, who in *Vibrant Matter* dedicates several pages to thinking through the political efficacy of fat. There may be others,[11] but most political theory focuses on words, concepts, ideas, ideologies, and the making of arguments. On the other side of the gap, nutritional psychologists and public health nutritionists, from what I have seen, rarely situate their work in larger debates about, say, the *telos* of the city, or the purpose of shared political life. Drew Ramsey places the onus of good nutrition on the individual, and the word *democracy* does not appear in *Public Health Nutrition*. The book has a few passing references to social justice and body mass index (BMI), but there is little explicit reflection on the purpose of public health policy. Political theorists can act as intermediaries between these literatures and imagine new research agendas and public policies.

Drew Ramsey describes a randomized control trial that showed that replacing junk food with fruits, vegetables, fish, whole grains, and healthy fats—in other words, the Mediterranean diet—led to lower reported rates of depression and anxiety (Ramsey 2021: 29–32). Political theorists, reading about this work, can wonder how public health nutrition interventions could address the problem of antagonistic politics. What can liberal democracies do to facilitate eating healthy food without becoming paternalistic or oppressive? How can democracies counteract a capitalist business model that sometimes profits from selling food that puts people in a bad mood? What can technological advances, say, in the study of the GI tract reveal about eating disorders and the way to treat them (Monti 2021)? Ask your students what they think. Put them in a position to draw from three literatures—nutrition, public policy, and political theory—and do research to share with the class. It is fine to read great books; it is also exhilarating to do political theory on the edge of the discipline.

ATTEND TO SMELL

In *Thus Spoke Zarathustra*, Nietzsche argues that the main tradition of philosophy privileges reason, spirit, intellect, ideas, concepts, and so forth, and neglects the fact that the material body is the soil from which cognition grows. In a section entitled, "On the Despisers of the Body," Zarathustra says, "Behind your thoughts and feelings, my brother, stands a powerful commander, an unknown wise man—he is called self. He lives in your body, he is your body" (Nietzsche 2011: 23). I situate myself in a minor tradition of political philosophy that includes Nietzsche, John Dewey, Maurice Merleau-Ponty, William E. Connolly, and Jane Bennett, which holds that the body—a term that can encompass GI processes, blood pressure, hormones, posture, exercise, food, the weather, sunlight, physical co-presence, and so on—affects our ethico-political decisions. The major tradition of philosophy tends to use visual metaphors to describe thinking and knowing; the minor tradition argues that we learn as much from our hands, ears, proprioceptive organs, and so forth, as we do with our eyes. For political philosophers in this camp, A. S. Barwich's new book, *Smellosophy: What the Nose Tells the Mind*, provides much food for thought. Drawing on recent research on olfaction, Barwich extracts philosophical lessons that have implications for political theory. In a word, political theorists should attend to smell as a factor in our own thinking and in political and social life in general.

If the Western philosophical tradition thinks of smell, according to Barwich, it is something that occurs independently of or after the hard work of cogitation. Western philosophy, like much of Western culture in general, exhibits a kind of "sensory chauvinism" that "routinely fuels neglect, especially of the more hidden systems. There are vital senses of which you are not consciously aware until you have a severe brain lesion. Contrary to popular opinion, we have more than five senses" (Barwich 2020: 308). What is surprising about this analysis is that neuroscientists have been working for over a century on lesion studies and have produced maps of the brain that identify regions primarily responsible for vision, speech, emotion, hearing, and so forth. And yet, as neurobiologist Alan Jasanoff explains in *The Biological Mind*, scientists and the public have smuggled old assumptions about the mind–body dualism into research on the brain that identifies it as "the seat of the soul" or "the mechanism of the mind" (Jasanoff 2018: 12). The *cerebral mystique* persists because people can point to a part of the brain—particularly in the cerebral cortex—and give it a role that used to be assigned to the mind. Smell confounds the *cerebral mystique* because it does not follow a linear path that can be traced in the same way as vision or hearing from waves to organs to brain. Researching olfaction forces us to reconsider how human beings know anything about themselves or their environment at all.

Rather than review the process by which human beings smell, I will discuss a quote in which Barwich summarizes the perceptual content of smell:

> Odor situations represent a perceptual measure of neural decision-making in context, where input cues are integrated in terms of their temporal and learned associations. From this perspective, sensory perception constitutes a measure of changing signal ratios in an environment informed by expectancy effects from top-down processes. (Barwich 2020: 306)

People make certain assumptions about how the mind relates to the body and the world that the extant science on vision supports. This is that a human being (subject) receives and processes visual stimuli from the world (objects) in a specific neural pathway that culminates in the sensory cortex. Vision and the science of it supports a metaphysics of subjects and objects with solid boundaries between them. Olfaction has some resemblance in that a sense organ, the nose, sniffs molecules from the world and sends a signal that goes to the olfactory bulb and then to the olfactory cortex. A major difference, though, is that "the olfactory signal gets scrambled, so much so that the neural topology bears absolutely no resemblance to the topology of the chemical stimulus. The idea that our mental life is, in one way or another, a representational expression of physical structures breaks down" (Barwich 2020: 11). Smell does not provide a mirror of the world. Instead, a mix of molecules reaches the nose, olfactory receptors independently of our volition select what signals to send along neural pathways, which the brain then interprets and evaluates based on context, anticipation, desires, fears, and other factors. Smell makes clear that human perception is a contactenation of chemicals and electrical impulses that do not provide an especially accurate map of the world; sense organs do not discern the truth so much as processes that may help human beings survive and reproduce; and brains with histories and biological, chemical, and electrical interactions are prone to notice some things and misinterpret or ignore other things.

Why does this matter for political theorists? One reason is that smell moves human beings. We are drawn to things that smell good and repulsed by things that smell bad. Though *Smellosophy* does not foreground the ethical and political stakes of smell, there are passages that make clear that smell plays a role in how human beings mate, make friends, purchase things, decide where to live, get angry, or stay calm:

> The nose guides value judgments about our surroundings all the time. We actively choose and decide with our nose. Many underestimate the influence of smell on their minds. Not all decisions based on smell happen in awareness or evoke conceptual images. Smells can instruct behavior without residing at the forefront of consciousness. (Barwich 2020: 120)

Smellosophy's opening paragraph includes a quote from Immanuel Kant saying that the sense of smell is dispensable and that "there are more disgusting objects than pleasant ones" (Barwich 2020: ix). This illustrates Nietzsche's point that philosophers can be "despisers of the body" who minimize the role of senses like smell in thinking and get squeamish around smells that remind them of bodily functions like sweating, sex, defecating, or dying. Philosophers like Hegel use the word sense (*Sinn*) to describe the inner essence of a thing; Barwich's point is that we ought to appreciate the role that smell plays in our sense of what a thing is or if it is good or bad. You cannot understand mating, friendships, social life, or parenting very well unless you attend to smell.

Based on my research so far, I have found more examples of how smells lead to disgust and contempt than any positive emotion. In "Smell in the City: Smoking and Olfactory Politics," Qian Hui Tan explains how political authorities in Singapore have licensed, or rather encouraged, people to express their contempt for the smells of cigarette smoking and smokers. With signs, advertising campaigns, and fines, authorities have nudged urban dwellers to view a modern city as odor-free and smokers as social deviants. "Smokers and non-smokers are drawn into antagonistic relations that are suffused with affective charges, the most dominant one being that of frustration" (Tan 2013: 62). One can find other examples of scholars documenting the majority hating the smell of out-groups.

In principle, however, odors could generate feelings of warmth among people who are presently cold to each other. "Many hotel chains…employ perfumers to create a house scent, a pleasant background to sentience that customers come to associate with their brand" (Barwich 2020: 121). When I gave a series of lectures at the Indian Institute of Technology-Kharagpur in January 2018, the hosts opened the event by filling the room with flowers and lighting a ceremonial lamp. If hotels and Indian academics know that smells can support positive feelings and memories, then policymakers may explore how smells can improve the political atmosphere.

Where to begin? In *Revelations in Air: A Guidebook to Smell*, journalist Jude Stewart describes the popularity, scent, and benefits of lavender:

> Lavender can supposedly calm anxiety, promote relaxation, and encourage sleep… A growing body of scientific studies…suggest lavender may indeed have super-powers. In one study, lavender oil beat the placebo handily in helping participants suffering with anxiety disorder; participants slept better and felt less restless and out of sorts. Lavender helped quell anxiety and depression in a group of high-risk postpartum mothers. It allayed the fears of dental patients awaiting potentially painful treatments. It soothed the low-anxiety nerves of people who'd just watched anxiety-inducing film clips. (Stewart 2021: 182)

People place lavender in their clothes drawers and in their sheets. If the therapeutic uses of lavender are on the right track, then maybe policymakers could infuse the air with lavender in mass transit systems, departments of motor vehicles, schools, prisons, and other public places that can be sites of anger and conflict. Policymakers could also recognize that air pollution leads to anosmia, loss of smell, which in turn leads to depression, anxiety, weight loss, and decreased social interaction (Zhang et al. 2021). That stinks.

The idea of using smells for political ends—political aromatherapy, if you will—is beyond the pale for many political thinkers and actors. But political theorists may contribute to political science writ large by floating ideas that are new, some might say crazy, and that have not yet been operationalized for experiments. Barwich cites a neuroscientist who explains that "odor communicates essential social cues in human life," and then adds her own view that "a variety of interesting, underexplored research topics are up for grabs" (Barwich 2020: 141). I think that political scientists should run experiments in which they gauge people's political attitudes with different smells in the room. Then, they could run the same experiments but this time telling the participants to either enjoy or excuse the smell. And so forth. As with diet, students can do their own research looking at the relationship between smells, brains, public policies, and political attitudes.

GO TO SLEEP

It's good, in political theory classes, to assign new articles so that you and the students stay abreast of developments in the field. One such article that draws upon neuroscience to address a real-world problem is Jonathan White's article on "Circadian Justice" published in *The Journal of Political Philosophy* in the fall of 2021. White's article prompts readers to consider sleep as not just a matter of mental, emotional, and physical health, but also of political justice. You do not need to study neurology to know that sleep matters, but it provides evidence why sleep performs an essential role in a healthy life and democratic politics.

White's article identities several reasons why people are sleeping poorly these days because of factors outside their control. People are sleeping for shorter amounts of time because of intense work schedules, artificial light coming from inside and outside the sleeping space, and cell phones that beep and flash at all hours. People, particularly those who work in the gig economy, are not sleeping on a regular schedule. And people do not sleep as soundly when they know that other people, particularly those competing with them in the global economy, are working. In short, modern, fast-paced, capitalist, urban life is leading to the *shortening*, *irregularization*, and *desynchronization* of sleep. People tend to assume that individuals are responsible for their own sleep habits, but people's time to rest is affected by things like noise pollution, night flights, and employers who expect workers to respond to messages immediately. "Holding individuals responsible for collective problems is generally a bad idea, but especially in an area like sleep, where feelings of personal responsibility can generate added anxiety, exacerbating the situation" (White 2021: 17).

White cites an article from the *Journal of Integrative Neuroscience* that details the effects of a poor night's sleep on mood, cognition, and biometric measures. In the study, individuals who slept less than six hours of sleep, compared to the other individuals, had higher depression and anxiety, made more errors in simple cognitive tasks, and had an increase in heart rate and EEG alpha and beta power at rest (Barnett and Cooper 2008). Poor sleep over a sustained period of time compromises one's well-being and life-chances.

White's more interesting claim, and the one that adds a political theory angle to research about sleep, is that sleep deprivation creates and exacerbates social and political inequality. People who are sleep deprived suffer health problems; cannot access banks, voting booths, or libraries that are only open when they are sleeping; and lose social status because of their irregular sleep schedule. On a political level, "Those whose sleep is curtailed, disrupted, or timed differently from the majority find themselves disadvantaged in terms of their capacity to participate as citizens" (White 2021: 2). There is a vicious cycle at work. The sleep deprived suffer from social segregation and interpersonal mistrust, but they do not have the energy or access to resources to change the system. White cites depressing research that those who work on the night shift exhibit limited solidarity with other workers because they are so tired and rarely meet the daytime crew. The article is filled with data about why people sleep poorly these days and how hard it is to change the basic structure of society to allow people to get good sleep. The situation is not hopeless. White observes that labor unions succeeded in the past in limiting worker hours, and there are similar campaigns one could launch today to give workers more control of the working week and the length of shifts, a right of employees to have a say in their schedule, a right to disconnect from work, and so forth. "Reducing the pressure to cut sleep, and increasing control over its timing and location, seem essential to alleviating the problems that arise" (White 2021: 18). I agree with White that *circadian justice* ought to be something that political theorists, policymakers, and the public take seriously.

Here is the aspect of the article that I would want to discuss with my students. White observes that the *homorhythmic* model of social life may have been the norm in pre-industrial, agrarian societies, but electricity, urbanization, all-night mass transit systems, and the global economy have created a polyrhythmic model of society. To address circadian injustice in polyrhythmic societies, White suggests "reconfiguring public institutions so that they can be accessed at all hours—turning day institutions into day-and-night institutions" (White 2021: 20). My question is whether this accommodation to people working the night shift will make things better or worse. Immediately, more janitors, bus drivers, call center workers, and so forth will be able to access public institutions. But employers will also feel less pressure to maintain daytime hours now that employees can work more easily at night.

Political theorists do not teach neuroscience because they want to add to expert knowledge in the field. Rather, we teach neuroscience so that we can have informed conversations about things like how to ensure people are sleeping enough to be healthy, think clearly, and participate in democratic politics if they wish.

THE RISK AND REWARD OF INTERDISCIPLINARY TEACHING

As political theorists, our primary responsibility is to keep alive a tradition. When I was a graduate student at Johns Hopkins University, I used to work on B-level, a floor of the library with many of the books in the social sciences and humanities. I found myself reading books with call numbers that started with the same letters, and when I started writing books, they started with the same letters. That is how a tradition works. My job at my university is to teach books that offer profound accounts of political life. In a healthy higher education environment, other people specialize in other areas.

At the same time, colleges and universities can be wonderful places for cross-pollination, as ideas from one discipline drift into another. At Hopkins, I attended the seminar for the history of moral and political thought with participants from the classics, history, philosophy, English, modern languages and literatures, and other departments. I would sometimes sit in on lectures and seminars hosted by the art history, sociology, and economics departments, and I would often go to events for the entire university community. At all the schools where I have taught, departments host events where they hope that people from other corners of the college or university attend. There are countervailing forces in higher education that incentivize academics to drill down into one area. But at its best, higher education can create a community where academics from different disciplines share ideas, critiques, book recommendations, requests for clarification, and so forth with one another. In this chapter, I hope to have shown that political theorists and neuroscientists may work alongside one another to address real-world problems such as in-your-face politics.

NOTES

1. On how developments in the natural sciences—including epigenetics, the interaction between an organism's environment and its genes—problematize any attempt to draw a sharp line between the human and the nonhuman, see Frost (2016).
2. On how the popular video game *Fortnite* enables young people to meet other gamers but isolates them from the wider community, see Tampio (2018a). A political scientist at Denison University, Ohio, ran an experiment to see the relationship between video game preferences and democratic traits (Harrington 2019). This is the kind of productive interplay I envision between political theory and political science, and there is more work to do examining the relationship between childhood habits and adult political dispositions.
3. One could also discuss with students the Korean television series *Squid Game.* The show dramatizes the parallels between the games played as children and the competitive nature of modern capitalist societies in which one's success depends on defeating one's peers.
4. I wish that Minton and Faber had gone farther in thinking about how movement affects thinking. For example, they encourage dance teachers to teach students about typographies, cultures, and dance around the world and then ask: "How do these movements reflect the environment of each culture?" (Minton and Faber 2016: 17). I think that the more interesting question is how movement offers insights into other cultures. What do you learn through dance, or other somatic rituals, about another culture that you cannot learn from books?
5. My philosophy professor at New College of Florida, Douglas Berggren, used to share a story that Joan of Arc told one of her frightened lieutenants before battle to act brave to become brave.
6. The yoga taught in a U.S. public school physical exercise class is likely to eschew the rich philosophical resources of the yogic tradition (Godrej 2017b). I would like to see public schools have these conversations rather than avoid physical exercises associated with diverse cultures.
7. I thank political scientist Katherine Goktepe for discussions about the place of dance and music in political theory.
8. Breastfeeding is another topic that deserves the attention of political theorists. "Breastfeeding may induce long-term effects on biopsychosocial systems implicated in brain health" (Fox et al. 2021: 322).
9. Gandhi thought that food justice was crucial to Indian independence, politically and ethically, from the British. He argued that the British took and retained India

using food, intoxicants, and medications, and in *Diet and Diet Reform*, he wrote about the adulteration of *ghee* (clarified butter) with vegetable oil, the health benefits of uncooked foods, the difference between cow and goat milk, and how many kilos of greens each member of his *ashram* consumed (Godrej 2017a: 897).

10. Kennan Ferguson's *Cookbook Politics* offers a fascinating account of how cookbooks create national cultures and political identities (Ferguson 2020). The research agenda I am proposing in this section is more earthy: how material foodstuffs compose the bodies of people and their ethico-political dispositions.

11. Laura Ephraim argues that human waste posed a problem for John Locke and other seventeenth-century agricultural reformers who believed that "all should be used." She has opened up a promising research agenda on what she calls, with a nod to Jacques Rancière, the "partition of the digestible" (Ephraim 2021).

REFERENCES

Abernathy, C. and J. Forestal (2020), "Civics Across Campus: Designing Effective Extracurricular Programming," *Journal of Political Science Education*, **16** (1), 3–27.

Altindag, D. T., D. Baek, H. Lee and J. Merkle (2020), "Free Lunch for All? The Impact of Universal School Lunch on Student Misbehavior," *Economics of Education Review*, **74**, Article 101945.

Barnett, K. J. and N. J. Cooper (2008), "The Effects of a Poor Night Sleep on Mood, Cognitive, Autonomic and Electrophysiological Measures," *Journal of Integrative Neuroscience*, **7** (3), 405–20.

Barwich, A. S. (2020), *Smellosophy: What the Nose Tells the Mind*, Cambridge, MA: Harvard University Press.

Beausoleil, E. and M. LeBaron (2013), "What Moves Us: Dance and Neuroscience Implications for Conflict Approaches," *Conflict Resolution Quarterly*, **31** (2), 133–58.

Bennett, J. (2010), *Vibrant Matter: A Political Ecology of Things*, Durham, NC: Duke University Press.

Connolly, W. E. (2002), *Neuropolitics: Thinking, Culture, Speed*, Minneapolis, MN: University of Minnesota Press.

Dotson, T. and N. Tampio (2021), "Vaccine Mandates Will Backfire. People Will Resist Even More," *The Washington Post*, July 31.

Ephraim, L. (2021), "Everyone Poops: Consumer Virtues and Excretory Anxieties in Locke's Theory of Property," *Political Theory*, accessed November 22, 2021 at https://doi.org/10.1177/00905917211048420.

Ferguson, K. (2020), *Cookbook Politics*, Philadelphia, PA: University of Pennsylvania Press.

Fishkin, J., A. Siu, L. Diamond and N. Bradburn (2021), "Is Deliberation an Antidote to Extreme Partisan Polarization? Reflections on 'America in One Room'," *American Political Science Review*, **115** (4), 1464–81.

Fox, M., P. Siddarth and H. A. Oughli et al. (2021), "Women Who Breastfeed Exhibit Cognitive Benefits after Age 50," *Evolution, Medicine, and Public Health*, **9** (1), 322–31.

Frost, S. (2016), *Biocultural Creatures: Toward a New Theory of the Human*, Durham, NC: Duke University Press.

Godrej, F. (2017a), "Gandhi, Foucault, and the Politics of Self-Care," *Theory & Event*, **20** (4), 894–922.

Godrej, F. (2017b), "The Neoliberal Yogi and the Politics of Yoga," *Political Theory*, **45** (6), 772–800.

Grafton, S. (2020), *Physical Intelligence: The Science of How the Body and the Mind Guide Each Other Through Life*, New York: Pantheon.

Groopman, J. (2021), "What Does the Microbiome Do?," *The New York Review of Books*, October 21.

Harrington, D. (2019), "If You Play Video Games, Are You a Terrible Democratic Citizen?," *One twenty seven* [blog], accessed November 21, 2021 at https://onetwentyseven.blog/2019/01/28/if-you-play-video-games/.

Hill, S. R. (2019), "Hannah Arendt's Syllabus for 'Thinking'," *Twitter*, accessed November 11, 2021 at https://twitter.com/Samantharhill/status/1120742416858918912.

Holbein, J. B., J. P. Schafer and D. L. Dickinson (2019), "Insufficient Sleep Reduces Voting and Other Prosocial Behaviours," *Nature Human Behaviour*, **3** (5), 492–500.

Jasanoff, A. (2018), *The Biological Mind: How Brain, Body, and Environment Collaborate to Make Us Who We Are*, New York: Basic Books.

Jones-Smith, J. (ed.) (2020), *Public Health Nutrition: Essentials for Practitioners*, Baltimore, MD: Johns Hopkins University Press.

Ksiazkiewicz, A. (2020), "Conservative Larks, Liberal Owls: The Relationship between Chronotype and Political Ideology," *The Journal of Politics*, **82** (1), 367–71.

Latour, B. (1993), *We Have Never Been Modern*, Cambridge, MA: Harvard University Press.

Lee, E.-Y., A. Bains and S. Hunter et al. (2021), "Systematic Review of the Correlates of Outdoor Play and Time Among Children Aged 3–12 Years," *International Journal of Behavioral Nutrition and Physical Activity*, **18** (1), Article 41.

Minton, S. C. and R. Faber (2016), *Thinking with the Dancing Brain: Embodying Neuroscience*, Lanham, MD: Rowman & Littlefield.

Monti, A. (2021), "A Stable Sense of Self Is Rooted in the Lungs, Heart and Gut," *Psyche*, December 6, accessed December 7, 2021 at https://psyche.co/ideas/a-stable-sense-of-self-is-rooted-in-the-lungs-heart-and-gut.

Mutz, D. C. (2015), *In-Your-Face Politics: The Consequences of Uncivil Media* (1st edition), Princeton, NJ: Princeton University Press.

Nietzsche, F. (2011), *Nietzsche: Thus Spoke Zarathustra*, eds A. Del Caro and R. Pipplin, New York: Cambridge University Press.

Panagia, D. (2009), *The Political Life of Sensation*, Durham, NC: Duke University Press.

Ramsey, D. (2021), *Eat to Beat Depression and Anxiety: Nourish Your Way to Better Mental Health in Six Weeks*, New York: Harper Wave.

Ronto, P. (2021), "Hiking in the US Has Never Been More Popular," *RunRepeat*, August 6, accessed November 22, 2021 at https://runrepeat.com/hiking-never-more-popular.

Rousseau, J.-J. (1985), *The Government of Poland*, trans. W. Kendall, Indianapolis, IN: Hackett Publishing.

Sokoloff, W. W. (2014), "Teaching Political Theory at a Prison in South Texas," *PS: Political Science & Politics*, **47** (2), 518–22.

Stewart, J. (2021), *Revelations in Air: A Guidebook to Smell*, New York: Penguin Books.

Tampio, N. (2016), "Teaching Grit Is Bad for Children, and Bad for Democracy," *Aeon*, June 2, accessed November 21, 2021 at https://aeon.co/ideas/teaching-grit-is-bad-for-children-and-bad-for-democracy.

Tampio, N. (2018a), "'Fortnite' Teaches the Wrong Lessons," *The Conversation*, October 12, accessed June 18, 2020 at http://theconversation.com/fortnite-teaches-the-wrong-lessons-104443.

Tampio, N. (2018b), "Look Up From Your Screen," *Aeon*, August 2, accessed September 22, 2021 at https://aeon.co/essays/children-learn-best-when-engaged-in-the-living-world-not-on-screens.

Tampio, N. (2021), "A Weakness in the Argument for Vaccine Mandates," *The Boston Globe*, August 25.

Tan, Q. H. (2013), "Smell in the City: Smoking and Olfactory Politics," *Urban Studies*, **50** (1), 55–71.

Taylor, F. (2021), "Michael and Catherine Zuckert on Leo Strauss's 'What is Liberal Education?' and 'Liberal Education and Responsibility'," *Enduring Interest*, November 1, accessed November 21, 2021 at https://enduringinterest.podbean.com/e/michael-and-catherine-zuckert-on-leo-strauss-s-what-is-liberal-education-and-liberal-education-and-responsibility/.

van den Berg, M. E. L., M. Winsall and S. M. Dyer et al. (2020), "Understanding the Barriers and Enablers to Using Outdoor Spaces in Nursing Homes: A Systematic Review," *The Gerontologist*, **60** (4), e254–e269.

White, J. (2021), "Circadian Justice," *Journal of Political Philosophy*, accessed November 10, 2021 at https://doi.org/10.1111/jopp.12271.

Zhang, Z., N. R. Rowan and J. M. Pinto et al. (2021), "Exposure to Particulate Matter Air Pollution and Anosmia," *JAMA Network Open*, **4** (5), Article e2111606.

Zwald, M. L. and C. L. Ogden (2020), "Population Surveillance and Monitoring," in J. Jones-Smith (ed.), *Public Health Nutrition: Essentials for Practitioners*, Baltimore, MD: Johns Hopkins University Press, pp. 7–32.

8. Teaching the public, with examples from education policy

INTRODUCTION

How can political theorists teach the public? In this chapter, I share advice based upon my public intellectual work in the past decade in which I have published in high-profile outlets such as *The Boston Globe*, *The Conversation*, and *The Washington Post*, appeared on national television programming on CNN and C-SPAN, recorded dozens of radio interviews and podcasts, given many public talks, communicated regularly with think tank researchers, and met with politicians to discuss education policy. One purpose of this chapter is to argue that political theorists should aspire to become what Michel Foucault calls *specific intellectuals* who combine training in political theory with expertise about specific policy arenas. A second purpose is to share advice about how to do that in the Internet age.

THE SPECIFIC INTELLECTUAL

Michel Foucault gives us a distinction that clarifies how political theorists may contribute to changing the world.

A political theorist may aspire to become a *universal intellectual*. The universal intellectual presents themselves as a "master of truth and justice" and "the spokesman of the universal" (Foucault 1980b: 126). Foucault likely had the French existentialist Jean-Paul Sartre in mind as the paradigmatic universal intellectual. In *What is Literature?*, Sartre asserted that the writer could lead a revolutionary movement through the force of their words. "It is up to us," Sartre explains, "to convert the city of ends into a concrete and open society—and this by the very content of our words" (Poster 1989: 47). Sartre wrote philosophy books such as *Being and Nothingness*, became a celebrity in France and the rest of the world, and communicated with the public via radio, newspapers, and films. Leftists still applaud Sartre for using his public platform to expose French war crimes in Algeria and defend the country's right to self-determination (Birchall 2021). Another universal intellectual is Noam Chomsky, who became famous as a linguist and then called upon intellectuals to speak unpopular truths, including about the hypocrisy surrounding U.S. foreign policy in Vietnam (Chomsky 1967). The appeal of universal intellectuals is that they present a utopian vision to explain the present and provide a roadmap for a better future.

A political theorist may also aspire to become a *specific intellectual*. Specific intellectuals inhabit and write about a particular place where power and knowledge interact, such as a hospital, asylum, or laboratory. This location gives specific intellectuals a "more immediate and concrete awareness of struggles" (Foucault 1980b: 126). Specific intellectuals do not speak for the proletariat and are not striving for a communist revolution. Rather, specific intellectuals may fight multinational corporations, predatory lenders, and the capitalist state that oppresses people. Even if specific intellectuals do not march under a communist banner, they work to improve the lives of people who are tortured in prisons, live in neighborhoods without clean tap water, and are enlisted to serve in unjust wars. An example of a specific intellectual is the atomic scientist J. Robert Oppenheimer. "It's because he had a direct and localized relation to scientific knowledge and institutions that the atomic scientist could make his intervention; but, since the nuclear threat affected the whole human race and the fate of the world, his discourse could at the same time be the discourse of the universal" (Foucault 1980b: 128). Foucault participated in the Groupe d'Information sur les Prisons in which he attended events but was silent while inmates, social workers, and family members spoke (Demers 2016). Specific intellectuals possess first-hand knowledge of concrete situations, and they try to ameliorate those situations. Rather than advocate a comprehensive redesign of society, specific intellectuals wage a "guerilla warfare" against local injustices (Poster 1989: 49).

So where does this leave political theorists? Political theorists talk, read, and write at seminar tables and in libraries, not in nuclear laboratories or prisons. May political theorists act as specific intellectuals? Foucault leaves open this possibility with his notion of *exchangers*, or "privileged points of intersection" (Foucault 1980b: 127). Psychiatrists, doctors, social workers, laboratory technicians and so forth have their expert knowledge, but they still need a way to exchange their knowledge with others in ways that enable people to see patterns. The political theorist may act as somebody who brings the insights of the local expert into larger academic and public conversations. In a 1972 interview with Foucault, Gilles Deleuze says that "theory is a relay from one practice to another. No theory can develop without eventually encountering a wall, and practice is necessary for piercing this wall" (Foucault 1980a: 206). I take Foucault and Deleuze to mean that specialists know their own situation and area of expertise, but they may not have explored the deepest philosophical issues at play. Political theorists undergo an apprenticeship in how to use ideas, but they need to listen carefully to people in the world to refine their ideas and ensure they have traction outside of the academy. Political theorists do not need to become nuclear physicists or regularly visit prisons to comment on those areas, but they do need to learn about those worlds if they wish to contribute to policy debates about them.

The political scientist and television host Melissa Harris-Perry says that political science needs to fund *ambassadors* and find *translators* to bring the insights of political science to a public audience (Harris-Perry and Friess 2015). Similarly, a 2015 American Political Science Association task force suggests that political scientists could better communicate with the public through a video library, a speaker's bureau, electronic journals, ungated articles on newsworthy content, and communications training (Lupia and Aldrich 2015). The risk of these proposals, from a Foucaultian perspective, is that they involve experts talking down to people who are not professional political scientists. Political scientists and theorists are tempted to act as if they are smarter than other people because of their degrees, jobs, or reputations. Foucault cautions intellectuals against using their accomplishments in one area to justify their public pronouncements on another topic. There is no such thing as a smart person as such. Stated positively: Foucault enjoins theorists to do as much homework as they can before they speak in public about matters of public concern. Political theorists can add to public conversations *if* they bring insights gleaned from training in political theory, deep knowledge of a narrow field of empirical scholarship, and conversations with people affected by specific policies.

Jürgen Habermas, according to Peter Verovšek, differentiates the roles of the theorist and the public intellectual. The theorist is a professional researcher, committed to finding the truth, and willing to subject themselves to peer review. The public intellectual amplifies the voice of the marginalized, acts as an early warning system about troublesome developments, speaks about things that are close to their heart, and performs the role of a citizen deliberating with their peers. Habermas defends "the independence and objectivity of social and political philosophy as an enterprise oriented towards truth" and allows "the theorist to participate in political debate as a critic of existing proposals and contemporary affairs more generally" (Verovšek 2021: 3). I see Habermas's point that the rules of the game differ for academics and people acting in the public sphere. I, for one, do not think that public-facing work ought to count for tenure and promotion. Scholarship is written for scholars, and if you want to stay in academia, then you need to earn the respect of other academics. Writing for the public, too, has its own norms and expectations, including being active on social media and allowing editors to write the titles. Nevertheless, I disagree that it is possible to draw "a hard line between the voice of the truth-oriented theorist and the critical, engaged public intellectual" (Verovšek 2021: 13). Political theorists doing public intellectual work ought to bring their scholarly habits into the public sphere, and they ought to return to their scholarly work with insights gained from real-world debates. Political theorists teach the public just as they do their students in the classroom, and, if they are democratic, then they ought to learn from the public and other experts as well. There is a membrane between academic and public intellectual roles, but it is a permeable one.

Foucault's writings on the specific intellectual inform how I have participated in debates about education policy for the past decade. In the rest of the chapter, I share advice about how political theorists may bring their insights to bear on public debates.

And on the topic of public speaking, Box 8.1 discusses the importance of talking to the back of the room.

BOX 8.1   PLAY TO THE BACK OF THE ROOM

I learned about the importance of public speaking on the job market. After giving a talk for a job that I was not offered, I asked for help from the Hamilton College Oral Communication Center. The speaking coach told me that the audience wants to see you thinking on your feet. He also suggested that I begin every lecture with a map of the argument and pace myself so that the audience can follow along. Philosophers since Plato have disparaged rhetoric, but the fact of the matter is that teachers are performers, and we can either get good at our craft or not. Use every class as an opportunity to develop good public speaking skills, not least because you want them to be second nature when you present at conferences or to the public.

One tip I have picked up along the way is from Johnny Ramone, the guitarist of the punk band, the Ramones. "Always play to the back of the room" (McCarthy 2011). In general, strong students sit in the front of the classroom, and it is tempting to call on them whenever their hands are raised. The danger to this approach is that you talk with a handful of students in a class, while all students deserve to share their thoughts and participate in the classroom discussion. When I am lecturing, I project my voice to the back row, and I call on students whose eyes are flashing even if their hands are down. I rarely end class without every student speaking at least once.

If you want to be a stellar teacher, learn a few tricks from rock stars.

RESEARCH THE POLICY AREA

In "Nietzsche, Genealogy, History," Foucault recommends a method that is "gray, meticulous, and patiently documentary" (Foucault 1984: 76). A universal intellectual starts with abstract concepts about right, law, justice, equality, or virtue and then looks for material to impress the pattern. Foucault advises specific intellectuals to attain knowledge of the specific situation at hand, which may include visiting locations, talking with experts and people affected by policies, reading sources in the archives, taking notes on legislation, and other activities that help you discover what Machiavelli called the effectual truth of things.

Here is an example. In 2010, I entered the public debate about the Common Core, a national set of education standards championed by the Obama administration to reform instruction in reading, writing, and mathematics. At the peak of the debate about whether states should adopt the standards (2013–14), in one six-month period there were 190,000 tweets from 53,000 distinct actors that used the hashtag #CommonCore (Supovitz, Daly and Del Fresno, 2018). What could I say about the Common Core that other people were not saying? Two things. First, I was one of the few public intellectuals to discuss the standards themselves (Tampio 2018a, 2019). I printed copies of the standards, the founding documents, think tank reports about the standards, and scholarship about education standards, education reform, and federalism. I followed the path by which policy entrepreneurs partnered with billionaires and politicians to drive the national adoption of the standards, including through the Obama administration's Race to the Top program. Additionally, I shared insights from the history of philosophy about the relationship between politics and education.

STAY ABREAST OF DEVELOPMENTS

If one wants to jump into a debate at the right time, one needs to know about meetings, grants, reports, statements, laws, and so forth that lead up to the crystallization of an event.

When I became aware of the Common Core in the spring of 2012, the plan had already been in motion for years. The architect of the Common Core, David Coleman, used to work as a McKinsey consultant, and one McKinsey strategy—"deliverology" (Tampio 2016)—is to change the facts on the ground before possible opponents can respond. After the 1989 Governor's Summit in Charlottesville, Virginia, education reformers created an organization in Washington, D.C.—Achieve, Inc.—that would push the standards, testing, and accountability agenda throughout electoral cycles. In the 1990s and 2000s, Achieve, Inc. and other groups published reports and promoted initiatives—including the American Diploma Project—that anticipated the Common Core State Standards Initiative. Even if the Common Core came as a surprise to parents, if you had been following behind-the-scenes developments in education reform, you would have been ready to respond to it. I resolved to stay ahead of the curve for future education developments, and many of my education articles have been on topics before they have burst through to public consciousness.

One example of this is entering the debate about higher education account-ability. One way that education reformers transformed American primary and secondary education is through holding schools, administrators, teachers, and students accountable for test scores. Many of the same individuals and groups that lobbied for No Child Left Behind and Race to the Top have moved on to higher education accountability, including using graduates' salaries as a measure to determine whether students at certain universities or in certain programs may access federal financial aid. By listening to podcasts, following key actors on Twitter, reading dozens of education articles a week, joining webinars, communicating with journalists and policy insiders, and reading bills, I was able to write articles alerting people, for instance, to legislation that would create a national student database that would make it harder for students to major in nonlucrative fields (Tampio 2021a, 2021b).

Sometimes, keeping your eyes open for ongoing developments means being "critically receptive" to conspiracy theories (Hayward 2022). A conspiracy is a plan that people want to keep a secret. Sometimes insiders share things that maybe they are not supposed to share on social media, and sometimes outsiders piece together things that are happening in different places but which may be connected. Between 2012 and 2014, I read many blogs by parents arguing that Microsoft co-founder Bill Gates was funding and coordinating the Common Core State Standards Initiative. On June 7, 2014, *The Washington Post* pub-lished a front-page article, "How Bill Gates Pulled Off the Swift Common Core Revolution," that included a timeline of events, an interview with Bill Gates, and information about grants that the Bill and Melinda Gates Foundation gave to the Council of Chief State School Officers, the Kentucky Department of Education, the James B. Hunt, Jr. Institute for Educational Leadership and Policy Foundation, The NEA Foundation for the Improvement of Education, and other think tanks, civil rights groups, and schools of education (Layton 2014). In a blink, Bill Gates's connection to the Common Core moved from the shadows to the light. Sometimes staying on top of developments in one's policy area means collecting open-source intelligence, imagining possibilities, and anticipating moves like a chess player.

CHOOSE YOUR INTERVENTION

Political theorists, following Marx's advice to change the world and not just interpret it, may either work with organizations in civil society or write for the public. I have chosen the second option, but there is value in the first.

The first option is civically engaged political science. This is research that seeks to inform the public, address community-grounded concerns, contribute to civic problem solving, and model "reciprocal and respectful engage-ment with various communities and groups" (Rasmussen et al. 2021: 707). American Political Science Association (APSA) President Rogers M. Smith has called political scientists to enter into "respectful partnerships with social groups, organizations, and governmental bodies, in ways that both shape our research questions and our investigations of answers" (Smith 2020: 21). Tufts University political scientist Peter Levine, a leader of APSA's newly created Institute for Civically Engaged Research (ICER), and Harvard professor Danielle Allen have worked together on Educating for American Democracy (EAD), an initiative to improve how American schools teach civics and history (Educating for American Democracy 2021). Smith, Levine, and Allen are all trained political theorists recovering an ancient conception of political science that seeks to inform public policy.

I see the value of this work, but I feel more comfortable playing the role of a gadfly who speaks the truth outside the halls of power. For example, I have publicly criticized plans to reform civics education that work within the standards, testing, and accountability paradigm (Tampio 2020a). As a reader of John Dewey, I favor other ways to teach civics—namely, by raising children in a democratic educational environment where they can exercise their voice in the classroom and with their representatives. I see the value of working with established political parties, think tanks, and foundations, but I would rather play the role of a "first mover" who is willing "to first deviate from an established norm" (Bicchieri 2016: 165). Political theorists with job security have a precious opportunity to use their platform to challenge and change social norms.

WATCH AND LEARN

For the rest of this chapter, I will speak to those who wish to write for the public. As an editor and reviewer, I often tell authors to study articles pub-lished in the journals where they are submitting. If every published article has six to eight sections, 40 to 60 sources, and around 9000 words, then your sub-mission should do the same (Tampio 2005). I offer similar advice to academics who wish to write for newspapers or magazines.

I was fortunate to take a workshop with the OpEd Project, a nonprofit dedicated to helping individuals learn the craft of writing opinion essays for the public. I learned about the template that most op-eds use. Open by bringing the reader up to speed quickly about a news story. In the second or third paragraph—what editors sometimes call the "nut graf"—state your thesis. Offer three or four pieces of evidence to support your thesis. Have a "to be clear" paragraph in which you acknowledge the valid points of your opponents. Restate your thesis. Do not go over word count. Use the simplest language you can. Use hyperlinks rather than notes. The OpEd Project has a webpage dedicated to "tips and tricks" that offer these and other suggestions (The OpEd Project 2021).

I also find it rewarding to write longer essays for outlets such as JSTOR *Daily* and *Aeon*. An academic article can take years from initial intuition until publication. Though the peer-review process tends to strengthen your argument, reviewers can also set unreasonable conditions for acceptance. I sometimes want to get ideas out into the world in a timely fashion even if the piece is not as developed as if it had been double-blind peer reviewed. My *Aeon* essay, "Look Up from Your Screen" (Tampio 2018c) has been shared on social media thousands of times, translated into Hebrew, and is included in *The Norton Reader* alongside essays by Maya Angelou, Frederick Douglass, and Benjamin Franklin (Tampio 2020b). I am still researching the relationship between corporeality, education, and democracy, but I am glad that I could enter the debate about education technology sooner rather than later.

TWO CRITERIA FOR WHERE TO PITCH AN OP-ED

In the Internet age, it does not matter as much as it once did where you publish an article. Even the etymology of op-ed—opposite the editorial page—reveals that the term no longer makes sense for opinion essays published exclusively on the Internet. Today, many people choose what articles to read based on what people share on social media, and the outlet alone will not guarantee that many people will read your article. I understand why academics sometimes self-publish on Medium or Substack. However, I want sharp minds to edit my piece before it is published, and I appreciate the legitimacy provided by publishing in a respectable outlet. Here, then, are my two criteria for where I pitch op-ed ideas.

First, pitch an editor you respect. Editors write the title, choose the images, and sometimes add their own words and examples. My university has a communications department and hires a communications firm to help faculty place op-eds. I am grateful that they have helped me place pieces in high-profile outlets such as MarketWatch (Tampio and Rossi 2020). In general, though, I prefer to choose the editors with whom I work. For outlets like *The Conversation*, authors work with one editor but several comment on drafts before the article is accepted. In this way, authors acquire some of the advantages of the peer-review process.

Second, find outlets that help you reach the target audience. Sometimes, you just want to reach a large audience and contribute to a societal conversation about, say, how video games influence civic habits. My article on the video game *Fortnite* in *The Conversation* has been read over 125,000 times, was translated into Spanish, and was syndicated by *Navy Times* and *Business*

Insider (Tampio 2018b). Other times, however, you publish in places because they are read by a specific audience. For instance, the editor of a blog about philanthropy invited me to send him an essay, and I used this as an opportunity to discuss a niche topic—namely, the political and educational ramifications of the Bill and Melinda Gates Foundation's Measures of Effective Teaching Project (Tampio 2018d).

COMMUNICATE AS CLEARLY AS POSSIBLE

Political scientist Peter DeScioli and cognitive psychologist Steven Pinker have documented how *American Political Science Review* articles include stylistic devices—"piled modifiers, needless words, nebulous nouns, missing prepositions, and buried verbs"—that make the argument unnecessarily hard to follow (DeScioli and Pinker 2022: 123). I agree with Rose McDermott: "Messages should use clear, clean language using colorful metaphors" (McDermott 2015: 86). Think about how you could write in such a way that it is easy to translate.[1]

Public intellectuals "play a key role in the agenda-setting function of the informal public sphere, by ensuring that the public opinions generated within this anarchic communicative realm 'has benefited from information, thoughtfulness, and the exchange of ideas'" (Verovšek 2021: 11). I once gave a public talk on the Common Core on Long Island, and a parent printed and distributed one of my articles for everyone attending the event. She told me that she had read my piece eight times. If you write clearly about a topic that people care about, they will read political theory.

GET A FEEL FOR THE GAME

Michael Oakeshott famously argued that you cannot hand somebody a cookbook and expect them to make a soufflé. "A cookery book presupposes somebody who knows how to cook" (Oakeshott 1991: 119). Likewise, there is no rule book for being a public intellectual, just rules of thumb you learn from thinking out loud in public. Here are a just a few things I have learned from doing political theory in public.

Join the Conversation

Every day, journalists, policymakers, academics, teachers, parents, and citizens share articles and observations on Twitter. If you Tweet to people, they often reply immediately. I have, for instance, had Twitter exchanges with President Bush's congressional liaison officer on No Child Left Behind, New York City's school chancellor, many education journalists, and countless academics. Diane Ravitch, a respected education scholar with a popular blog, has shared many of my articles on her blog and on Twitter. If you want influential people to engage your work and share it, then you may need to be active on social media. Jennifer Forestal argues that different platforms facilitate different kinds of conversations, with Facebook facilitating conversations within ideological groups, for good or ill, and Reddit facilitating "critical, diverse, and *collaborative* engagement" among people from different backgrounds addressing matters of public concern (Forestal 2021: 315; original emphasis).

Write to and Meet with People

I correspond with reporters, academics, think tank fellows and researchers, politicians, and policymakers. Also, when I can, I attend in person events and meet policymakers, politicians, and the influencers shaping the debate. I have had a meal or coffee with many of the key education policymakers in New York. Diplomats meet in person when they can to discuss important topics, and neuroscientists have shown that face-to-face interactions can generate trust (Holmes 2018). It helps if you live in a metropolis like Washington, D.C. or New York City, but you can still find ways to establish a personal connection with people.

Work on Timing

Machiavelli recommends that rulers hunt so that they know how to move swiftly over unfamiliar terrain (Machiavelli 1998: 59). One can adjust this advice to becoming a public intellectual. If a news story breaks, it is usually too late to write an opinion essay on it. You need to be on the lookout for the story in advance and start preparing your arguments and thinking about outlets.

LOOK THE PART

When I was on a book tour for *Common Core* (Tampio 2018a), I did a live radio interview that started at about 2 am. Afterwards, somebody wrote to me and chastised me for using many filler words such as *um* and *like*. Another time, I participated in a debate on CNN, and afterwards, people tweeted at me that I was looking down when the other person was speaking. You can ask people to overlook your mistakes in public communication because you are a head-in-the-clouds academic, or you can learn public communication skills. Here are just a few pointers I would make.

Invest in Good Equipment

I have done dozens of radio interviews, and I kick myself that I did not get a landline phone earlier. A cheap phone with wires from the phone to the base to the wall provides better sound quality for interviews than cell phones or wireless phones. For interviews using videoconferencing calls, I have bought a professional-grade microphone. If you appear on television, get a good lamp or lighting arrangement, and you may want to get a sound-dampening background so that there is no echo. Make an attractive background for Zoom interviews, including hiding wires and putting plants in your room.

Teach Yourself, Take Classes, or Hire a Coach

There are professionals who prepare people for radio and television appearances. If you are an academic, your school may pay for lessons. It is good to learn from your mistakes; it is better to learn from other people how to avoid those mistakes. In "Learning to Communicate Better with the Press and the Public," Brown University professor Rose McDermott shares pointers that she learned from the head of voice and speech at the American Repertory Theater in Cambridge, Massachusetts (McDermott 2015).

USE PUBLIC INTELLECTUAL WORK TO ENERGIZE YOUR SCHOLARSHIP

The vocation of political theory entails studying the deepest currents of political life. Rising to the surface of the ocean to participate in a timely debate can be an exhilarating experience. But political theorists find satisfaction and meaning in probing the depths of political life. After you make a timely intervention, you might realize that there is a philosophical problem that you need to research in more depth. When you tweet about education, you have 280 characters to say something pithy. It is hard to build a sustained argument in that amount of space. When you write op-eds, you normally get 600 to 1000 words to drive home your thesis. There is room for a little complexity, but the point of an op-ed is to convince somebody that your position is right. If you want to investigate an issue in depth, there are few better ways to do it than to write books and articles that you rethink and refine after peer review.

Do public intellectual work because you care about the world, but then return to your calling of exploring the ocean flows of politics.

NOTE

1. Here is the opening of my essay, "Look Up from Your Screen," from *Aeon* that has been translated into Hebrew and published in *The Norton Reader*:

   A rooster crows and awakens my family at the farm where we are staying for a long weekend. The air is crisp, and stars twinkle in the sky as the Sun rises over the hill. We walk to the barn, where horses, cows, chickens, pigs, dogs and cats vie for our attention. We wash and replenish water bowls, and carry hay to the cows and horses. The kids collect eggs for breakfast. (Tampio 2018c)

REFERENCES

Bicchieri, C. (2016), *Norms in the Wild: How to Diagnose, Measure, and Change Social Norms*, New York: Oxford University Press.

Birchall, I. (2021), "How Jean-Paul Sartre and *Les Temps Modernes* Supported Algeria's Struggle for Freedom," *Jacobin*, March 25.

Chomsky, N. (1967), "A Special Supplement: The Responsibility of Intellectuals," *New York Review of Books*, **8** (1), February 23.

Demers, J. (2016), "Prison Liberation by Association: Michel Foucault and the George Jackson Atlantic," *Atlantic Studies*, **13** (2), 165–86.

DeScioli, P. and S. Pinker (2022), "Piled Modifiers, Buried Verbs, and Other Turgid Prose in the *American Political Science Review*," *PS: Political Science & Politics*, **55** (1), 123–8.

Educating for American Democracy (EAD) (2021), "Excellence in History and Civics for All Learners," accessed September 21, 2021 at https://www.educatingforamericandemocracy.org/our-vision/.

Forestal, J. (2021), "Beyond Gatekeeping: Propaganda, Democracy, and the Organization of Digital Publics," *The Journal of Politics*, **83** (1), 306–20.

Foucault, M. (1980a), *Language, Counter-Memory, Practice: Selected Essays and Interviews* (1st edition), ed. D. F. Bouchard, Ithaca, NY: Cornell University Press.

Foucault, M. (1980b), *Power/Knowledge: Selected Interviews and Other Writings, 1972–1977*, ed. C. Gordon, trans. C. Gordon, L. Marshall, J. Mepham and K. Soper, New York: Pantheon Books.

Foucault, M. (1984), *The Foucault Reader*, ed. P. Rabinow, New York: Pantheon.

Harris-Perry, M. and S. Friess (2015), "An Interview with Melissa Harris-Perry," *PS: Political Science & Politics*, **48** (S1), 26–30.

Hayward, T. (2022), "'Conspiracy Theory': The Case for Being Critically Receptive," *Journal of Social Philosophy*, **53** (2), 148–67.

Holmes, M. (2018), *Face-to-Face Diplomacy: Social Neuroscience and International Relations*, New York: Cambridge University Press.

Layton, L. (2014), "How Bill Gates Pulled Off the Swift Common Core Revolution," *The Washington Post*, June 7.

Lupia, A. and J. H. Aldrich (2015), "How Political Science Can Better Communicate Its Value: 12 Recommendations from the APSA Task Force," *PS: Political Science & Politics*, **48** (S1), 1–19.

Machiavelli, N. (1998), *The Prince*, trans. H. C. Mansfield, Chicago, IL: University of Chicago Press.

McCarthy, T. (2011), "Johnny Ramone's Advice to Performing Musicians," *Mac Tracts*, June 17, accessed October 26, 2021 at https://tmc102464.wordpress.com/2011/06/17/johnny-ramone%e2%80%99s-advice-to-performing-musicians/.

McDermott, R. (2015), "Learning to Communicate Better with the Press and the Public," *PS: Political Science & Politics*, **48** (S1), 85–9.

Oakeshott, M. (1991), *Rationalism in Politics and Other Essays*, Indianapolis, IN: Liberty Fund.

Poster, M. (1989), "Sartre's Concept of the Intellectual," in M. Poster, *Critical Theory and Poststructuralism: In Search of a Context*, Ithaca, NY: Cornell University Press, pp. 34–52.

Rasmussen, A. C., P. Levine and R. Lieberman et al. (2021), "Preface," *PS: Political Science & Politics*, **54** (4), 707–10.

Smith, R. M. (2020), "What Good Can Political Science Do? From Pluralism to Partnerships," *Perspectives on Politics*, **18** (1), 10–26.

Supovitz, J., A. J. Daly and M. Del Fresno (2018), "The Common Core Debate on Twitter and the Rise of the Activist Public," *Journal of Educational Change*, **19** (4), 419–40.

Tampio, N. (2005), "Writing Political Theory: Lessons from an Apprenticeship," *PS: Political Science & Politics*, **38** (3), 391–2.

Tampio, N. (2016), "Democracy, Federal Power, and Education Reform," *Perspectives on Politics*, **14** (2), 461–7.

Tampio, N. (2018a), *Common Core: National Education Standards and the Threat to Democracy*, Baltimore, MD: Johns Hopkins University Press.

Tampio, N. (2018b), "'Fortnite' Teaches the Wrong Lessons," *The Conversation*, October 12, accessed June 18, 2020 at http://theconversation.com/fortnite-teaches-the-wrong-lessons-104443.

Tampio, N. (2018c), "Look Up from Your Screen," *Aeon*, August 2, accessed September 22, 2021 at https://aeon.co/essays/children-learn-best-when-engaged-in-the-living-world-not-on-screens.

Tampio, N. (2018d), "Philanthropy and the End of Teacher Autonomy," *HistPhil*, June 8, accessed September 22, 2021 at https://histphil.org/2018/06/08/philanthropy-and-the-end-of-teacher-autonomy/.

Tampio, N. (2019), *Learning versus the Common Core*, Minneapolis: MN: University of Minnesota Press.

Tampio, N. (2020a), "Keep the Feds Out of Civics Education," *The Boston Globe*, September 23.

Tampio, N. (2020b), "Look Up from Your Screen," in M. A. Goldthwaite, J. Bizup and A. Fernald et al. (eds), *The Norton Reader: An Anthology of Nonfiction* (15th edition), New York: W. W. Norton & Company, pp. 325–32.

Tampio, N. (2021a), "How a National Student Database Could Cheapen the College Experience," *The Conversation*, June 1, accessed September 21, 2021 at https://theconversation.com/how-a-national-student-database-could-cheapen-the-college-experience-161228.

Tampio, N. (2021b), "How Much Money Do English Majors Make? Don't Ask," *The Boston Globe*, May 2.

Tampio, N. and E. Rossi (2020), "Opinion: Taking the Racism Out of Capitalism Isn't Good Enough," *MarketWatch*, August 27, accessed September 22, 2021 at https://www.marketwatch.com/story/taking-the-racism-out-of-capitalism-isnt-good-enough-11598555456.

The OpEd Project (2021), "Op-Ed Writing: Tips and Tricks," accessed September 22, 2021 at https://www.theopedproject.org/oped-basics.

Verovšek, P. J. (2021), "The Philosopher as Engaged Citizen: Habermas on the Role of the Public Intellectual in the Modern Democratic Public Sphere," *European Journal of Social Theory*, accessed June 14, 2022 at https://eprints.whiterose.ac.uk/172849/1/Verovsek%20EJST%20Accepted.pdf.

Index

abolitionist movement 37
Achilles 124
active-learning approach, running
    simulations 142–3
Adams, John 9
African American political thought *see*
    Indian and African American
    political thought
*Against Political Equality: The
    Confucian Case* 3, 161
Against the Ethicists 134
Allen, Danielle 196
Amazon Mechanical Turk 8
Ambedkar, Bhimrao Ramji
    "Annihilation of Caste" 88–9
    caste discrimination 88–9
    Constitution of India, architect of 91
    Dalits to Buddhism, conversion 88
    democracy 91
    physical degeneration and
        regeneration 89–90
    provisions against discrimination,
        Constitution of India 91–2
American Diploma Project 194–5
American Political Science Association
    *(*APSA) 8, 23, 192, 196
American Political Science Review 9,
    198
American political thought 37–8 *see also*
    Apess, William; Du Bois, WEB;
    Garvey, Marcus; King, Martin
    Luther, Jr.; Hartmann, Saidiya;
    hemispheric political thought
    code-switching 37
    questions for teaching 26
    Republicans of Nacogdoches 37–8
    Republic of Texas, founding of 37
American politics 24
American race relations 1
amino acid 177
amygdala 166
anhedonia 177

animality 147
Antidepressant Food Scale (AFS) 177
anxiety 177
Apess, William 23
    acts of treachery and violence by
        Pilgrims 30
    colonization and racialized slavery
        31
    European/American culture. 30
    indigenous counter-actualization 31
    on native Americans 29–31
    Pilgrims and American identity
        29–30
    A Son of the Forest 29
apology 122
apraxia 126
Arendt, Hannah 166
Aristotelianism 124
Aristotelian or Christian principles 57
Aristotle 12, 154, 166
Arsenio Hall Show, The 169
authors on reading list 24–7
    African American thinkers 25
    Democrat or Republican 25
Ayyar, Varsha 109–10

Bacon 13
Bai, Tongdong 161
Barwich, A. S. 167, 180, 183
Bayle, Pierre 135
Bennett, Jane 166, 179–80
Bergson, Henri 150
Bifidobacterium infantis 177
"big data" 7
biography 47–8
Biological Mind, The 180
Blau, Adrian 12
Blight, David W. 34
body mass index (BMI) 179
body thinking 174
Botticelli, Sandro 53

Brahminism 91
bringing politics into classroom 26–7
British imperialism 13
Brown, Wendy 10, 24
Brown v. *Board of Education* 104
Butler, Judith 131

calm perseverance 135
cannibalism 126
carbohydrates 177
cerebral mystique 158, 180–1
Chavismo 38
China, political developments in 1, 124
Chinese political thought
    animality 147
    comparative political theory 160–1
    Confucius 144–5
    Han Feizi 47–8
        on Confucians 50–2
        on cruelty 60–3
        evaluation of 69–72
        on human nature 55–7
        on justification 67–9
        and the problem of political
            chaos 49–50
    humanity 147
    Mozi 145
    pre-Confucian warrior ethics 144
    right and wrong 150–1
    Zhuangzi 146–7, 151–60
Chomsky, Noam 190–1
Christianity 132
Cicero 13
circadian justice 185
circulation pumps 2
Civil Rights Act of 1964 25
classical political philosophy 120
Clinton, Bill 169
Closing of the American Mind, The 130
cognitive neuroscience 167–8
Coleman, David 194
colonialism 28
Common Core 194–5, 198
community-grounded concerns 195–6
comparative political theory 13, 140,
    160–1
Comparative Political Theory 13
Confucians/Confucianism 141
    ethico-political visions 148
    principle of 49

Confucius 50–1, 144–5, 155
Connolly, William E. 14–15, 44, 151,
    166, 170, 180
conspiracy theories 195
constructing a dialogue 44–7
contemporary American political debates
    1, 23
contextual studies 11–12
COVID-19 1
Creative Evolution 150
Creole elites 38
cross-fertilization 3

Daily Show, The 169
Dalit women 109
    capitalism 109
    caste 109–10
    difficulties facing 109–10
    resisting oppression 110
Dallmayr, Fred 141
dance education programs 175
Dandi Salt March 98, 101
Dark Princess: A Romance 95
Deleuze, Gilles 159, 191
deliverology 194
democracy/democratic 140
    Caesarism 38
    educational environment 196
    study of 3
depression 177
Descartes 126
*Designing Social Inquiry: Scientific
    Inference in Qualitative Research*
    6
Design of the University, The 44
desynchronization of sleep 184
Dewey, John 7, 125, 180, 196
*Divide: How Fanatical Certitude is
    Destroying Democracy, The* 136
dopamine 178
Dotson, Taylor 136–7
Douglass, Frederick 23
    1852 speech 32
    1869 speech 34
    on Black Americans 31–3
    Burlingame Treaty 34
    on Chinese Americans 34–5
    egalitarian society 33
    race 35
    republicanism and Christianity 32–3

response against nativist sentiment
34–5
"Self-Made Men" (1894), 33
Dreber, Anna 8
drunkenness 129
Du Bois, W. E. B 78
Conservation of Races, The 93
Dusk of Dawn 94
racism 93–5
Souls of Black Folk, The 93–5, 97
vision to end racism 96–7

Eat to Beat Depression and Anxiety:
Nourish Your Way to Better
Mental Health in Six Weeks 176
economic debates 1
Economics 2
Educating for American Democracy
(EAD) 196
education 23
accountability 195
politics and policy 1–2, 4, 190, 193
Emerson, Ralph Waldo 13
empiricist methodology 69
endorphins 175
epic political theorists 9
Epicurus 125
equal strength 130
ethico-political sensibility 176
ethnography 16–17
Euben, Roxanne L. 141
European fascism 84
evaluation 69–72
extraordinary artistic precision 122

Faber, Rima 174–5
Feuerbach, Ludwig 178
field trips 167
Flathman, Richard E. 126
folate 177–8
Food and Drug Administration (FDA)
179
Foreign policy 2
Fortune and the Dao: A Comparative
Study of Machiavelli, the
Daodejing, and the Han Feizi 59
Foucault, Michel 10, 131, 168, 190
Frazer, Michael 11
Freeden, Michael 13, 141

Freud, Sigmund 129
fund ambassadors 192

Gandhi, Mohandas
Dandi Salt March 98, 101
Gandhi–Irwin Pact 100
Home rule (*swaraj*) 98–9
leader of Indian National Congress
90
nonviolence (*ahimsa*) 99–100
against political oppression 103
practice of untouchability 90
reconciliation
with Bahujans 102
with Muslims 103
satyagraha ("truth force") 98–102
and Savarkar 102
swaraj ("freedom from the English
yoke") 98–9
Gandhi–Irwin Pact 100
Garvey, Marcus 78, 83–4
1923 speech 85
controversies 85–6
discrimination 84
forward-looking orientation 85
International Convention of the
Negroes, 1920 86
our blood or Negro blood in writings
85
strategies to consolidate Black
identity 84–5
gastrointestinal (GI) tract 177
Gates, Bill 195, 198
global climate change 2
Goodin, Robert E. 9
Government of Poland, The 170
Grafton, Scott 171, 174
Grant, Jacquelyn 36
Greek antiquity 136
Greek political thought
Sextus Empiricus 124–6
skeptical language 132–3
skepticism, political implications of
133–6
teaching 119–21
guerilla warfare 191
Gunnell, John G. 3

Habermas, Jürgen 192

Haitian Revolution 38
Hamilton, Alexander 11
Han Feizi 12
    and Confucians 51–2
    on cruelty 60–3
        conception of a political order
            63
        doctrine of "performance and
            title" 62
        good laws 61
        rewards and punishments 62
        Xunzi's position 61
    lectures on 47–8
    legalist political theory 48
    power of position (*shi*) 51
    regime 71
    rules of statecraft 52
    strengthen and protect state of Han
        49
Haraway, Donna 36
Harris-Perry, Melissa 192
Hartman, Saidiya 111–12
#CommonCore 194
hemispheric political thought 37–8
heteronormative resolution 131
hierarchical cultures 28
Hiero 120
Hinduism 81, 90, 103
Hindutva 80
Hobbes, Thomas 11, 166
Homer 120–2, 124, 128, 144
Home rule (*swaraj*) 98–9
homocysteine 177
homoerotic panic-titillation 131
homorhythmic model 185
Honig, Bonnie 152
Housing policy 2
How Social Science Got Better 2
human capabilities theory 132
Human Condition, The 3, 43, 69, 124
humanity 147
human nature 2, 54–9
    desire for individuals to acquire
        pleasure 56
    and human beings, difference
        between 57
    moralistic accounts of 59
    private-minded individuals 56
    public-spirited people 55
    selfishness of 55

Hume, David 4, 126, 133, 135

I Could Not Be Hindu 90
images, use of 46–7
immigration 23
incest 126
Indian and African American political
    thought, assignments with
    illustrations from
    assignment on ends *see* Ambedkar,
        Bhimrao Ramji; Du Bois, W.
        E. B
    assignment on forging identity *see*
        Garvey, Marcus; Savarkar,
        Vinayak Damodar
    assignment on intersectionality
        109–13 *see also* Dalit
        women; riotous black girls
    assignment on means 98–108 *see*
        also Gandhi, Mohandas;
        King, Martin Luther, Jr.
inflammation 177
inflammatory proteins 177
influenza pandemic (1918) 1
Institute for Civically Engaged Research
    (ICER) 196
institutionalizing discord, idea of 72
intellectual autonomy 77
intellectual-practical tradition 141
interconnectedness of cortical systems
    172
Interpretation of Dreams, The 129
Invisible Man 96
in-your-face politics 167–9
In-Your-Face Politics: The
    Consequences of Uncivil Media
    168
iron 178
irregularization of sleep 184
Isaac, Jeffrey C. 10, 14
Italian Renaissance 48, 70

Jasanoff, Alan 158, 180
Jati, common blood or race 81
Jiang, Tao 154
Jim Crow segregation 84
Johnson, Mark 141–2
Journal of Political Philosophy, The 9
junzi 51

justification 66–9
  empiricist methodology 69
  Machiavelli's realism and Plato's
    idealism 68
  Mohism and Confucianism 69
  philosophical doctrine 66
  sage-kings for guidance on good
    governance 67

Kant, Immanuel 11, 119–20, 126, 167
Keohane, Robert O. 6
King, Gary 6
King, Martin Luther, Jr. 83
Ku Klux Klan 84
Kwek, Dorothy 155–6

Lakoff, George 141–2
Latin American independence
  movements 38
Laursen, John Christian 126, 135
learning objectives 136–7
lectures
  biography 47–8
  constructing a dialogue 44–7
  cruelty 60–6
  evaluation 69–72
  human nature 54–9
  justification 66–9
  philosophical problems 50–4
  plurality 70
  political principles 59–66
  real-world political problems 49–50
Ledoux, Joseph 170
Legalism 46, 49 *see also* Han Feizi
Letter to the Romans 12
liberalism 15, 140, 154
Lippmann, Walter 123
Locke, John 11, 13
Longo, Matthew 16
Lucretius 125
  1962 speech 108
  civil rights movement 103, 107–8
  doctorate in systematic theology 104
  Nobel Peace Prize 104
  nonviolent resistance to racial
    inequality 104–6
  The Strength to Love 107
lynching 84

Machiavelli, Niccolò 11
  apocalypticism 52
  collaborated with Leonardo da Vinci
    48
  on cruelty 63–6
    cruel means to stop robberies
      and quarrels 64
    doctrine of cruelty 64–5
    *Machiavelli and the Orders of
      Violence* 64
  discovery of "new modes and
    orders" 52
  egalitarian 58
  freeing oneself from moralistic or
    religious frameworks 53–4
  human nature 57–9
  idealism, 52
  moralistic accounts of human nature
    57–9
  radical realist 72
  realism and Plato's idealism 68
  Strauss, about 55
Madison, James 4, 11, 168
magnesium 178
Mandela, Nelson 135
Manusmriti 91
MarketWatch 197
May Fourth Movement 72
McDermott, Rose 198
mental tranquility 127
Merleau-Ponty, Maurice 170, 180
metaphysical faith 123
methodism 7–8
microbiome 177
mind–body dualism 180
Minton, Sandra 174–5
Modi, Narendra 80
Mohism and Confucianism 69
Mohists 148
Monroe, Kristen Renwick 8
Montaigne, Michel de 126, 132, 140
mood-enhancing chemical 177
Moon, Meenakshi 110
motor cortex neurons 172
movies, watching 78–9
Mozi 145
Mutz, Diana C. 168–9

NAACP Legal Defense and Educational
  Fund 105

naïve barbarism 122
National Association for the
    Advancement of Colored People
    (NAACP) 87
National Health and Nutrition
    Examination Survey (NHANES)
    179
naturalization 23
Natural Right and History 3, 124
Natural science 2
Nature Human Behaviour 8
neo-Darwinism 57
neoliberalism 10
Neuropolitics: Thinking, Culture, Speed
    170
neuroscience in political theory course
    dance 174–6
    eat well 176–80
    interdisciplinary teaching 185–6
    in-your-face politics 168–9
    reasons to teach 166–8
    Rousseau's insight on political
        attachments 170
    sleep 183–5
    smell 180–3
    walk outdoors 171–3
neurotransmitters 177–8
Nietzsche, Friedrich 168, 170, 176
nonviolence 99–100, 106
non-Western political thought 161
normative political theory 166
North Atlantic political theorists 13
Nussbaum, Martha 131, 134

Oakeshott, Michael 126, 135–6
Odysseus 124
omega-3 fatty acids 166
online deliberation with video-based
    discussions 169
OpEd Project 196–7
open-source intelligence 195
Oppenheimer, J. Robert 191
Ordorealists, 70
Outlines of Pyrrhonism 126–7, 132–3

Panagia, Davide 167
Pan-American emancipation 37
Pan-Islamism 82
paradox of difference 151

Pascal, Blaise 126
patriarchal Christianity 36
PATRIOT Act 72
Pawar, Urmila 110
pedagogy 15, 26, 64
Peloponnesian War, 45
Peng Yu 147, 155
personal identity 151
Philadelphia Negro, The 111–12
philosophical doctrine 66
philosophical problems 50–4
philosophic education 77
Physical Intelligence 171
Plato 12, 166–7
Platonic idealism 125
Platonic Ideas 125
pluralism 15, 140
Pluralists 15
plurality 70
political and educational ramifications
    198
Political Liberalism 37
Political Life of Sensation, The 167
political moralism 50
political passivity 153
political philosophy 4
    analytic 16
    Straussian history of 12–13
    understanding of political affairs 24
political polarization 169
political principles 59–66
    cruelty 60–6
    Han Feizi and *The Prince* 60–6
political science 3–10, 16
    and political theory 5–11
    "vending machine" model of 8
political scientists 2–3
political sensibilities 176
political theorists 3–10, 13–15, 17,
    166–7, 190–1
    political affairs, 3
Political Theory 131
*Political Theory and the Displacement of
    Politics* 152
Politics 123, 133
politics of skepticism 126, 135
Popkin, Richard 126
populism 2, 38
practice of untouchability 90
pre-Confucian warrior ethics 144

Prince, The 3, 12, 43, 47–8, 50, 52–4,
        57–8, 63–6, 68, 71, 86
Prison Lectures 44
professional-grade microphone 200
*Prophet of Discontent: Martin Luther
        King, Jr. and the Critique of
        Racial Capitalism* 104
public communication 199
public intellectuals 192, 198
public teaching
        communication 198
        conversation 198–9
        criteria for where to pitch an OpEd
                197–8
        developments 194–5
        equipment 200
        intervention 195–6
        policy area research 193–4
        public intellectual work 200
        specific intellectual 190–3
        watch and learn 196–7
        work on timing 199
Pyrrhonism of Sextus 126

Qin dynasty 63, 145
Quest of the Silver Fleece, The 95

race riots 84
racism 28
Ramsey, Drew 176
Rashtra, love of fatherland 81–2
Rawls, John 131
realism 54
real-world political problems 49–50
Records of the Grand Historian 47
regional diversity 144
religious fundamentalists, 1970s and
        1980s 8
remainders of politics 152
reproducibility crisis 8
Republic 3, 43, 123–5, 133
Republicans of Nacogdoches 37–8
ressentiment 149
Review of Politics, The 141
Ribeiro, Brian C. 126
riotous black girls 111–12
Romantic thinkers 16
Rorty, Richard 133–4
Rousseau, Jean-Jacques 169

RuMo 148

sage-kings 67
sageliness 156–7
Sanskriti, culture or civilization 82
Sartre, Jean-Paul 190
satyagraha ("truth force") 98–102
Savarkar, Vinayak Damodar 80
        conflict of life and death between
                Hindus and Muslims 83
        Essentials of Hindutva 80
        Hindus 81–2
        The Indian War of Independence 81
        ultranationalism in India 83
        uniting Hindus to oppose British
                rule 80–1
Scottish Enlightenment 4
Seeing Like a State 156
self-determination 190–1
self-governance 124
sense-impressions 129
serotonin 177–8
Sesame Street 169
settler colonialism 31
Sex and Social Justice 3
Sextus Empiricus 124–6, 147
Shays' Rebellion in Massachusetts 11
Shklar, Judith 4, 23
shortening of sleep 184
Sima Qian 145
skeptical language 132–3
skepticism 15, 126–7, 140
        argument
                based on circumstances 128–30
                from customs 130–2
                from differences in animals
                        127–8
        command from tyrant 134
        contemporary relevance of 135
        guidance of nature 133
        moral or religious orthodoxies 135
        political implications of 133–6
        skeptical tradition 134–5
        technocrats 136
        traditions of laws and customs
                133–4
skeptics 134
Skinner, Quentin 11–12
sleep 183–5
Slingerland, Edward 154, 159

smell 180–3
smellosophy 167
Smellosophy: What the Nose Tells the Mind 180, 182
Smiet, Katrine 36
Smith, Rogers M. 8, 196
Social Justice in Islam 3
Social media 169
social sciences 1, 8
Socrates 122–3
Sojourner Truth and Intersectionality 36
Sokoloff, William 168
Souls of Black Folk, The 3
specific intellectual 191, 193
spiritual exercises 10
Sri Aurobindo 99
Strauss, Leo 12, 120, 124
suspension of judgment 127
swaraj 98–9
sympathy 170

tacit knowledge 7
Talking Heads 170
Tata Institute for Social Sciences 88
techniques of the self (Foucault) 10
television programming 169
Their Eyes Were Watching God 96
Theory of Justice, A 3
Thoreau, Henry David 176
Thoughts on Machiavelli 12
Thus Spoke Zarathustra 152–3, 180
Tilak, Bal Gangadhar 81
timely interventions 13–14, 197, 200
Tocqueville, Alexis De 23, 27–9
    American and European identities, difference 27–8
    American Christian *mores,* 28
    condemned slavery 29
    ideal American 28–9
    journey to America in 1831–32 27
    on White Americans 23, 27–9
Toward Perpetual Peace 3
training students to think for themselves 76–9
    intellectual autonomy 77
    philosophic education 77
trans fats 177
translators 192
Treatise of Human Nature, A 4
Truth, Sojourner 23

precursor to intersectional theorists 36
on religious Americans 35–7
violence to free enslaved people 35
Trying Not to Try 154

ultranationalism 87
uncivil media 169
United States, founding of 9
universal intellectual 190
Universal Negro Improvement Association (UNIA) 83

Van Norden, Bryan W. 142
Varela, Francisco 170
Verba, Sidney 6
Verovšek, Peter 192
videoconferencing calls 200
vitamin B12 177
Voting Rights Act of 1965 25

Warring States period 49
Washington Post, The 195
Wayward Lives, Beautiful Experiments 111
We Also Made History: Women in the Ambedkarite Movement 110
Whiskey Rebellion in Pennsylvania 11
wisdom 122
Witherspoon, John 4
Wolin, Sheldon 7, 10

Yousafzai, Malala 167

Zacka, Bernardo 16
Zhou dynasty 145
Zhuangzi 146–7
    cultural spirit 146
    knowledge and control 149
    paradox 152
    people sleeping and dreaming 149
    philosophy 146
    political theory 155–60
    politics, critiques of 153–5
    Qiwulun 147–8, 160
    Sextus Empiricus and 146–7
    style 151–3
    as teacher of tolerance 153–4

xiaoyao, free and easy wandering   Ziporyn, Brook 147
    158